Communications
in Computer and Information Science 1404

More information about this series at http://www.springer.com/series/7899

Udo R. Krieger · Gerald Eichler ·
Christian Erfurth · Günter Fahrnberger (Eds.)

Innovations for Community Services

21st International Conference, I4CS 2021
Bamberg, Germany, May 26–28, 2021
Proceedings

 Springer

Editors
Udo R. Krieger (iD)
University of Bamberg
Bamberg, Germany

Christian Erfurth (iD)
University of Applied Sciences Jena
Jena, Germany

Gerald Eichler (iD)
Deutsche Telekom
Technology & Innovation
Darmstadt, Germany

Günter Fahrnberger (iD)
University of Hagen
Hagen, Germany

ISSN 1865-0929   ISSN 1865-0937 (electronic)
Communications in Computer and Information Science
ISBN 978-3-030-75003-9   ISBN 978-3-030-75004-6 (eBook)
https://doi.org/10.1007/978-3-030-75004-6

This Springer imprint is published by the registered company Springer Nature Switzerland AG
The registered company address is: Gewerbestrasse 11, 6330 Cham, Switzerland

Foreword

The International Conference on Innovations for Community Services (I4CS) was back in Germany for its 21st edition in 2021. When scheduling the date, we looked for availability at one of the largest auditoriums at the University of Bamberg to have a high probability of carrying out the event in person. However, for the first time in history, we supported a hybrid conference to cover all situations owing to the unpredictability of the ongoing COVID-19 outbreak.

In June 2001, Herwig Unger and Thomas Böhme at the Technical University of Ilmenau, Germany, founded the Workshop on Innovative Internet Community Systems (IICS). It has continued its success story under its revised name of I4CS since 2014. IICS/I2CS published its proceedings in Springer's Lecture Notes in Computer Science (LNCS) series until 2005, followed by Gesellschaft für Informatik (GI) and Verein Deutscher Ingenieure (VDI). I4CS commenced with the Institute of Electrical and Electronics Engineers (IEEE) before it switched back to Springer's Communications in Computer and Information Science (CCIS) series in 2016, creating a permanent partnership with Springer in 2018. The unique combination of the printed proceedings and the SpringerLink online edition generates substantial interest from external readers, with increasing numbers of downloads.

The selection of conference locations (alternating international and German venues) reflects the conference concept: members of the Program Committee (PC) can propose suitable locations to host our community. For 2021, the Steering Committee had the honor to hand over the organizational responsibility to Udo R. Krieger and, therefore, to select the city of Bamberg in Germany as the venue. Located on both banks of the River Regnitz, the city perfectly reflects this year's motto "Bridging Digital Communities".

We were proud to achieve the envisaged number of scientific presentations, combined with a keynote, two invited talks, and a great social conference program to strengthen the cultural community spirit. The proceedings of I4CS 2021 comprised six sessions that covered the 14 full papers and 2 short papers selected out of the 43 submissions, received from authors in ten countries. Furthermore, three invited papers were added. Interdisciplinary thinking is a key success factor for any community. Hence, I4CS 2021 covered the established plurality of scientific, academic, and industrial topics, bundled into three key areas: "Technology", "Applications", and "Socialization".

Technology: Distributed Architectures and Frameworks

- Data architectures and models for community services
- Mobile collaboration and learning infrastructures
- 5G technologies and ad-hoc mobile networks
- Search, information retrieval, and artificial intelligence
- Common data models and big data analytics

Applications: Communities on the Move

- Social networks, news, and open collaboration
- Block chain for business and social life
- Recommender solutions and context awareness
- Augmented reality, robotics, and location-based gaming
- Intelligent transportation, logistics, and connected cars

Socialization: Ambient Work and Living

- Pandemic-related challenges, eHealth, and ambient assisted living
- Smart energy and home control
- Smart cities and municipal infrastructure
- Digitalization, IoT, and cyber physical systems
- Security, identity, and GDPR privacy protection

Many thanks to the 26 members of the current Program Committee, representing 14 countries worldwide, for their 153 worthwhile reviews, especially to its chair, Christian Erfurth, and to the Publication Chair, Günter Fahrnberger, who challenges a very successful cooperation with the Springer publishing board and high reputation of I4CS.

Following the established precedent, the 22nd I4CS will take place outside of Germany around June 2022. The location has not yet been determined by the Steering Committee. Please check regularly the permanent conference URL http://www.i4cs-conference.org/ for more details! Proposals on emerging topics as well as applications from prospective Program Committee members and potential conference hosts are kindly welcome at request@i4cs-conference.org.

Please stay healthy! Kind regards on behalf of the entire Steering Committee and the Editors' Board.

May 2021   Gerald Eichler

Preface

As Conference Chair, it is my pleasure to present this CCIS volume with its unique contributions on distributed architectures and software frameworks, advanced applications and services supporting digital communities, and digital socialization covering ambient work and living. The related papers were presented at the 21st International Conference on Innovations for Community Services (I4CS) 2021, held during May 26–28, 2021, at Otto-Friedrich-Universität in the UNESCO World Heritage Site of Bamberg, Germany. This ancient medieval residence with its marvellous Romanesque cathedral is located between the beautiful arms of the River Regnitz and represents one of the most attractive places in the Bavarian region of Upper Franconia.

Inspired by the exciting cultural heritage of Europe, I4CS again continued its reflection on a multi-dimensional, interdisciplinary approach to assist the digital evolution of modern societies. During a difficult period of the COVID-19 pandemic in 2021, the conference theme *Bridging Digital Communities* expresses the hope of many people in today's digital world that the rapid evolution of Internet and web technologies, as well as the outstanding capabilities of mobile Internet devices, will enable us to effectively support each other within a united global society during the daily challenges of our lives. The conceptual identity and mission statement of the University of Bamberg as well as its research and teaching efforts are dedicated to this unique multi-dimensional, interdisciplinary evolution of digital societies toward a new global identity of humans that is derived from the existing strong cultural backgrounds of the involved communities.

Following a thorough review procedure, with at least three reviewers for each submission, the Program Committee of I4CS compiled an interesting scientific program. It included 14 full papers, two short papers, and one keynote speech:

- "Security, Trust and Privacy: Challenges for Community-Oriented ICT Support" by Professor Dr. Gerald Quirchmayr, Deputy Head of Research Group Multimedia Information Systems, University of Vienna.

There were also two invited talks:

- "The Third Wave of Artificial Intelligence - From Blackbox Machine Learning to Explanation-Based Cooperation" by distinguished Professor Dr. Ute Schmid, Head of Cognitive Systems Group, University of Bamberg. Her scientific achievements in the area of artificial intelligence and her outstanding activities with respect to a systematic transfer of computer science knowledge to young children and school students have been honored with the Rainer-Markgraf Award 2020.
- "Ubiquitous Computing as a Seventh Sense: How Real-Time Feedback Can Make Resource Use Salient and Enable Resource Conservation" by Professor Dr. Thorsten Staake, Chair of Information Systems and Energy Efficient Systems, University of Bamberg.

As Conference Chair, I express my gratitude to all members of the Program Committee and all external reviewers for their dedicated service, maintaining the quality objectives of the conference, and for the timely provision of their valuable reviews. I thank all the authors for their submitted contributions, all the speakers for their vivid presentations, and all the participants for their contributions and interesting discussions. I express my sincere appreciation to the University of Bamberg as conference host, as well as to all the members of the Steering Committee and the local Organization Committee. Their great efforts were devoted to the success of this conference during a challenging period. Moreover, I acknowledge the support of the EasyChair conference system and express my gratitude to its management team that always serves the scientific community in an altruistic manner. Further, I thank Springer for unceasing support and excellent management of the CCIS publishing project.

Finally, it is my hope that readers will find the I4CS 2021 proceedings informative and useful with respect to their research and development activities in the near future. It may effectively assist them in building new, resilient bridges within digital communities that continue to exist hundreds of years from now, in a way similar to the bridges across River Regnitz that are located at Altes Rathaus.

May 2021   Udo R. Krieger

Organization

Program Committee

Sebastian Apel	Technical University of Applied Sciences Ingolstadt, Germany
Amr Tarek Azzam	Cairo University, Egypt
Gilbert Babin	University of Montréal, Canada
Gerald Eichler	Deutsche Telekom, Germany
Christian Erfurth	University of Applied Sciences Jena, Germany
Günter Fahrnberger	University of Hagen, Germany
Hacène Fouchal	University of Reims Champagne-Ardenne, France
Sapna Ponaraseri Gopinathan	Coimbatore Institute of Technology, India
Michal Hodoň	University of Žilina, Slovakia
Kathrin Kirchner	Technical University of Denmark, Denmark
Udo Krieger	University of Bamberg, Germany
Peter Kropf	University of Neuchâtel, Switzerland
Ulrike Lechner	Bundeswehr University Munich, Germany
Andreas Lommatzsch	Technical University of Berlin, Germany
Karl-Heinz Lüke	Ostfalia University of Applied Sciences, Germany
Raja Natarajan	Tata Institute of Fundamental Research, India
Deveeshree Nayak	University of Washington Tacoma, USA
George Papadopoulos	University of Cyprus, Cyprus
Dana Petcu	West University of Timisoara, Romania
Frank Phillipson	Netherlands Organisation for Applied Scientific Research, Netherlands
Siddharth Rautaray	Kalinga Institute of Industrial Technology, India
Joerg Roth	Nuremberg Institute of Technology, Germany
Amardeo Sarma	NEC Laboratories Europe, Germany
Pranav Kumar Singh	Indian Institute of Technology Guwahati and Central Institute of Technology Kokrajhar, India
Julian Szymański	Gdansk University of Technology, Poland
Leendert W. M. Wienhofen	City of Trondheim, Norway

Additional Reviewers

Achilleos, Achilleas
Mettouris, Christos
Vanezi, Evangelia
Yeratziotis, Alexandros

Abstracts of Invited Papers

Security, Trust and Privacy: Challenges for Community-Oriented ICT Support

Gerald Quirchmayr[ID]

University of Vienna, Vienna, Austria
gerald.quirchmayr@univie.ac.at

Abstract. With ICT increasingly becoming the main basis for community communication and cooperation, security, trust, and privacy protection are commonly accepted as core aspects of system design and operations. Starting with a representative example illustrating the resulting challenges, this talk will then give an overview of major legal requirements with the focus on privacy protection. Against this background the feasibility of security and trust mechanisms will be discussed in the context of communities that need to share information and have to cooperate in multiple ways to reach their common goals.

Keywords: Communities · ICT support · Legislation · Privacy · Security · Trust

The Third Wave of Artificial Intelligence

From Blackbox Machine Learning to Explanation-Based Cooperation

Ute Schmid 🆔

University of Bamberg, Bamberg, Bavaria, Germany
ute.schmid@uni-bamberg.de

Abstract. Machine learning is considered as an important technology with high potential for many application domains in industry as well as society. Impressive results of deep neural networks, for instance for image classification, promise that complex decision models can be derived from raw data without the need of feature engineering (end-to-end learning). However, there is an increasing awareness of the short-comings of data-intensive black box machine learning approaches: For many application domains it is either impossible or very expensive to provide the amount an quality of data necessary for deep learning. Furthermore, legal or ethical or simply practical considerations often make it necessary that decisions of learned models are transparent and comprehensible to human decision makers. Consequently, AI researchers and practitioners alike proclaim the need for the so-called 3rd Wave of AI to overcome the problems and restrictions of an AI which is focusing on purely data-driven approaches. In the talk, it is shown that machine learning research offers many alternative, often less data-intensive, approaches. Current topics and approaches for explainable and interactive machine learning will be introduced and illustrated with some example applications.

Keywords: Data engineering bottleneck · Explainability · Interactive machine learning

Ubiquitous Computing as a Seventh Sense

How Real-Time Feedback Can Make Resource Use Salient and Enable Resource Conservation

Thorsten Staake

University of Bamberg, Bamberg, Bavaria, Germany
thorsten.staake@uni-bamberg.de

Abstract. Behavior change has been identified as a powerful tool to curb energy consumption. In this context, information and communication technology (ICT) and especially consumption feedback can trigger behavior change on a large scale. Yet, many such feedback tools fail to produce the hoped-for energy saving effectsmostly as they fall short in triggering an initial adaption and recurrent application. In order to overcome this problem, we describe and empirically test a scalable and cost efficient solution that relies on "in-situ" real-time feedback. In several randomized controlled trials, the IT artifact demonstrated savings of over 500 kWh per year and household by enabling users to relate current behavior to personal resource use. The contribution also outlines how the artifact has been developed into a successful product that is already been installed in over 75 000 households and how the technology became an integral part of a commercially successful IoT infrastructure for drinking water systems.

Keywords: IoT for drinking water systems · Real-time feedback · Smart faucets

Contents

Community Data and Visualization

Technology Empowers Industry Processes

Future Community Support

Invited Paper

Security, Trust and Privacy: Challenges for Community-Oriented ICT Support

Gerald Quirchmayr[(⊠)] [iD]

University of Vienna, Vienna, Austria
gerald.quirchmayr@univie.ac.at

Abstract. With ICT increasingly becoming the main basis for community communication and cooperation, security, trust, and privacy protection are commonly accepted as core aspects of system design and operations. Starting with a representative example illustrating the resulting challenges, this talk will then give an overview of major legal requirements with the focus on privacy protection. Against this background the feasibility of security and trust mechanisms will be discussed in the context of communities that need to share information and have to cooperate in multiple ways to reach their common goals.

Keywords: Communities · ICT support · Legislation · Privacy · Security · Trust

1 Motivation and Background

Community support platforms ranging from messengers, social media platforms, group wikis and shared websites to fully developed computer supported cooperative work (CSCW) systems are deeply embedded in personal environments, in the workplace and in private life (cf. [1]). Communities that want to make full use of current and emerging technologies need to embark on the many sharing options these systems offer. Information sharing, resource sharing, and task sharing, to name only a few very central ones, do all require a high level of trust between the participants, and the assurance of security and privacy through system architecture and operational safeguards. The more sensitive the confidentiality of the shared information is, the higher of course also the required level of protection. In this context patient communities and the remote provision of medical services are one of the most challenging settings (cf. [2]). While for other communities the potential impact of data loss or data leakage might be far less severe, the basic concerns regarding privacy, security and trust are always present (cf. [3]). That is why they have to be addressed as integral aspects of requirements engineering and system design, if not for legal reasons, at least in the interest of user and management acceptance. Special attention needs to be given to communities of volunteers, who often provide essential services to society with limited resources. Even when being reasonably equipped and highly competent, privacy discussions and the concerns they cause are known to jeopardize even the most valuable projects (cf. the recent examples from the current pandemic [4]).

© Springer Nature Switzerland AG 2021
U. R. Krieger et al. (Eds.): I4CS 2021, CCIS 1404, pp. 3–6, 2021.
https://doi.org/10.1007/978-3-030-75004-6_1

2 Information Sharing Needs in the Light of Privacy, Security, and Trust

Privacy issues, security requirements, and trust between community members and in the used systems are often dealt with in separate projects, leading to stressful situation for system designers and operators. This approach culminates in cases where GDPR and NIS compliance are implemented without coordination between these two areas, thereby missing a unique opportunity to significantly raise security and trust levels while at the same time avoiding redundant developments (Fig. 1).

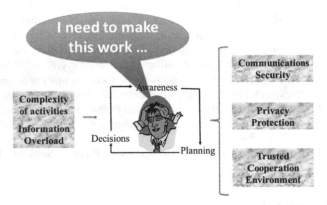

Fig. 1. Challenges influencing system design and operations.

Trust as prerequisite for information sharing can be considered as a multi-faceted user requirement that can cover several areas, mainly (for trust in cloud computing cf. [5]):

- trust in the community as a whole,
- trust in individuals,
- trust in the legal environment, especially in laws and regulations being enforced and adhered to,
- trust in the privacy protection mechanisms provided by a system, and
- trust in the security protection mechanisms provided by a system.

Given the above list, trust does to a large extent depend on the proper integration of legal requirements, organizational concepts, and technological capabilities in the system development process from the requirements analysis phase to rollout, test, operation, and maintenance. In an agile development process this might initially be considered as fully incompatible with the very paradigms of agile development, but this barrier can be overcome, as for example shown in the "Handbook of the Secure Agile Software Development Life Cycle" [6].

3 A Cascading View on Design Requirements

As adequate privacy protection is one of the major building blocks of a trusted system environment, getting a clear picture of possible privacy concerns and potential impacts of any group or community support system must be an integral part of the requirements analysis. While user acceptance already is an important driver for including trust and security, Art. 25 GDPR [7] even mandates privacy by design and by default. It therefore is helpful to look at privacy, security and trust as a triad depending on each other (Fig. 2).

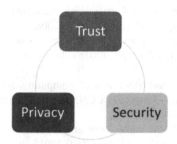

Fig. 2. Interdependency of trust, privacy, and security

However suitable this triad model might be, from a development viewpoint it might be even better to consider trust as a driver for privacy and security and privacy as a driver for security (Fig. 3).

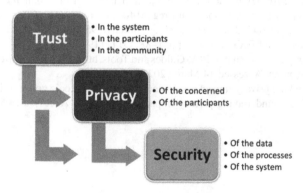

Fig. 3. Towards a cascading view on privacy and security

Once this cascade has become part of the development process through integrating it by means of dedicated user stories, DPIA (data processing impact analysis) approaches can be built on, such as the CNIL PIA Guide [8] and its Australian counterpart [9].

4 Some Core Lessons for System Development and Operations

Adequate privacy protection is one of the major building blocks of a trusted system environment, and so are trust mechanisms and security. While agile development is geared towards speed and efficiency, these factors can still be covered, as leading examples show (cf. [6]). Guidelines and templates for security- and privacy-related requirements are well-developed and ready for use. Legislation and user acceptance, especially when servicing volunteer communities, need to be considered as major drivers. Continuous deployment and function creep remain a constant challenge.

References

1. Koch, M.: CSCW and enterprise 2.0 - towards an integrated perspective. In: BLED 2008 Proceedings, p. 15 (2008). http://aisel.aisnet.org/bled2008/15
2. Azencott, C.-A.: Machine learning and genomics: precision medicine versus patient privacy. Phil. Trans. R. Soc. A. **376**(2128) (2018). http://dx.doi.org/10.1098/rsta.2017.0350. 3762017035020170350
3. Pearson, S.: Privacy, security and trust in cloud computing. In: Pearson, S., Yee, G. (eds.) Privacy and Security for Cloud Computing. CCN, pp. 3–42. Springer, London (2013). https://doi.org/10.1007/978-1-4471-4189-1_1
4. Labs, J., Terry, S.: Privacy in the coronavirus era. Genet. Testing Mol. Biomarkers **24**(9), 535–536 (2020). https://doi.org/10.1089/gtmb.2020.29055.sjt
5. Dragoni, N.: A survey on trust-based web service provision approaches. In: 2010 Third International Conference on Dependability, Venice, Italy, pp. 83–91 (2010). https://doi.org/10.1109/depend.2010.21
6. Pietikäinen, P., Röning, J. (eds.): Handbook of the Secure Agile Software Development Life Cycle. University of Oulu, Finland (2014). ISBN number: 978-952-62-0341-6, Juvenes Print Oulu
7. Regulation (EU) 2016/679 of the European Parliament and of the Council of 27 April 2016 on the protection of natural persons with regard to the processing of personal data and on the free movement of such data, and repealing Directive 95/46/EC (General Data Protection Regulation) (Text with EEA relevance), pp. 1–88. OJ L 119 (2016)
8. CNIL Privacy Impact Assessment (PIA) Guides and Tools. https://www.cnil.fr/en/PIA-privacy-impact-assessment-en. Accessed 14 March 2021
9. Guide to undertaking privacy impact assessments. https://www.oaic.gov.au/privacy/guidance-and-advice/guide-to-undertaking-privacy-impact-assessments/. Accessed 14 March 2021

Services for Critical Infrastructure

Threshold Pair Selection for the Reliable Condition Monitoring of Telecommunication Services

Günter Fahrnberger$^{(\boxtimes)}$ iD

University of Hagen, Hagen, North Rhine-Westphalia, Germany
guenter.fahrnberger@studium.fernuni-hagen.de

Abstract. A service provider usually measures the conditions of its service(s) via Key Performance Indicators (KPIs) and lets a Condition Monitoring System (CMS) continuously oversee them. A CMS additionally notifies the responsible workforce of abnormal KPI values. Telecommunication services often show time-varying load characteristic, i.e. their amplitudes of use fluctuate time-dependently. On account of that, a CMS has to cope the Condition Monitoring (CM) of such telecommunication services by dint of fluctuating thresholds. A couple of existing disquisitions have pioneered the calculation of dynamical thresholds to this end. Aside from the *normal* condition, contemporary CMSs can typically classify into the two measurable abnormal states *warning* and *critical* by way of two collaborating thresholds. Up to now, nobody has publicized a mechanism to extract the two ideal thresholds from an array that comprises at least three available ones. This contribution closes this gap by introducing three threshold extraction strategies, scrutinizing their reliability, and recommending ideas for further ones.

Keywords: Condition Monitoring · Damage detection · Nagios · Novelty dection · Supervision · Surveillance

1 Introduction

Irrespective of the currently coexisting mobile telephony generations (2G, 3G, 4G, 5G), telecommunication services enabled by them mostly feature time-varying load characteristic. This means that their magnitude of utilization oscillates, e.g. depending on the time of the day, day of the week, and/or week of the year. Just as independent of the bearer technology is the necessity to monitor these services to make their providers aware of their condition (changes). For this purpose, the service administrators select significant, quantifiable values as so-called KPIs and let a CMS incessantly observe them. When a CMS detects abnormal KPI values, it changes the KPI condition and alerts the responsible personnel.

Two scholarly pieces especially deal with the CM of telecommunication services with time-varying load characteristic [2,3].

© Springer Nature Switzerland AG 2021
U. R. Krieger et al. (Eds.): I4CS 2021, CCIS 1404, pp. 9–21, 2021.
https://doi.org/10.1007/978-3-030-75004-6_2

The first of them introduces a comprehensive CMS based upon a Nagios plugin with Friedrich Pukelsheim's three sigma rule [2,4].

The second ameliorates its ancestor with an outlier removal technique and a further automatic threshold calculation method, which do their job for any statistical distribution of the KPI history [3]. The latter also places a guideline at disposal how to supervise new services. It advises to initially utilize Friedrich Pukelsheim's three sigma rule without outlier erasure as a robust threshold computation algorithm against false condition changes. If missing notifications impend or have already taken place, variance-diminishing outlier eradication must happen prior to the threshold evaluation. If this does not entirely help, the guideline suggests to ultimately adopt the minimum or maximum value of an outlier-free array of historical KPI values as a yet stricter threshold.

The choice of the optimum threshold calculation technique seems to be a manual action at first glance, which contradicts the objective of both preceding publications. Therefore, this disquisition pursues the idea of calculating and applying combinations of the three introduced threshold algorithms in the paper about outlier removal for the reliable CM of telecommunication services. Nagios, its derivative Icinga, and also other CMSs support two co-existing thresholds to distinguish the three conditions *normal*, *warning*, and *critical*. A fourth condition *unknown* just emerges in the case of an unmeasurable KPI and, hence, does not depend on any threshold. While the laxer warning threshold represents the boundary between the normal and the warning condition, the stricter critical threshold separates the warning and the critical state.

Since the alluded CMSs can merely make use of two out of the three available thresholds, a static approach would be to renounce one of them and, thus, reduce the threshold triplet to a pair. The decision on the best renunciation candidate again requires manual efforts. More flexibility promises the dynamic way in this publication that calculates all three thresholds and steadily ignores either the minimal, central, or maximal value of them. If a CMS has to report too low KPI values, it sets the higher of the two unignored thresholds as warning and the lower as critical threshold. Reversely, for the reporting of too high KPI values, the warning threshold assumes the lower of the two unignored thresholds, and the critical threshold takes on the higher. The literature surveys in both predecessors substantiate the novelty of this flexible digest.

Section 2 recapitulates the necessary algorithms for the annihilation of outliers and the computation of the three above-mentioned thresholds. Section 3 adds pseudocode for the automatical reduction of a threshold triplet to a pair. Section 4 empirically determines the optimal abdicable threshold by means of real-world KPIs. Based on the findings, Sect. 5 draws conclusions for worthwhile future work.

2   Related Work

The sections about related work in both ancestors of this scholarly piece cite abundant literature about outlier exclusion respectively threshold evaluation [2,3].

That is why this section does rather well by familiarizing readers with the utilized techniques for outlier deletion in Subsect. 2.1 and threshold obtainment in Subsect. 2.2 as preparation for Sect. 3. Furthermore, the audience possibly benefits from collaterally perusing CM fundamentals of the engineering area, such as Davies's Handbook of Condition Monitoring [1].

2.1 Outlier Removal

In 1950, John Edward Walsh published some nonparametric statistical tests of whether the largest observations of a set are too large or too small [3,5]. Nonparametric statistics covers techniques that do not depend on any particular probability distribution in order to function appropriately. That is why such tests can be readily applied without incipient distribution determination, which makes them more lightweight. In 1953, Walsh felt obliged to issue an amendment to Theorem 4 of his original publication [3,6].

The null hypothesis of Walsh's nonparametric tests H_0 assumes a count of zero outliers in an input KPI history. More precisely, they act on the assumptions H_0^{min} (not all of the r_{min} lowest values are too small) and H_0^{max} (not all of the r_{max} highest values are too large). In contrast, if Walsh's nonparametric tests identify outliers, i.e. all r_{min} lowest values as too small or all r_{max} highest values as too large, they reject H_0^{min} respectively H_0^{max} and, thereby, H_0.

Algorithm 1. Outlier Recognition Based on Walsh's Idea

Require: $X = \{x_i \in \mathbb{R} | 1 \leq i \leq n \wedge (\nexists i) x_i > x_{i+1} \wedge i, n \in \mathbb{N}\}$

1: **if** $n < 3$ **then** {KPI history size smaller than 3 $(\mathcal{O}(1))$}
2:    **return** X {$\mathcal{O}(1)$}
3: **else** {KPI history size larger than 2 $(\mathcal{O}(1))$}
4:    $c = \lfloor \sqrt{2 * n} \rfloor$ {$\mathcal{O}(1)$}
5:    $b = \sqrt{c - 2}$ {$\mathcal{O}(1)$}
6:    $a = \frac{1 + b * \sqrt{(\frac{c-b^2}{c-1})}}{c - b^2 - 1} = 1 + b * \sqrt{(\frac{2}{c-1})}$ {$\mathcal{O}(1)$}
7:    $r_{max} = 1$ {Initialization of r_{max} $(\mathcal{O}(1))$}
8:    **while** $x_{n+1-r_{max}} - (1 + a) * x_{n-r_{max}} + a * x_{n+1-r_{max}-c} > 0$ **do** {Iteration over r_{max} $(\mathcal{O}(n))$}
9:        $r_{max} = r_{max} + 1$ {$\mathcal{O}(1)$}
10:    **end while**
11:    $r_{min} = 1$ {Initialization of r_{min} $\mathcal{O}(1)$}
12:    **while** $x_{r_{min}} - (1+a) * x_{r_{min}+1} + a * x_{r_{min}+c} < 0$ **do** {Iteration over r_{min} $(\mathcal{O}(n))$}
13:        $r_{min} = r_{min} + 1$ {$\mathcal{O}(1)$}
14:    **end while**
15:    **return** $X_{red} = \{x_i \in \mathbb{R} | r_{min} \leq i \leq n + 1 - r_{max} \wedge i, n, r_{max}, r_{min} \in \mathbb{N}\}$ {$\mathcal{O}(1)$}
16: **end if**

Algorithm 1 adapts Walsh's idea since it merely depends on a KPI history array X sorted in ascending order as input [3]. Walsh's original calculation of

$b_{orig} = \sqrt{\frac{1}{\alpha}}$ necessitates the additional specification of a probability of error α, which demands an X with a cardinality of $|X| = n \geq \lceil \frac{\lceil \frac{1+\alpha}{\alpha} \rceil^2}{2} \rceil$. For example, a desired $\alpha < 0.1$ would demand a cardinality $|X| = n \geq \lceil \frac{\lceil \frac{1+0.1}{0.1} \rceil^2}{2} \rceil = 61$, or $\alpha < 0.05$ a cardinality of $|X| = n \geq \lceil \frac{\lceil \frac{1+0.05}{0.05} \rceil^2}{2} \rceil = 221$.

To make Algorithm 1 applicable for $\forall n \in \mathbb{N}$, line 2 returns the unmodified X if the inequation $n < 3$ in line 1 applies, and line 5 in the else branch between line 3 and 16 evaluates $b = \sqrt{c-2}$ without a specified α. This conversion from the original $b_{orig} = \sqrt{\frac{1}{\alpha}}$ to the current $b = \sqrt{c-2}$ succeeds by automatically adopting $\alpha = \frac{1}{c-2}$ for the sake of computability.

After the preparatory computation of c, b, and a in the lines from 4 to 6, line 7 initializes r_{max} with 1 to test H_0^{max} for the highest historic KPI value x_n. As long as the inequation in line 8 applies, H_0^{max} must be rejected for the current value of r_{max} and tested for $r_{max} + 1$ (incrementation performed in line 9). Once the inequation in line 8 does not apply, the while-loop from line 8 to 10 immediately ends. In almost the same manner as lines 7 to 10 appraise the lowest r_{max} that supports H_0^{max}, the pseudocode in the lines numbered from 11 to 14 determines the lowest r_{min} that corroborates H_0^{min}. Line 15 finally outputs the outlier-free array X_{red} as the subset of X that misses the $r_{min} - 1$ lowest and the $r_{max} - 1$ highest values, which are deemed to be outliers.

2.2   Threshold Computation

In 1994, Friedrich Pukelsheim proved his three sigma rule for random variables with a unimodal Lebesgue density by elementary calculus [3,4]. While the first of the three methods hereinafter instantly employs his rule without attempting to exclude any outlier, the second gets rid of all outliers beforehand by means of Algorithm 1. The third also eliminates all outliers in an array of historical KPI values with the help of Algorithm 1 prior to a very frugal and efficient threshold evaluation.

Three Sigma Rule without Prior Outlier Removal The three sigma rule optimally performs if the input KPI history does not deviate too much from the normal distribution. Let $\bar{x}$ denote the arithmetic mean and σ the standard deviation of a KPI history array X, then (1) shows the computation of the threshold $t_{3\sigma}$ based on the three sigma rule. The arithmetical operator $\mp$ within them makes clear that thresholds below or above the arithmetic average may be calculated.

$$t_{3\sigma} = \bar{x} \mp 3*\sigma = \bar{x} \mp 3*\sqrt{\frac{\sum_{i=1}^{n}(x_i - \bar{x})^2}{n}} = \frac{\sum_{i=1}^{n} x_i}{n} \mp 3*\sqrt{\frac{\sum_{i=1}^{n}(x_i - \frac{\sum_{i=1}^{n} x_i}{n})^2}{n}} \quad (1)$$

The reliability analysis in the document about the reliable CM of telecommunication services with time-varying load characteristic assesses the three sigma rule without prior outlier annihilation as the most permissive threshold calculation method [2,3]. This upshot does not astonish considering that a large array of historic KPI values, and particularly outliers among them, drive up the standard deviation σ and, accordingly, the distance between the arithmetic mean $\bar{x}$ and the threshold $t_{3\sigma}$ [3]. On the one hand, this provides a high robustness against false condition changes. On the other hand, it increases the probability of missing condition changes.

Three Sigma Rule with Prior Outlier Removal A forerunning search and eradication of outliers with Algorithm 1 suppresses their erratic influence on the standard deviation σ_{red}. Let $\bar{x}_{red}$ denote the arithmetic mean and σ_{red} the standard deviation of the outlier-free array X_{red}, then (2) evaluates the threshold $t_{3\sigma_{red}}$ with the aid of the three sigma rule.

$$
t_{3\sigma_{red}} = \bar{x}_{red} \mp 3 * \sigma_{red} = \bar{x}_{red} \mp 3 * \sqrt{\frac{\sum_{i=r_{min}}^{n+1-r_{max}} (x_i - \bar{x}_{red})^2}{n+2-r_{max}-r_{min}}}
$$

$$
= \frac{\sum_{i=r_{min}}^{n+1-r_{max}} x_i}{n+2-r_{max}-r_{min}} \mp 3 * \sqrt{\frac{\sum_{i=r_{min}}^{n+1-r_{max}} (x_i - \frac{\sum_{i=r_{min}}^{n+1-r_{max}} x_i}{n+2-r_{max}-r_{min}})^2}{n+2-r_{max}-r_{min}}} \qquad (2)
$$

It must not be inferred that the elements of the outlier-free array X_{red} are normally distributed. If anybody prefers not to apply an algorithm (like the three sigma rule), which fits for input sets based on the Gaussian distribution, to arrays without knowing their distributions, the below-mentioned approach might be a feasible alternative.

Minimum or Maximum Value. After the outlier extinction with Algorithm 1, a very simple threshold evaluation considers all elements of the outlier-free array X_{red} as the bandwidth of KPI values that represents the normal condition of the monitored service. On this basis, the boundary values of X_{red} barely occurred within the normal condition. If too low KPI values signify an abnormal condition, (3) determines the smallest element of X_{red} as the threshold t_{min}. Conversely, (4) stipulates the largest element of X_{red} as t_{max} if too high KPI values stand for an abnormal condition.

$$
t_{min} = min(X_{red}) \qquad (3)
$$

$$
t_{max} = max(X_{red}) \qquad (4)
$$

It goes without saying that this technique mandatorily requires foregoing prudential outlier obliteration. Otherwise, abnormal KPI values would become thresholds and might prevent condition changes.

In a broader sense, all three threshold computation techniques belong to the type of unsupervised machine learning since they are supposed to compute unlabeled data sets. This saves training stages and even enables their proper operation with only one historical KPI value.

The undermentioned section elaborates a warning and a critical threshold out of the three previously evaluated thresholds.

3   Threshold Selection

The pick of a warning and a critical threshold needs $t_{3\sigma}$, $t_{3\sigma_{red}}$, and t_{min} respectively t_{max} as a sorted array. The CM of too low KPI values desires their ascending sorting, viz. $T_{min} = \{t_1, t_2, t_3 | t_1 \leq t_2 \leq t_3\}$. Inversely, the CM of too high KPI values requisitions their descending order, i.e. $T_{max} = \{t_1, t_2, t_3 | t_1 \geq t_2 \geq t_3\}$. The time complexity of this reordering in either direction does not exceed $\mathcal{O}(3 * log(3)) = \mathcal{O}(1)$ and, therewith, consequently continues the lightweight behavior of the outlier elimination in Subsect. 2.1 and the threshold computation methods in Subsect. 2.2. Each of the approaches in the Subsects. 3.1, 3.2, and 3.3 disregards one element of T_{min} respectively T_{max}.

3.1   The Tolerant Approach

This approach leaves t_3 of T_{min} and T_{max} out of further consideration. This omission concerns the highest threshold of T_{min} and the lowest of T_{max}. In accordance with (5) and (6), t_2 becomes the warning threshold t_{warn} and t_1 the critical threshold t_{crit}. Because t_1 and t_2 typify the lowest elements of T_{min} and the highest of T_{max}, the chance of (wrong) condition changes remains minimal.

$$t_{warn} = t_2 \tag{5}$$

$$t_{crit} = t_1 \tag{6}$$

It must be remarked that (5) and (6) could miss the creation of needful condition changes due to too much tolerance. For this reason, one might resort to more rigor in the subsequent subsection.

3.2   The Balanced Approach

This option omits t_2 rather than t_3 and, thence, (7) adopts t_3 as the warning threshold t_{warn} instead of t_2. As aforementioned, t_3 serves as the highest threshold of T_{min} and as the lowest of T_{max}. It can be expected that any imminent incident entails KPI values that facilely undershoot t_3 of T_{min} respectively overshoot t_3 of T_{max}. Compared to (6), (8) again assigns t_1 to t_{crit} and, with it, proffers the longest warning period.

$$t_{warn} = t_3 \tag{7}$$

$$t_{crit} = t_1 \tag{8}$$

If the responsible staff has become desensitized and generally dismisses warning signals as annoying nuisances, then the balanced approach turns out to be suboptimal. The higher strictness in the next subsection offers a possible remedy.

3.3   The Strict Approach

The least tolerance ensues with the omittance of t_1 rather than of t_2 or t_3. Omitting t_1 allows t_3 staying the warning threshold t_{warn} according to (9). In relation to the balanced approach, t_2 takes over the role of the critical threshold t_{crit} from the omitted t_1 as per (10). This swap shortens the warning period and declares abnormal KPI values as critical faster.

$$t_{warn} = t_3 \tag{9}$$

$$t_{crit} = t_2 \tag{10}$$

In consummation of this section, it can be tacitly assumed that the tolerant approach causes the lowermost number of condition changes among all threshold choosing options. This perfectly avoids false condition changes but is rather prone to missing ones.

The duration of exceptional conditions determined by the balanced and the strict approach ought to coincide because of their identical warning threshold. The tighter critical threshold of the strict approach gives rise to expectations of longer critical and shorter warning phases than the balanced approach.

The following section reports on the suitability of the three competitors.

4   Reliability Analysis

This section scrutinizes the reliability of the three threshold selecting alternatives for two exemplary telecommunication services. The investigation results probably differ for other examinable service candidates.

A viable threshold picking procedure has to fulfill the knock-out-criterion of causing neither false hard states nor misses of absolutely essential hard conditions for a scrutinized service. If several strategies comply with this must-have, then the amount of caused soft states decides their ranking.

A freshly emerged aberrant condition stays soft for a predefined retention period before it enters the hard state with an obligatory notification to the responsible administration folks. This protective mechanism ensures that short-time threshold exceedances during this time span do not wreak unnecessary hard states and, as a consequence, desensitizing notifications.

Apart from the already presumed policy of nary a false or missing hard condition, the threshold culling strategy with the most triggered soft states wins because of the best sensitivity to hard conditions in case of KPI deterioration.

For the sake of consistency, the CMS of the references [2] and [3] again measured both KPIs, computed their thresholds, and documented their state (transitions). The key data of the CMS can be abstracted as follows.

- **Hardware:** 2 HP ProLiant DL360 G6, each with 32 2.4 GHz CPU-cores and 36 GB main memory
- **Operating System:** Fedora Linux release 33 64-bit
- **Cluster Engine:** Corosync with Pacemaker

- **Condition Monitoring System:** Nagios 4.4.5
- **Plug-in Programming Language:** PHP 7.4.15

As aforementioned, the CMS sensed two independent, non-publicly available KPIs and exerted all three threshold selection strategies of Sect. 3 on each of them [3].

The first KPI displays the received requests of a Domain Name Service (DNS). The second does the same for an Intelligent Network (IN) service. Each of these telecommunication services is intended for incessant duty and, thereto, hosted on a highly available infrastructure. Nonetheless, they diametrically differ in terms of their usage patterns. The DNS never idles, whereby its KPI does not assume the zero value under normal circumstances. On the contrary, the IN service oftentimes remains unused during nightly minutes and regularly causes zeros in its KPI history. The screenshots in Fig. 1 and Fig. 2 zoom in on the amount of inbound requests (vertical axes) during a paradigmatic time slot from midnight to 6 a.m. (horizontal axes) of an ordinary weekday in order to clearly illustrate the dissimilarity of both services.

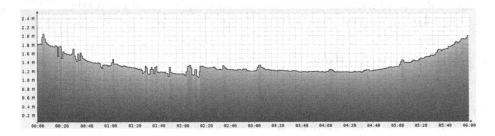

Fig. 1. DNS KPI

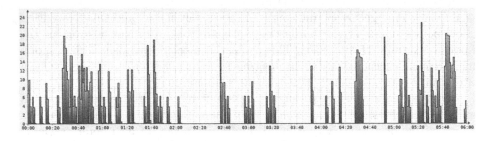

Fig. 2. IN KPI

Despite their disparity, an identical test configuration applied to both KPIs for the sake of comparability.

The CMS polled every KPI at intervals of 60 s, i.e. the system maintained a granularity of one minute.

For the threshold evaluations, it loaded those 52 historic values of each KPI from the correspondent Round Robin Database (RRD) that a KPI had assumed exactly a week ago, exactly two weeks ago, ..., exactly 51 weeks ago, and exactly 52 weeks ago. This period of a year was chosen because it better covers all conceivable low and high usage seasons than any other period.

For the sake of comparableness with the predecessor [3], the examination outcome in this section also includes the statistics for single (critical) thresholds based upon Sect. 2 rather than only for pairs of warning and critical thresholds in compliance with Sect. 3. For the same reason, the retention interval of ten consecutive threshold exceedances between a first soft and a potentially resulting hard condition persists.

Table 1 reveals the number of nil threshold exceedances for the DNS during an observed calendar month.

Table 1. Threshold Exceedances/Notifications of DNS

	Warning	Critical
Three sigma rule without prior outlier removal	N/A	0/0
Three sigma rule with prior outlier removal	N/A	0/0
Minimum value	N/A	0/0
Tolerant approach	0/0	0/0
Balanced approach	0/0	0/0
Strict approach	0/0	0/0

Accordingly, the DNS neither caused a single notification. This result should not amaze readers since this permanently accessed service all but uninterruptedly operates owing to the underlying high-availability infrastructure. The antecedent disquisition just as well discloses the absence of any notifications [3]. Albeit such a finding delights the users and the owner of this DNS, its scientific usefulness leaves something to be desired. In this case, there is nothing else for it but to choose as little permissiveness as doable by dint of the minimum value method. Proponents of two-threshold-approaches would rather continue the DNS monitoring with the strict approach.

As opposed to Table 1, Table 2 refers to the IN service and presents different amounts of condition changes for each threshold (pair).

The figures of the single-threshold-ways in the upper three rows resemble those in the paper about outlier removal for the reliable CM of telecommunication services [3]. All detected a multitude of soft condition changes to a greater or lesser extent. The three sigma rule without and with prior outlier effacement did not trigger any notification. In contrast, the more rigorous minimum value technique has shaped up as unfeasible for the IN service with a plurality of 272 obviously false notifications.

Table 2. Threshold Exceedances/Notifications of IN Service

	Warning	Critical
Three sigma rule without prior outlier removal	N/A	1,683/0
Three sigma rule with prior outlier removal	N/A	2,112/0
Minimum value	N/A	10,922/272
Tolerant approach	509/0	1,572/2
Balanced approach	9,466/275	1,552/9
Strict approach	9,003/271	2,064/10

The numbers in the underpart of Table 2 acknowledge the three two-threshold-methods as hybrids of their origins in the upper half. The 2,112 threshold exceedances of the three sigma rule with prior outlier extermination roughly split into 509 soft warning and 1,572 soft critical states of the tolerant approach. The approximately 11,000 soft condition changes of the balanced and of the strict approach similarly evolve from the 10,922 threshold exceedances of the minimum value policy. The zero warning notifications of the tolerant approach stem from the absent critical hard states of the three sigma rule. Likewise, the 275 of the balanced and 271 warning notifications of the strict approach originate from the 272 critical hard states in the third line. There is nothing left but to verify the two, nine, and ten critical notifications in the right column of the lower three rows for their validity. A scrutiny of the IN service unveils its perfect availability of 100 percent during the observed calendar month and, as a result, outs all critical hard states in Table 2 as false alarms.

Both the balanced and the strict approach with hundreds of warning and few critical notifications definitely impart a wrong picture of the fully working IN service and, for that reason, do not suit in this case. The tolerant approach falls in the category *borderline*. Undoubtedly, it twice let the IN service enter the hard critical state by mistake. A closer inspection descries that the first of these false alerts only lasted one minute, and the second two minutes. A slightly longer retention time of twelve in lieu of ten minutes would easily have averted them in that case. The tolerant approach apparently appears as an expedient, but more rigorous substitute for both single-threshold-methods that are based upon the three sigma rule.

However service administrators eventually design their decision-making process for a suitable threshold computation and selection strategy, they are well advised to start with the top of the itemization afterward and gradually descend to stricter methods whenever absent notifications impend or have already happened.

- Three sigma rule without prior outlier removal
- Three sigma rule with prior outlier removal
- Tolerant approach
- Balanced approach
- Strict approach
- Minimum value

Although the pairing of a warning and a critical threshold distinctly extend the range of possibilities, the successional section unambiguously defines this scholarly piece as a scientific snapshot, which doubtlessly deserves continuation.

5 Conclusion

The field test in Sect. 4 demonstrates the utility of the three two-threshold-techniques explicated in Sect. 3 for a decision-maker who deems the three sigma rule with prior outlier removal as too lax and the minimum value technique as too stern for the CM of a KPI.

While Sect. 3 proposes three ilks to cull two out of three thresholds, it behooves at this point to abstractly present how to condense an array, which contains m arbitrary thresholds, to a pair. The CM of too low KPI values again calls for its ascending sorting to $T_{min} = \{t_1, \cdots, t_m | 1 \leq i < m \wedge (\forall i)t_1 \leq t_{i+1}\}$. Vice versa, the CM of too high KPI values presupposes descendingly reordered elements in $T_{max} = \{t_1, \cdots, t_m | 1 \leq i < m \wedge (\forall i)t_1 \geq t_{i+1}\}$. Whilst $m \ll n$, the reordering time costs $\mathcal{O}(m*log(m))$ do not violate the requirement of algorithmic lightweightness.

5.1 The Generalized Tolerant Approach

Equation 11 generalizes the warning threshold of the tolerant approach t_{warn} by using the median of T_{min} or T_{max} as warning threshold. For instance, $m = 3$ leads to $t_{warn} = t_{\lceil \frac{3}{2} \rceil} = t_2$ in agreement with (5).

$$t_{warn} = \begin{cases} t_{\lceil \frac{m}{2} \rceil} & \text{if } m \equiv 1 \mod 2 \\ \frac{t_{\frac{m}{2}} + t_{\frac{m}{2}+1}}{2} & \text{if } m \equiv 0 \mod 2 \end{cases} \tag{11}$$

Because the critical threshold of the tolerant approach t_{crit} always equals the foremost element t_1 of T_{min} or T_{max}, (12) accords with (6).

$$t_{crit} = t_1 \tag{12}$$

5.2 The Generalized Balanced Approach

Equation 13 uses the hindmost element t_m of T_{min} or T_{max} as the warning threshold of the balanced approach t_{warn}. Equation 7 proves that for $m = 3$ with $t_{warn} = t_3$.

$$t_{warn} = t_m \tag{13}$$

As the tolerant approach, the balanced one assigns the leading t_1 of T_{min} or T_{max} to its critical threshold t_{crit}. On this account, (14) conforms to (8).

$$t_{crit} = t_1 \tag{14}$$

5.3   The Generalized Strict Approach

The strict approach inherits the rearmost element t_m of T_{min} or T_{max} as its warning threshold t_{warn} from the tolerant approach as shown in (15). On that account, $t_{warn} = t_3$ for $m = 3$ in 9.

$$t_{warn} = t_m \tag{15}$$

The critical threshold of the strict approach t_{crit} equates to the warning threshold of the tolerant one. On account of this, (16) again exhibits the calculation of the median of T_{min} or T_{max}, and (10) yields $t_{crit} = t_{\lceil \frac{3}{2} \rceil} = t_2$ for $m = 3$.

$$t_{crit} = \begin{cases} t_{\lceil \frac{m}{2} \rceil} & \text{if } m \equiv 1 \mod 2 \\ \frac{t_{\frac{m}{2}} + t_{\frac{m}{2}+1}}{2} & \text{if } m \equiv 0 \mod 2 \end{cases} \tag{16}$$

5.4   Future Work

This work can be readily continued in three dimensions.

Firstly, the lightweight outlier expunction in Subsect. 2.1 evidentially does a good job. Hopefully, prospective research will educe ameliorated successors that can perform even better.

Secondly, Subsect. 2.2 showcases merely three threshold calculation techniques that excel at the reliable CM of telecommunication services. Adequate enhancements are certainly developable. If sufficiently lightweight, all kinds of machine learning algorithms (supervised, semi-supervised, and unsupervised) can qualify for it.

Thirdly, the same applies to the three two-threshold-strategies presented in Sect. 3 and universalized in this section. The arithmetic average of T_{min} or T_{max} as a threshold could be an unsophisticated amelioration. In addition, even the prior application of the outlier erasement in Subsect. 2.1 on T_{min} or T_{max} (to dispose of outlying thresholds) might deserve study.

Acknowledgments. Many thanks to Bettina Baumgartner from the University of Vienna for proofreading this paper!

References

1. Davies, A.W.: Handbook of Condition Monitoring-Techniques and Methodology. Springer, Dordrecht (1996). https://doi.org/10.1007/978-94-011-4924-2
2. Fahrnberger, G.: Reliable condition monitoring of telecommunication services with time-varying load characteristic. In: Negi, A., Bhatnagar, R., Parida, L. (eds.) ICD-CIT 2018. LNCS, vol. 10722, pp. 173–188. Springer, Cham (2018). https://doi.org/10.1007/978-3-319-72344-0_14
3. Fahrnberger, G.: Outlier removal for the reliable condition monitoring of telecommunication services. In: 2019 20th International Conference on Parallel and Distributed Computing, Applications and Technologies (PDCAT), pp. 240–246 (2019). https://doi.org/10.1109/PDCAT46702.2019.00052

4. Pukelsheim, F.: The three sigma rule. Am. Stat. **48**(2), 88–91 (1994). https://doi. org/10.2307/2684253
5. Walsh, J.E.: Some nonparametric tests of whether the largest observations of a set are too large or too small. Ann. Math. Stat. **21**(4), 583–592 (1950). https://doi.org/ 10.1214/aoms/1177729753
6. Walsh, J.E.: Correction to "some nonparametric tests of whether the largest observations of a set are too large or too small". Ann. Math. Stat. **24**(1), 134–135 (1953). https://doi.org/10.1214/aoms/1177729095

A Blockchain to Bridge Business Information Systems and Industrial Automation Environments in Supply Chains

Karl Seidenfad, Tim Hoiss[(⊠)], and Ulrike Lechner[(⊠)]

Computer Science Department, Universität der Bundeswehr München, Munich, Germany
{karl.seidenfad,tim.hoiss,ulrike.lechner}@unibw.de

Abstract. The design of information systems using distributed ledger technologies needs to balance the potential of disruptive technologies with community needs. The NutriSafe project implements a blockchain-based infrastructure for food supply chains using the Hyperledger Fabric framework. The paper presents results from engineering a blockchain-based solution for food production and logistics with process models, architecture, and concepts and two focus areas: the bridges between business information systems to blockchain and from Internet of Things technology to blockchain. The article discusses the concepts of integrating the blockchain infrastructure across all layers of the automation pyramid, with the implications of integrating operational technology and storing semantics between products and machinery on a distributed ledger. Throughout, ideas and designs take the needs of small and medium-sized organizations into account and aim for an open, distributed approach inspired by the edge computing philosophy.

Keywords: Blockchain · Industrial automation · Semantic IoT · Architecture

1 Introduction and Motivation

Distributed Ledger Technology, also known as blockchain technology, is an innovative technology for online communities of all kinds: cryptocurrencies, educational certificates, or supply chain tracing and tracking are example applications in which blockchain brings benefits to a community. Distributed ledger technologies come with the promises of effortless information sharing and high levels of information security. However, unlocking the potential of Distributed Ledger Technology for everyday business cases and ecosystems with business information systems and operational technologies is an endeavor that calls for software engineering considerations. The use case considered here is the supply chain and, in particular, the food production and logistics.

A supply chain can be seen as a community with a shared interest in delivering value to the customer and the safety and security of products and services. A primary driver in designing the blockchain infrastructure is the tracking & tracing capability to ensure food safety.

This paper contributes to software engineering and, in particular, software engineering of business information systems with distributed ledger technologies with the

© Springer Nature Switzerland AG 2021
U. R. Krieger et al. (Eds.): I4CS 2021, CCIS 1404, pp. 22–40, 2021.
https://doi.org/10.1007/978-3-030-75004-6_3

business requirements of small and mediums sized organizations in mind. Scenarios and models contribute to the understanding of benefits and use cases of the novel Distributed Ledger Technology and the integration path of operational technology and blockchains describes bridges between blockchain and operational technology for an efficient integration. The paper aims to increase effectiveness and efficiency of design of innovative information systems for communities that use blockchain.

The paper is organized as follows. Section 2 summarizes the state of the art in blockchain technology by referencing various blockchain-based projects in the field of supply chain, industrial production and IoT. Section 3 presents the research design which is guided by the design science paradigm and Sect. 4 introduces the supply chain business case of NutriSafe. Section 5 depicts the NutriSafe approach of integrating traditional information systems, such as ERP systems. Section 6 extends this approach by integrating operational technology, such as PLC, MQTT and semantic IoT. The focus lies on interoperability by the "bridges" between blockchain and business information systems and between blockchain and operational technology, to empower applications for advanced analytics. Section 7 concludes the paper and points out our next steps.

2 State of the Art

The article contributes to the design and development of blockchains and software architecture and considers first blockchain technology and, second, notable blockchain-driven projects in the fields of supply chain management (SCM) and IoT.

Current research is strongly focusing on pure technical improvements such as higher transaction performance and advanced cryptography. We identified a need regarding a better orchestration between off-chain and on-chain operations and a simpler integration of operations research disciplines, such as Process Mining [1], Machine Learning etc. The context of this research is project NutriSafe and we aim to increase maturity for SCM applications of blockchain technology within small and medium-sized organizations.

2.1 Blockchain Technology

Distributed ledger technologies are a family of technologies for decentralized data storage in a distributed structure of nodes, also called peers. Blockchain, a subset from DLT, describes a technology for distributed data storage in a peer-to-peer network, with the option of guaranteed code execution via smart contracts. Blocks structure data and transactions. The blocks are written to the so-called ledger, i.e., the blockchain, using consensus algorithms among network nodes. These blocks are validated and attached to the predecessor block in a tamper-proof manner by cryptographic concatenation. A new block has a header, is linked to the predecessor block by the hash value, and comprises selected transactions. The number of aggregated transactions into one block is determined by the blockchain protocol and may be configured. For a review of algorithms and mechanisms, see [2].

A classification of blockchain technologies can be made by the blockchain's exposure and the right to be part of the consensus. There are public, private, permissioned, or permissionless blockchains. "Public" defines the exposure of the blockchain itself, and everyone can access it, which is most common in cryptocurrencies. The possibility to be part of the consensus differentiates public blockchains. Popular cryptocurrencies like Bitcoin or Ethereum are permissionless, which allows, in theory, everyone to be a so-called miner and determine the next block. Private permissioned blockchains are often used in a business context or industrial consortiums. Blockchain frameworks used in supply chains range from private permissioned blockchains as Hyperledger Fabric [3] or Hyperledger Sawtooth [4] to public permissionless blockchains as Ethereum [5].

Various studies analyze business needs. Notable research is by Weking et al. [6] on taxonomy of blockchain-based business models. An essential contribution to blockchains' costs do Sedlmaier et al. [7] with their analysis of the energy consumption. The systematic review of applications of blockchain technology in supply chain management by Dietrich et al. [8] lists more than 40 blockchain projects in a structured analysis.

2.2 Design Elements and Projects

The widely known blockchain frameworks Hyperledger [9] and Ethereum [10] define core concepts as decentralized networks, cryptography, consensus algorithms, smart contracts, and data structures [11] to achieve certain governance and security levels.

In software engineering of blockchain-based information systems, there are various design pattern approaches. Fundamental conceptualization and design topics of blockchain technology for supply chains in Industry 4.0 scenarios discuss Epiphaniou et al. [12]. In [3] a commercial platform for tracking containers and their documentation and its benefit for global supply chains is described.

For the application domain supply chain, Liu et al. [13] identify design patterns grounded in a traceability system's design and development. Their design pattern language consists of creational patterns, structural patterns, inter-behavioral patterns, and intra-behavioral patterns. This pattern language goes beyond the technical level and addresses "traceability" as the primary use case of many blockchain implementation projects. Salah et al. [5] present a solution for tracing, tracking, and performing business transactions of soybeans in agriculture supply chains using the public blockchain Ethereum. Another SCM-based approach was introduced by Miehle et al. [14] in project PartChain. The project's scope is designing a Hyperledger-based network for the automotive supply chain and a corresponding tracing application for automotive parts.

Other implementation examples, utilizing blockchains, are in industrial automation [15] and IoT [16]. Schmiedel [17] introduces a project to retrofit an additive manufacturing machine by utilizing Hyperledger Fabric to serve a secure machine history to build business models like pay-per-use or predictive maintenance on top of it.

The majority of IoT applications rely on protocols like MQTT [18] using a publish-subscribe mechanism. This protocol utilizes a messaging broker that manages the communication. That centralized architecture turns a messaging broker into a primary target for tampering IoT data. Ramachandran et al. [19] introduce an approach to combine a publish-subscribe broker with blockchain-based immutability.

3 Method

The research is guided by the design science paradigm [20, 21] and the overall research project follows an iterative approach. Design of technology, scenario analysis goes hand in hand with the engineering of blockchain technology. The paper represents the design and experiences after conceptualization, design, and implementation of blockchain with core functionality, the advanced functionality of tracing and tracking, and the integration of various business information systems via a REST API and other interfaces, as well as the identification of design patterns [22]. This article is the result of reflection on the learnings in the design process. The second main part of the paper, the integration of operational technology with blockchain, is more conceptual with design and implementation as ongoing work.

This article extends previous work on the research design [23], IoT integration with blockchain [24], blockchain design patterns [22] and design principles [25]. The project contains 3 Docker repositories, 9 different Github repositories with about 200 k lines of code, and 12 contributors.

4 The NutriSafe Business Case

The design of blockchain infrastructures for the supply chain of food production and logistics is the objective of the research project NutriSafe (cf. nutrisafe.de, nutrisafe.at), which is the context. Increasing the resilience of the food supply chain is a goal of the project NutriSafe. The project uses blockchain as a means for seamless and secure information flows across the supply chain.

In this paper, we consider the increase of the level of resilience of a supply chain by leveraging tracing & tracking functionalities: blockchain enables identification of the source of a food safety issue and increases the effectiveness of both alerts and recalls. For this analysis, we use a scenario of the production of soft cheese from fresh milk. Examples for food safety issues include, e.g., failures of production lines that lead to quality issues in the final product, temperatures in transportation may be wrong. Again, the product's quality may not meet quality standards, or a zoonosis can infect a product in transport or maturation. An IT security issue may lead to faulty labels or documentation. Products need to be destroyed as their quality can no longer be guaranteed.

The supply chain and the increase of resilience of the supply chain is the topic of this research. Accordingly, the community considered includes not only producing-organizations as, e.g., farmers and logistics service providers but also public authorities as, e.g., food authorities and IT-service providers. The community uses a stakeholder map shown in Fig. 1 and the NutriSafe infrastructure as the central element of the design. The community comprises many actors typical for any food supply chain and actors specific for the scenario of soft cheese production, namely dairy and milk truck.

The supply chain depicted in Fig. 2 starts with the milk farm. The milk farm hands over the fresh milk to a milk truck, which transports milk to the dairy and takes a sample for quality checks. The dairy processes fresh milk to produce, e.g., soft cheese transported by a logistics service provider to a retailer. The end customer buys the product, the soft cheese, at a grocery store. We assume that all actors (as depicted in Figs. 2 and 3) use

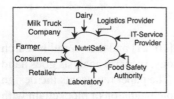

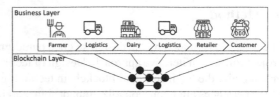

Fig. 1. Stakeholder map for the cheese supply chain

Fig. 2. Supply chain access to the blockchain

the blockchain to share information concerning production and logistics. A core user story is the creation of traceable product history. The product history is, e.g., providing information to the end-customer or for efficient tracking and tracing in a food safety issue.

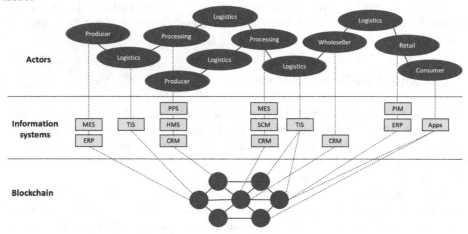

Fig. 3. Conceptual architecture of a DLT-based supply chain

The conceptual architecture of a blockchain as infrastructure is depicted in Fig. 3. Actors have their information systems: ERP Systems, customer relationship management systems (CRM), herd management systems (HMS), and systems used by logistics service providers to manage transportation.

Note that the depicted supply chain is quite linear. In reality, there are many farmers, logistics service providers, production facilities, wholesalers, and retailers that participate in a supply chain. An analysis of the scenarios resulted in requirements and design decisions.

- Cost-efficiency: Many actors in food production and logistics would be small and medium-sized companies with limited IT capabilities. Also, food production and logistics is a price-sensitive industry sector with small margins.
- Food safety: The numbers of alerts and recalls in the food sector are on the rise. Digital technologies may increase effectiveness and efficiency in identifying food safety causes, alarms, and recalls.

- Visibility and new services: while visibility throughout the supply chain is desirable for resilience, it is crucial who can access information: competitors may not see information about supplies, and customers, wrong information in the blockchain cannot stay there: blackmailing or human errors are perceived to be a threat. This discussion about visibility and confidentiality motivates our decision for the permissioned blockchain Hyperledger Fabric framework.

5 Information Systems and Blockchain Integration

This first main part presents the blockchain and its integration with the business information systems. The architecture with three layers is presented first, followed by a more detailed description of layers with integration components, the conceptual data model, and the necessary scripts for blockchain operations to manage the infrastructure.

5.1 The Architecture

The technical architecture is structured in three layers, as depicted in Fig. 4. The top "UI Layer" is populated by user-facing applications and enterprise applications. The applications enable end-users to store and access data in the blockchain.

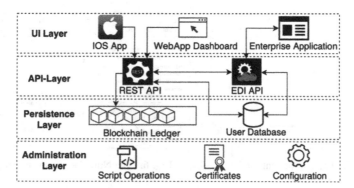

Fig. 4. The layered architecture to bridge between applications and blockchain network

The UI Layer contains the WebApp dashboard, an IOS application designed to enable mobile access and information provision to the blockchain state. The web application and the IOS app use JSON over HTTP to send REST-Calls to the NutriSafe REST-API.

The API-layer is the middle layer of the technical architecture. The REST API and the EDI API provide the connectivity of user faced applications and the blockchain infrastructure. In small and medium-sized enterprises, EDI is a common standard for communication with business partners. REST is the de-facto standard for web-interfaces. We propose an EDI-API which enables accessibility by enterprise applications.

The third layer is the "Persistence Layer" with the blockchain ledger and a shared user database. The shared user database enables the authenticity of users or systems for all APIs. The web application provides user management with an interface for adding, deleting, and changing user details and rights to invoke chaincode. Note that the current implementation uses whitelisting to define rights for function calls. Hyperledger Fabric in the 2.2 LTS version is used as the technical platform for the blockchain.

The fourth layer contains the operational support and necessities for configuring and maintaining a Hyperledger Fabric network. The designed scripts for creating update transactions enable a fast way to expand the network. Configuration files are inherent by the blockchain framework and are customized for our scenario.

5.2 API-Layer: REST API and Meta Model

The REST API provides the interface for all web applications to the blockchain. Note that the first design iteration of NutriSafe utilizes a REST API for each organization.

The RESTful interface (cf. Fig. 5) provides a set of functions to enable the interaction with the NutriSafe Hyperledger Fabric network. To authenticate the transaction proposals to the blockchain network, the user's organization's certificate and the corresponding key have to be accessible for the REST API. Custom clients transfer username and password to receive a JSON Web Token (JWT) per session on the REST API. Since the REST API hosts its own user database, user management is also part of its feature set. Customizable whitelists define the function calls per user and are adjustable to chaincode updates.

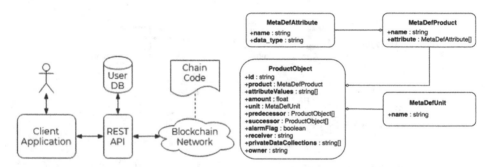

Fig. 5. The component model   **Fig. 6.** The NutriSafe meta-model pattern

The meta definition (cf. Fig. 6) consists of a flexible data model populated after the deployment of the chaincode on the blockchain. Product templates of different types (e.g., milk or cheese) can be defined. Each template consists of a fixed set of values and a set of optional attributes. Unique product lots are created with this template. A lot always contains a system-wide unique id, the current owner, the amount, the unit in which the amount is measured, the product template name, an alarm flag, a possible receiver, a list of attribute Values, a list of identifiers of predecessor and successor lot, a list of private data collections, and a list of previous owners with timestamps. The tracking of predecessor and successor lots enables an efficient forward and backward tracing of products. The alarm flag allows signaling a incident with the product lot.

Each optional attribute has a name field and type, which can be an integer or string. This approach enables a highly customizable data model depending on the products reflected on the blockchain, adjusted to the participants' needs. The meta-model can be updated on a running blockchain, and the REST API provides the functionality for updating. Note that an update of the meta-model can be done without chaincode deployment or restarting the blockchain.

5.3 Persistence Layer: Network Topology and Data Model

In Hyperledger Fabric, there are ordering nodes, endorsing, and committing peers. Ordering nodes are the central component that orders incoming transactions in blocks using the RAFT consensus algorithm. Endorsing peers have chaincode installed and are responsible for creating so-called Read-Write-Sets by executing the chaincode for a transaction proposal send by a client. After calculation, the result is sent back to the client without the transaction's commitment to the ledger. The Read-Write-Set is then sent to the ordering nodes for the transaction record and block creation.

Channels organize the peers. Each channel has its chaincode deployed and contains its blockchain. Transactions are only visible for all participants in the same channel.

In our scenario shown in Fig. 7, we instantiate two application channels: the first one provides a track-and-trace functionality for products of all kinds; the second one implements functions and data models for organizing shipments by a logistics network. In our scenario, one supply chain participant is part of both channels and, thus, sees all transactions. The construct of private data collections ensures confidentiality inside a channel. This allows sharing of information on a peer-to-peer basis without a recording of the data in the blockchain. To ensure private data integrity, a hash-value of the data is committed and stored in the blockchain. In general, the channel topology and private data collection structure depend on the consortium.

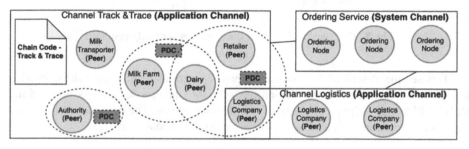

Fig. 7. Network topology and the channel configuration of the "soft cheese" scenario

5.4 Operations: Script Environment

The Hyperledger Fabric framework provides a set of scripts for basic network management operations by default [26]. A toolchain for the generation, configuration, and administration of fabric-based networks is realized using the Hyperledger Fabric framework's client software. However, most of the administrative operations require long sequences of commands executed in a strict order. Scripting those operations is fundamental for efficient network deployment and operation. This section introduces three advanced operations that are important for the dynamic customization of a large network with complex relations:

1. Create a new consortium. Creates an empty consortium in a system channel.[1]
2. Organization joins a consortium. The existence of a consortium and a representation of the joining organization with the necessary certificates are prerequisites.
3. Organization joins a channel. An application channel and a representation of the joining organization with the necessary certificates are prerequisites.

All scripts are applicable to all setups of Hyperledger Fabric networks (Version 2.2). The scripts simplify the operation by extracting all setup dependent information to variables inside the scripts, which also can be set by flags. Each script operation generates a configuration-update transaction and is not further proceeded. The generated file is distributed to the participants to sign. After fulfilling the network policy of necessary signatures, it can be committed to the network.

Our model of scripts for network management operations is depicted in Fig. 8: the script operations title, goal, parameters, environmental prerequisites, required files, and the desired output. The model empowers users to visualize the correlations between script operation and the surrounding environment.

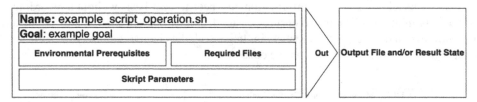

Fig. 8. Graphical approach for documenting scripted operations

This section described how to use scripted operations to configure the network's topology. We introduced a meta-definition, a flexible data model for products and the REST API as our endpoint to existing information systems. The next section discusses aspects of integrating assets of an industrial production ecosystem.

6   To New Shores - The Automation Ecosystem

The integration of blockchain into a system architecture with business information systems is now extended by integrating devices from industrial automation. Note that this section reports on concepts and works in progress. It refers to the automation pyramid, according to Siepmann et al. [27] and points out the need for more connectivity.

---

[1] Note that the consortium itself as an element in a Hyperledger Fabric network is depreciated in newer versions and Fabric version 2.2 (LTS) is the last one supporting this feature.

6.1 The Architecture

Our work, which is grounded in scenarios, business model analysis, and stakeholder interviews, identifies the potential of increased connectivity: for more secure and seamless information flows and more effective tracking and tracing. To exemplify this: in the production of soft cheese, it might be convenient to have the farm's information system as the system that first provides information about the fresh milk to the supply chain by storing it in the blockchain. This is probably sufficient for information about production conditions and the essential parameters, as, e.g., fat or protein in milk. It might be better for food safety reasons when cow and milking parlor provide information to the blockchain immediately – such that, e.g., hygiene issues at this level can be traced back to the origin. The same applies to transportation: E.g., the stability of temperature is often essential for food safety, and temperature information can be sent to the blockchain directly from an autonomous sensor, while CO_2 emissions associated with the transport would be calculated and sent by a business information system.

Therefore, it occurs to be the next logical step to provide advanced connectivity to the blockchain for "smart farming" infrastructures. We identified several heterogeneous systems like auto-ID solutions with RFID, conveyor systems, and robotics applications as candidates to be integrated in stakeholder interviews. These applications are firmly grounded in industrial automation, and the automation pyramid, as depicted in Fig. 9 is the reference model for our integration path.

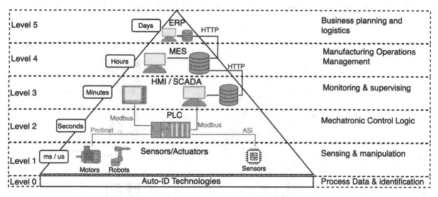

Fig. 9. The automation pyramid [27] and extend by time frames and sample devices

6.2 The Integration Path

The architecture of blockchain integrated with business information systems is the starting point. Business information systems, e.g., ERP systems, are located in level 5 of the automation pyramid. We present an integration path into the levels 4 to 0 and discuss use cases for each by inspecting a milk farm as a classical NutriSafe participant.

According to the analysis of Hofmeier [28], we characterize the milk farm as a participant in the food supply chain. The infrastructure of a farm with an administrative office and several stables is depicted in Fig. 10. Each stable has a PC running on Windows and utilizes herd management software (HMS) and software for robotic milking. Further Windows PC are in the office using the MS Office toolchain and running accounting software. Cows wear collars with RFID sensors, and robotic milking parlors collect data. A milk farm has many obligations for detailed documentation, which needs to be shared with authorities on demand.

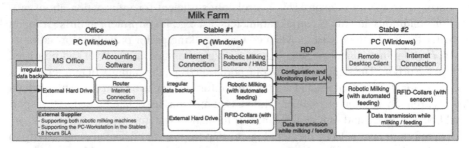

Fig. 10. The simplified IT infrastructure of a milk farm, according to Hofmeier [28]

Subsequently, we go through the milk farm's IT infrastructure as we encountered it in interviews [28]. The automation pyramid guides us from the ERP systems down to the mechatronic devices in the production. The architecture as we developed it to integrate blockchain, information systems, and Internet-of-Things is presented in Fig. 11.

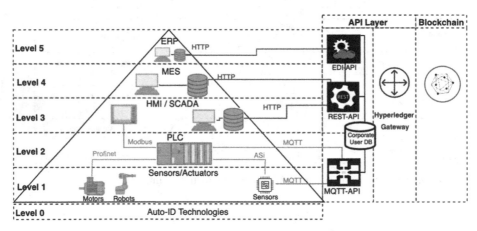

Fig. 11. The automation pyramid extended by a blockchain-based infrastructure and APIs

The blockchain is a collectively hosted infrastructure. The gateways are hosted locally by the organization and connect the organization to the blockchain infrastructure. Information systems on levels 5, 4, and 3 access the network via the Hyperledger gateway, which instantiates a REST API. To connect levels 2, 1, and 0 to the network, the Hyperledger gateway is instantiating an MQTT API that offers a Publish/Subscribe interface. Subsequently, we expose each level with practical integration examples.

Level 5 (Business Planning and Logistics). Level 5 is the core domain of NutriSafe and is shaped by ERP software systems. In our scenario, the milk farm's IT-systems can set HTTP-calls to the local REST API. This level is unchanged in terms of protocols and core connectivity elements (REST API) compared to Sect. 5.

Level 4 (Manufacturing Operations Management). The software in this architecture level is part of the manufacturing execution system (MES). The MES controls processes across multiple domains, such as performance analysis, quality management, track and trace, and product documentation. For example, milk farms use herd management systems (HMS) as an integrated solution that can be connected to the blockchain via a REST API in the same way as the information systems of level 5. Use cases for a milk farm are: sharing data with authorities, generation of trusted documentation, and tracing of products. The integration with blockchain enables the infrastructure for a trustworthy digital end-to-end process, which is a clear limitation of current solutions.

Level 3 (Monitoring and Supervising). This level is shaped by supervisory control and data acquisition (SCADA) and human-machine interfaces (HMI). SCADA systems gather data from a whole production line into a united view. Level 3 is the transition between managing and the execution level and provides data for the overlying MES. Tampering those data affects the farm's planning process, and since the time frame for MES ranges between hours and days, a manipulation is typically discovered late. SCADA systems are running in feature-rich environments such as desktop computers, allowing web applications to access the REST API. A use case in a milk farm is the visualization of the performance of each robotic milking system and committing valid overall equipment effectiveness (OEE) statements to NutriSafe.

Level 2 (Mechatronic Control Logic). This level is dominated by programable logic controllers (PLC). PLCs are used to control mechatronic functions in production. The devices are working closely with sensors and actuators on-site. In the case of a milk farm, applications are conveyor systems and robotic milking. PLC uses a wide range of Fieldbus technology, depending on the configuration and connected peripherals. Connecting an existing PLC-based solution with the blockchain in a non-invasive manner is a technical hurdle at this architecture level. PLC like SIEMENS S7 [29] can communicate over MQTT, a widely used protocol for Internet-of-Things. Therefore, an MQTT function block of the PLC supplier can be integrated, which is using the tag database of the PLC, without changing the existing control logic. Accordingly, the PLC is empowered to commit its data immediately to the blockchain network, without a vulnerable bypass [30] (p. 131). A milk farm-specific use case for the immediate bridging of PLC data into the blockchain can be the automated transfer of health parameters for each cow, read by the robotic milking. The feature empowers the farmer to monitor each animal's health and automatically generates a trustworthy history that can be shared with the food authority. Besides safety-relevant features, business models like pay-per-use and leasing contracts for robotic milking are enabled by this integration.

Level 1 (Sensing and Manipulation). Sensors and actuators are located in level one. Connecting devices of level one to the NutriSafe blockchain can be done by using the MQTT protocol again. Suppliers of industrial automation components offering specialized gateways to bridge telegrams from fieldbuses like IO-Link, to MQTT.

An architectural motivation for integrating level-one-devices into NutriSafe is to tackle a classical problem in the field of edge computing. Since PLC applications are designed to be cost-efficient, the capabilities are constrained by a lack of CPU-cycle-time [30] (p. 19). Shifting data of multiple IoT devices across one PLC, which bridges the payload between different protocols, can turn our PLC into a severe bottleneck. Therefore, balancing the load by empowering each sensor device to commit data is a strategy to keep mission-critical components like a PLC performing.

Level 0 (Process Data and Identification). The level is shaped by auto-ID technologies like RFID and optical markers like QR codes. A manual read can either integrate into NutriSafe with a smartphone using the REST API or an automated read by an industrial reader device that is MQTT enabled.

A milk farm-specific use case for the app-based solution can be the manual registration of goods. Utilizing the automated solution with an industrial RFID-reader, a use case in a milk farm can, e.g., identify animals in the stable. The feature empowers the farmer to provide a seamless record of the occupancy in each stable. Since we expect authorities to request those data more frequently, it will become a more common use case.

6.3 Integration of an MQTT API

The previous section elaborates the integration path for each architectural level with a REST API and an MQTT API as the endpoints for the integration on the client-side. Our approach is inspired by Ramachandran et al. [19] combining a network of MQTT-Brokers and blockchain-capabilities. Subsequently, we explain our architecture concept more in detail.

A setup with mechatronic components and an MES is depicted in Fig. 12. The MES is utilizing the REST API. The mechatronic components such as PLC and sensors are accessing our MQTT API, which consists of an MQTT broker and an MQTT-to-BC-Gateway. To increase interoperability, we propose all MQTT devices to be compliant with the Sparkplug B standard [31].

Since MQTT is offering a large flexibility for topic naming and payload encoding, this flexibility becomes a limitation when different organizations want to access distributed data of a less known OT-environment. Sparkplug is a standardization project by the Eclipse Foundation and a recent approach to reach more interoperability in the IoT, by making MQTT data more reasonable. It contains specifications for semantic topic naming, session states and payload management.

The concept shown in Fig. 12 utilizes two generic structures (cf. Figs. 6 and 13) as follows: The MES is aware of the machines' running jobs and knows the Sparkplug compliant namespace of each involved device. Each time a new job is finished, the MES adds the namespace of the active machine to the product-lot as a new attribute. Since the new lot is timestamped and contains a unique namespace, we can now query the ledger of the production machine precisely by the tuple of topic-domain and timestamp. Each

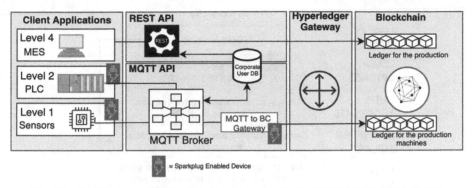

Fig. 12. Architecture with client applications accessing a REST API and MQTT API

device has its own ledger, and each ledger can be concatenated from top to down. I.e., a machine has its own ledger, which is referring to the ledgers of its subcomponents.

namespace/group_id/message_type/edge_node_id/[device_id]

Fig. 13. Template for a Sparkplug B compliant topic namespace

Our solution benefits from the combination of the generic structures of Sparkplug and the NutriSafe Meta Model. The flexible data model of NutriSafe (cf. Fig. 6) enables to address the full bandwidth of products in the food industry. Annotating predecessor and successor to each product-lot empowers, e.g., authorities to make a forward and backward tracing on the supply chain data. Within specific tracing cases, it is necessary to query data about the OT-environment which was involved in the production process.

Here Sparkplug comes into play. The semantic granularity ranges from production lines, over single machines and down to components such as actuators or sensors. Furthermore, industrial environments are shaped by patchworks of modern and also historically grown legacy infrastructures. Here our current data model faces limitations because it does not offer a means to integrate these infrastructural data.

According our approach, we plan to implement an MQTT-to-BC-Gateway, for the NutriSafe Software Toolkit, that is Sparkplug enabled and provides a configurable bridging functionality for OT-data to our blockchain-network. To fit the requirements of further analytics applications, using the gathered OT-data. The implementation addresses needs from the field of Data Science, which are depicted in a hierarchy of needs (cf. Fig. 14).

Our approach lays the foundation for further implementations regarding the layers Collect, Move/Store and Transform/Explore of Fig. 14. Following we are annotating open challenges for each layer.

COLLECT. The layer addresses connectivity of present sensors and the generation of context sensitive logs. While the usage of MQTT already increases connectivity, the problem of context sensitivity is still remaining. An example implementation guided by the philosophy of Sparkplug and a corresponding chaincode might be promising.

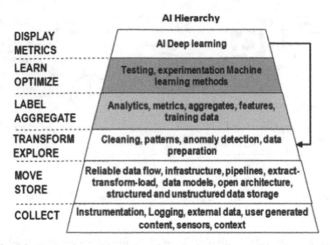

Fig. 14. Data science hierarchy of needs, according to Blasch et al. [32]

MOVE/STORE. The layer is targeting needs related to the consistency of data models, the presence of a trustworthy or at least reliable data pipeline, and the management of a reasonable storing. While supplying a trustworthy infrastructure is a core feature of blockchain technology, the system-wide rollout process for data models on-chain, needs to be extended by a strategy for annotating heterogenous data in a flexible way.

TRANSFORM/EXPLORE. The layer addresses tasks related to the cleaning of logs, pattern recognition and general preparation of data for further refining. Since data in the blockchain is immutable, cleaning up of data normally happens off-chain. To reduce the effort of post-processing off-chain, it might be interesting to outsource pattern recognition, anomaly detection and the cleaning up of data, to a corresponding chaincode. Since those refining tasks are encountered in multiple organizations, chaincode seems to be a good format to exchange algorithms inside a consortium.

Beside our main scenario of the tracking and tracing of products and the annotation of OT-data, the integration of an MQTT-based API with semantic structuring opens up the door for organizations in a consortium, to build advanced applications, utilizing the blockchain-network as a platform. Current research in the field of platform economies, especially for multi-sided markets, also identified the need of feature-rich API's and software artefacts, such as monitoring, filtering and analytics [33–35].

One question that needs to be resolved: Which functionality should be pushed to the chaincode? The functionality of the chaincode is available in the blockchain infrastructure. This might be convenient but increases the operational costs of the blockchain.

7 Conclusions and Next Steps

The paper introduces an architecture design approach for a blockchain-based infrastructure for communities. Supply chains in food production, logistics, and especially the production of soft cheese as scenario exemplifies and motivates the architecture decisions.

In the first part of the paper, we present our approach to connecting blockchain and business information systems as, e.g., ERP systems. Product lots are the central component handled in the blockchain, the meta-model allows for highly customizable data models, and the REST API uses a state-of-the-art interface to connect blockchain and business information systems. We also present our custom script operations for blockchain management and introduce a graphical notation for documenting script operations with parameters, prerequisites, and desired output.

In the second part, we present the integration path of operational technology to the blockchain. The automation pyramid guides this integration. While applications of levels 5, 4, and 3 are accessible by the REST API with small effort, layers 2 and 1 require a different solution. At this level, the integration faces constraints by limited hardware, the need for additional network components, and new reasonable data models. A Sparkplug compliant MQTT API is introduced in this context.

The edge computing paradigm guides the overall design – relying not on central structures as big databases or business information systems and central platform but leave autonomy to individual actors and devices as far as possible.

The blockchain increases the connectivity throughout all information systems across organizations and within organizations. Such increased visibility of the supply chain enables, e.g., seamless integration of information flows. We achieve cost efficiency through lightweight data models, the use of standards and technologies with strong community support (Hyperledger, REST, MQTT, Sparkplug, etc.), data models that can be seamlessly updated, and a collection of scripts to maintain the blockchain. We increase food safety through trustworthy documentation and protection against tampering by blockchain mechanisms. The Hyperledger Fabric framework provides us with permissions to tailor access to information according to business needs.

One of the next steps will be the technical implementation of the proposed software gateway, as a proof of concept and a platform for further evaluation, guided by a NutriSafe scenario in the food industry.

Our research aims at increasing resilience in food supply chains. Through information security within and across organizations, by digital, seamless information flows, the solution allows for better tracking & tracing and more effective notifications or recalls in case of food safety issues. In general, the COVID-19 pandemic shed light on supply chains' fragility: more and better services for supply chain management are needed and are expected to be implemented. Blockchain technologies are a candidate to contribute security and digital information integration to these new services to increase resilience.

Acknowledgments. We thank the German Federal Ministry of Education and Research (BMBF) for the funding of NutriSafe (FKZ: 13N15070). We would like to thank the German Federal Ministry of Education and Research (BMBF) and the Federal Ministry Republic of Austria – Agriculture, Regions and Tourism for funding the bilateral German-Austrian research project NutriSafe in the Sifo and Kiras Research programmes.

Furthermore, we want to thank Manfred Hofmeier for contributing information on the IT infrastructure in the food supply chain and Razvan Hrestic for discussions on the script environment of NutriSafe. We thank our colleagues Andreas Hermann, Tobias Wagner, Andreas Huber from

Universität der Bundeswehr, and Dennis Lamken from OTARIS GmbH for their contribution to the NutriSafe code base and their collaboration on the architecture. We also thank our German and Austrian project partners in NutriSafe for their interdisciplinary contributions and the reviewers of the I4CS conference for their careful and insightful comments.

References

1. Klinkmüller, C., Ponomarev, A., Tran, A.B., Weber, I., van der Aalst, W.: Mining blockchain processes: extracting process mining data from blockchain applications. In: Di Ciccio, C., et al. (eds.) BPM 2019. LNBIP, vol. 361, pp. 71–86. Springer, Cham (2019). https://doi.org/10.1007/978-3-030-30429-4_6
2. Yaga, D., Mell, P., Roby, N., Scarfone, K.: Blockchain technology overview (2018). https://doi.org/10.6028/NIST.IR.8202
3. Jensen, T., Hedman, J., Henningsson, S.: How TradeLens delivers business value with blockchain technology. MIS Q. Exec. **18**, 221–243 (2019). https://doi.org/10.17705/2msqe.00018
4. Caro, M.P., Ali, M.S., Vecchio, M., Giaffreda, R.: Blockchain-based traceability in Agri-Food supply chain management: a practical implementation. In: 2018 IoT Vertical and Topical Summit on Agriculture - Tuscany, IOT Tuscany 2018, pp. 1–4 (2018). https://doi.org/10.1109/IOT-TUSCANY.2018.8373021
5. Salah, K., Nizamuddin, N., Jayaraman, R., Omar, M.: Blockchain-based soybean traceability in agricultural supply chain. IEEE Access **7**, 73295–73305 (2019). https://doi.org/10.1109/ACCESS.2019.2918000
6. Weking, J., Mandalenakis, M., Hein, A., Hermes, S., Böhm, M., Krcmar, H.: The impact of blockchain technology on business models – a taxonomy and archetypal patterns. Electron. Mark. **30**, 285–305 (2020). https://doi.org/10.1007/s12525-019-00386-3
7. Sedlmeir, J., Buhl, H.U., Fridgen, G., Keller, R.: The energy consumption of blockchain technology: beyond myth. Bus. Inf. Syst. Eng. **62**, 599–608 (2020). https://doi.org/10.1007/s12599-020-00656-x
8. Dietrich, F., Ge, Y., Turgut, A., Louw, L., Palm, D.: Review and analysis of blockchain projects in supply chain management. Proc. Comput. Sci. **180**, 724–733 (2021). https://doi.org/10.1016/j.procs.2021.01.295
9. The Linux Foundation: Hyperledger Project
10. Diedrich, H.: Ethereum. Wildfire Publishing, Brookvale (2016)
11. Bundesamt für Sicherheit in der Informationstechnik: Blockchain sicher gestalten, 98 (2019)
12. Epiphaniou, G., Bottarelli, M., Al-Khateeb, H., Ersotelos, N.T., Kanyaru, J., Nahar, V.: Smart distributed ledger technologies in Industry 4.0: challenges and opportunities in supply chain management. In: Jahankhani, H., Kendzierskyj, S., Chelvachandran, N., Ibarra, J. (eds.) Cyber Defence in the Age of AI, Smart Societies and Augmented Humanity. ASTSA, pp. 319–345. Springer, Cham (2020). https://doi.org/10.1007/978-3-030-35746-7_15
13. Liu, Y., Lu, Q., Xu, X., Zhu, L., Yao, H.: Applying design patterns in smart contracts: a case study on a blockchain-based traceability application. In: Chen, S., Wang, H., Zhang, L.-J. (eds.) ICBC 2018. LNCS, vol. 10974, pp. 92–106. Springer, Cham (2018). https://doi.org/10.1007/978-3-319-94478-4_7
14. Miehle, D., Henze, D., Seitz, A., Luckow, A., Brügge, B.: PartChain: a decentralized traceability application for multi-tier supply chain networks in the automotive industry. In: 2019 IEEE International Conference on Decentralized Applications and Infrastructures, pp. 140–145 (2019)

15. Schorradt, S., Bajramovic, E., Freiling, F.: On the feasibility of secure logging for industrial control systems using blockchain. In: Proceedings of the Third Central European Cybersecurity Conference, CECC 2019 (2019). https://doi.org/10.1145/3360664.3360668

16. Singh, P.K., Singh, R., Nandi, S.K., Nandi, S.: Designing a blockchain based framework for IoT data trade. In: Rautaray, S.S., Eichler, G., Erfurth, C., Fahrnberger, G. (eds.) I4CS 2020. CCIS, vol. 1139, pp. 295–308. Springer, Cham (2020). https://doi.org/10.1007/978-3-030-37484-6_17

17. Schmiedel, C., Fraunhofer IPK: Die Hyperledger Fabric-Blockchain sorgt für Datensicherheit in der additiven Fertigung. https://www.ipk.fraunhofer.de/de/publikationen/futur/futur-online-exklusiv/vertrauen40.html. Accessed 09 Jan 2021

18. OASIS: MQTT Version 5.0. https://docs.oasis-open.org/mqtt/mqtt/v5.0/mqtt-v5.0.html. Accessed 10 Jan 2021

19. Ramachandran, G.S., et al.: Trinity: a byzantine fault-tolerant distributed publish-subscribe system with immutable blockchain-based persistence. In: 2019 IEEE International Conference on Blockchain and Cryptocurrency (ICBC), pp. 227–235 (2019). https://doi.org/10.1109/BLOC.2019.8751388

20. Hevner, A.R., March, S.T., Park, J., Ram, S.: Design science in information systems research. Des. Sci. IS Res. MIS Q. **28**, 75–105 (2004). https://doi.org/10.2307/25148625

21. Baskerville, R., Pries-Heje, J.: Explanatory design theory. Bus. Inf. Syst. Eng. **2**, 271–282 (2010). https://doi.org/10.1007/s12599-010-0118-4

22. Lamken, D., et al.: Design patterns and framework for blockchain integration in supply chains. In: 2021 IEEE International Conference on Blockchain and Cryptocurrency (ICBC) (2021, to appear)

23. Reimers, T., et al.: Absicherung von Wertschöpfungsketten in der Lebensmittelproduktion und -logistik mittels Distributed-Ledger-Technologie: Das Forschungsdesign. In: Bundesamt für Sicherheit in der Informationstechnik (eds.) Tagungsband zum 16. Deutschen IT-Sicherheitskongress, pp. 373–383. SecuMedia Verlag, Bonn (2019)

24. Reimers, T., Leber, F., Lechner, U.: Integration of blockchain and Internet of Things in a car supply chain. In: 2019 IEEE International Conference on Decentralized Applications and Infrastructures (DAPPCON), pp. 146–151 (2019). https://doi.org/10.1109/DAPPCON.2019.00028

25. Hoiß, T., et al.: Design of blockchain-based information systems – design principles from the NutriSafe project. In: Clohessy, T., Walsh, E., Treiblmaier, H., Stratopoulos, T. (eds.) "Blockchain beyond the Horizon" - Workshop at the European Conference on Information Systems, ECIS 2020 (2020)

26. Hyperledger Project: fabric-samples. https://github.com/hyperledger/fabric-samples. Accessed 22 Jan 2021

27. Siepmann, D., Graef, N.: Industrie 4.0 – Technologische Komponenten. In: Roth, A. (ed.) Einführung und Umsetzung von Industrie 4.0, pp. 47–72. Springer, Heidelberg (2016). https://doi.org/10.1007/978-3-662-48505-7

28. Hofmeier, M.: Beispiele für IT-Infrastrukturen in den Wertschöpfungsketten der NutriSafe-Szenarien, Neubiberg (2019)

29. SIEMENS AG: FB "MQTT_Client" für die SIMATIC S7-CPU. https://support.industry.siemens.com/cs/document/109748872/fb-mqtt_client-für-die-simatic-s7-cpu?dti=0&lc=de-WW. Accessed 09 Jan 2021

30. Niedermaier, M.: Security Challenges and Building Blocks for Robust Industrial Internet of Things Systems (2020). https://mediatum.ub.tum.de/doc/1533584/1533584.pdf

31. ECLIPSE Foundation: Sparkplug Specification Rev 2.2. https://www.eclipse.org/tahu/spec/Sparkplug Topic Namespace and State ManagementV2.2-with appendix B format - Eclipse.pdf. Accessed 11 Jan 2021

32. Blasch, E., Sung, J., Nguyen, T., Daniel, C., Mason, A.: Artificial intelligence strategies for national security and safety standards. In: AAAI Fall Symposium Series (2019)
33. Hein, A., Böhm, M., Krcmar, H.: Tight and loose coupling in evolving platform ecosystems: the cases of Airbnb and Uber. In: Abramowicz, W., Paschke, A. (eds.) BIS 2018. LNBIP, vol. 320, pp. 295–306. Springer, Cham (2018). https://doi.org/10.1007/978-3-319-93931-5_21
34. Hein, A., Scheiber, M., Böhm, M., Weking, J., Wittek, D., Krcmar, H.: Toward a design framework for service-platform ecosystems. In: Presented at the Twenty-Sixth European Conference on Information Systems, ECIS 2018 (2018)
35. Hein, A., Böhm, M., Krcmar, H.: Platform configurations within information systems research: a literature review on the example of IoT platforms. In: Presented at the Multikonferenz Wirtschaftsinformatik (2018)

An Approach to Supporting Militia Collaboration in Disaster Relief Through a Digital Environment

Philipp Hechenberger[1] (ID), Günter Fahrnberger[2](✉) (ID),
and Gerald Quirchmayr[3] (ID)

[1] University of Vienna, Vienna, Austria
[2] University of Hagen, Hagen, North Rhine-Westphalia, Germany
guenter.fahrnberger@studium.fernuni-hagen.de
[3] University of Vienna, Vienna, Austria
gerald.quirchmayr@univie.ac.at

Abstract. The continuously increasing frequency of natural disasters makes an efficient organization of relief missions an important target for public safety. In Austria, the regular armed forces, militia units as their reserve, and different civil first responder organizations support such missions. All of them represent important stakeholders for the restoration of public safety. Disaster relief missions need to fulfill demanding requirements and high standards, especially when considering (military) information security. Several digital processes during and after such operations already satisfy these norms, whereas preparatory ones still require improvement. The literature survey included in this paper is therefore intended to provide the foundation for further digitalization of disaster recovery operations by supporting collaboration between a variety of stakeholders. A typical collaboration stretches over several dimensions. This paper focuses on discussing the dimension *communication support*. The literature survey identifies the requirements, and is followed by a description of a prototype. Interested organizations can readily adopt or adapt the presented results for disaster recovery missions in Austria.

Keywords: Collaboration · Communication · Cooperation · Digitalization · Disaster relief · Infrastructure · Military · Militia · Protection · Security · Support

1 Introduction

As the global climate change results in highly demanding natural disasters, international communities (nations in particular) increasingly resort to armed forces to cope with the aftermath of devastation. To fulfill the tasks of disaster recovery, the efficient coordination of deployed units is necessary. Relevant preparation must already occur prior to missions.

© Springer Nature Switzerland AG 2021
U. R. Krieger et al. (Eds.): I4CS 2021, CCIS 1404, pp. 41–56, 2021.
https://doi.org/10.1007/978-3-030-75004-6_4

In Austria, militia troops[1] (as depicted in Fig. 1) support these operations. They need to be adequately informed about the current conditions and circumstances of an imminent mobilization. What is more, each militia soldier is required to get a mission order before their deployment. For this purpose, secure communication structures are required. Otherwise, saboteurs might perturb the convocation process. Nowadays, humanity generally has a multitude of possibilities in building infrastructure for such communication processes, especially supported by modern Information Technology (IT) solutions.

Fig. 1. Members of an Austrian Armed Forces militia unit disembark a relief operations boat during a flood fighting operation.

However, not many suitable solutions exist for the previously addressed scenario of secure communication channels for militia forces designated for mobilization. Hence, this paper lays the foundation for a solution prototype that satisfies internationally well-respected security and data protection requirements. It includes different conditions under which the stakeholders execute those missions. Moreover, it considers distinctive operation phases and roles during an entire mission.

---

[1] A military force that is raised from the civil population to supplement a regular army in an emergency (for details see https://www.bundesheer.at/sk/miliz/index.shtml).

Militia troops represent a special case in this consideration since they have no classified hardware available outside of operations. Since mission orders are usually classified, existing communication channels cannot be readily used for transmission. This work researches the special circumstances of transmitting, receiving, and processing classified data. In addition, it proposes a possible approach to support these processes. Furthermore, it also focuses on IT security standards established by military forces and the accompanying implications on general IT infrastructure and organizational measurements.

While this contribution can merely adumbrate ideas for a secure military collaboration platform, an associated master thesis with much more details is underway. This paper's merit comprises the elaboration and sketchy answering of research questions as well as the orchestration of a prototype. The work is of relevance as model for disaster relief support. The case study carried out in this paper can be generalized to different kinds of crisis management. Apart from the current section, the remainder of this document comprises four others. Section 2 as the centerpiece contains a comprehensive literature analysis for all parts of the envisaged solution prototype and concludes with the promulgation of three research questions. Section 3 proceeds by emphasizing the most important findings. A concise demonstration of a proper prototype follows in Sect. 4. The concluding Sect. 5 recapitulates this treatise, summarizes the answers to the research questions, and previews the master thesis as potential extension.

2 Disaster Relief Processes and Existing Support Environments

Disaster handling often challenges regular infrastructure resulting in federal institutions having to seek assistance from defense forces. In this situation, several requirements for the effective and efficient management of communication emerge. Furthermore, disaster control sometimes necessitates the exchange of classified data, e.g. for the mobilization of militia troops.

This section, therefore, provides a survey on the possibilities of sharing classified data among different stakeholders in real-time based on the requirements of the Austrian Armed Forces. It focuses on real-time messaging services and potential challenges in military environments.

2.1 Disaster Recovery Mission Process

To fully bring to bear an IT infrastructure, it is also important to consider the different phases of the disaster recovery mission process to identify possible issues during one or several of them. Different requirements ensue from the general splitting of such operations into phases. The subsequent discussion about military-assisted disaster recovery operations takes several different process phase models into consideration.

Figure 2 shows the phase model for joint operations performed by the United States (US) military [17]. It devotes itself to all sorts of military operations including humanitarian assistance. Simply described, it consists of the preliminary shaping phase and five main phases. The undervaluation of the operational layer and inelasticity diminish the value for modern mission planning and, particularly, for civil assistance operations [11].

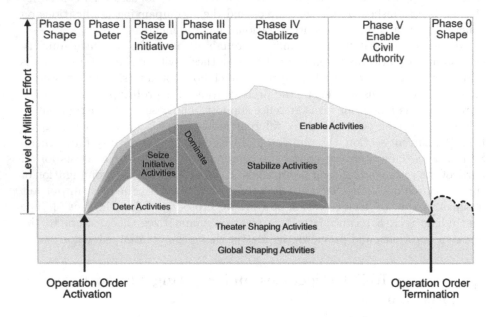

Fig. 2. Phase model for joint operations [17]

The Prevention-Preparedness-Response-Recovery (PPRR) model offers another viable option [5]. Its minimization of potential losses in case of an incident lets emergency management favor it. The shortcomings of this model lie in the transition between phases. However, the response and recovery phase of this model are of particular interest to support disaster recovery missions of the Austrian Armed Forces [12].

Although the discussed models are heavily used in military operations, none of them completely satisfies the modern requirements of disaster recovery operations. Nonetheless, the PPRR model delivers the relevant foundation for the support of the mobilization process during disaster recovery operations. It primarily addresses non-mobilized militia units as the most important group of stakeholders from an information security standpoint.

The US Disaster Response Staff Officer's Handbook describes simplified process phases for the mobilization of militia units as per Table 1 [20].

Its right column indicates special planning needs in the preparation phase as militia units are not yet mobilized and, therefore, considered as civilians. If their security clearance from former missions has expired, the renewal happens

Table 1. Simplified process phases for the mobilization of militia

Phase	Valid accreditation
Planning	Yes
Preparation	Maybe
Execution	Yes
Recovery (post processing)	Yes

in this phase. Unfortunately, even a valid accreditation does not automatically entail access to military equipment and, thus, to digital classified information. In particular, the preparation phase demands the provisioning of mission-critical information to these people without revelation to third parties.

That is why the intended prototype needs to incorporate these constraints for the utilization of (unclassified) equipment by militia forces [3,12]. Additionally, the contrivance must be able to provide classified information while maintaining data protection goals and the security levels established in distinct information domains. The other three phases can be conducted by utilizing classified systems and, as a consequence, be left out of scope in this contribution.

2.2 Existing Communication Infrastructure

In spite of an ongoing disaster scenario with a partial or full outage of civil communication channels, more robust military infrastructure is usually available and in use anyway. Regrettably, the latter cannot cover every use case. A disaster recovery mission command must accordingly assess the usefulness of all still deployable communication tools. This distinguishes missions with still working civil network infrastructure from those where pure military equipment (such as rugged devices) has to be used [7].

As this contribution provides the foundation for an independent collaboration solution, no dedicated communication bearer apart from the ubiquitous Internet will be considered. However, data throughput could be an issue in field operated (satellite) networks. Fulfilling the requirement of caching transmitted data also renders asynchronous communication possible.

Communication infrastructures can be of public or private nature. Public ones are accessible to everyone irrespective of involvement. On the contrary, internal networks or separated internal network access belong to the class of private communication infrastructures. Stakeholders are obliged to implement boundary protection gateways as access points to public infrastructure ensuring security across internal networks (a.k.a. intranets). On this account, intranets are considered as protected environments. In contrast, unprotected environments (such as smartphones connected to the Internet) are to be considered separately [2]. Generally, only public, unclassified, or at least declassified information may traverse such unmanaged channels [3].

The commanding disaster recovery units (by way of example governmental forces) commonly have their own internal (classified) infrastructure in place which they utilize during missions. Due to deliberately missing public access to such intranets, merely mobilized troops can make use of these sources. A general connection with external equipment must always fulfill several strict security requirements to prevent leaking contained classified data. Consequently, controlled gateways have to enforce these rules at network boundaries. Especially classification of data proves to be a challenging field. External stakeholders universally do not have access to sensitive data and, on that account, require a bilateral contract for the exchange of such data [3].

The implementation of unclassified infrastructure catches on more and more to provide access to a growing number of users. Such networks impose laxer provisions and are generally not intertwined with classified infrastructure. The only exception to this strict separation are, as mentioned before, controlled gateways to prevent unintended data leakage [2].

2.3 Roles and Stakeholders

A feasible solution requires distinct processes of operation. For that reason, it is mandatory to define different stakeholders and involved roles. A sufficient solution must aim at the possibility of utilization by both militia and professional military units.

The general hierarchization used in military standards classifies into strategic, tactical, and operational level. An adaption of these stages has also standardized them for Operations Security (OPSEC) planning [18]. On account of this, civil organizations can also apply this model.

Strategic Level. The highest level consists of all stakeholders involved in establishing the foundation for any disaster operation. This includes setting a certain mentality, structuring their underlying organizations, establishing general guidelines, and arranging cooperation with other organizations on the strategic level. Specifically, in disaster handling and recovery operations, those are Governmental Organizations (GOs) and Non-Governmental Organizations (NGOs) as well as corporate management [14]. The itemization below specifies the core objectives [7].

- Overview of the situation
- Strategic communication
- Information exchange
- Instructing, regulating, and legislative changes
- Financial control
- International cooperation

Operational Level. This level pursues the goal of planning and executing certain operations to achieve objectives, e.g. recovery in case of natural disasters.

Generally, this layer consists of special crisis committees constituted of representatives from relevant stakeholders. Depending on a mission, multiple committees can also be established on lower levels to better focus on the necessary work- and information flows [4]. The subsequent list encompasses the core objectives [7].

- Transregional alarming
- Transregional operational command
- Resource planning and balancing
- Psychological acute care
- Public relations

Tactical Level. The task forces as mission-specific stakeholders on this level conduct disaster recovery operations on site. They use the foundations laid by higher levels to handle disasters and help in recovery. For example, this level consists of actual soldiers, police forces, medical personnel, and firefighters [14]. The following listing covers the core objectives [7].

- Active defense[2]
- Rescue, recovery, and medical attention
- Evacuation and shelter
- Technical and administrative mission control

Besides the consideration of the different hierarchy levels, it is also necessary to differentiate between external (e.g. nonmilitary) and internal data recipients. The latter's handling apparently differs. While internal communications can be processed without any separate security mechanisms, additional boundary protection gateways need to enable external classified communication [2].

2.4 Necessary Communication Infrastructure

Communication infrastructure (necessary for collaboration) must enable data flows from an internal network to another (possibly external) infrastructure through channels accessible to all involved parties. Generally, the Internet facilitates these links. The same holds true for temporarily built networks for specific missions. Connections toward client networks shall always include controlled gateways to mitigate compromising of data or systems during transmission over such carrier networks [2]. Packets routed through the Internet can be handled with the most well-established solutions as the connection and data throughput are relatively stable. However, temporary (satellite) networks can have several issues with connectivity. Therefore, they have to be handled separately. A detailed view on these shall follow in later work as the current design and implementation of an initial working solution urges much more. It has to be noted that caching is relevant for chat transmissions to keep message communication up during unstable connections. Therefore, pure synchronous communication approaches might fail in several situations.

---

[2] Active defense in this case means establishing perimeter security, such as building up dams and securing objectives as well as arranging emergency shelters and deploying bases of operations.

2.5   Toward Possible Solutions

Teufel et al. analyze and compile different forms of collaboration in their 3K-Model that defines several dimensions to classify collaborating solutions as follows [15]:

- Communication support
- Coordination support
- Cooperation support

This model allows the classification of solutions depending on their respective functionality. It serves as the main source to orchestrate the approach necessary for supporting secure collaboration during disaster recovery operations.

This paper mainly brings the dimension of communication support into focus. It can be split into asynchronous and synchronous communication. As abovementioned, it is necessary for a feasible solution to simultaneously provide both ilks [13].

Coordination support is out of scope within this disquisition and, thereby, leaves room for future research.

Section 4 and the yet unpublished master thesis deal with cooperation support by utilizing the exchange of documents. This sort of collaboration differentiates the classes *file sharing (storage)* and *(simultaneous) document editing.*

Table 2 shows different requirements of collaboration for the previously mentioned stakeholders. One solution providing all three types may be optimal. However, multiple solutions, which fulfill all security requirements, can be considered as a possible prototype as well. The full or partial degree of fulfillment stems from general constraints in the availability of technology. The tactical level sometimes does not have access to regular computer hardware during missions. On account of that, the prototype does not need to fully satisfy every situation. For its planning, only solutions utilizing Internet Protocol (IP)-based network connections need heed since civil stakeholders normally take advantage of easily obtainable hardware, like smartphones or personal computers.

Table 2. Requirements per level

Level	File sharing	Document editing	Communication
Strategic level	Full	Full	Full
Operational level	Full	Full	Partial
Tactical level	Full	Partial	Partial

This work necessitates synchronous and asynchronous textual communication, as well as the sharing of different files, such as pictures or documents. Due to the necessary cooperation during disaster operations, some communication has to be established with external stakeholders. A satisfactory solution must provide access to resources across different security domains. Dynamically changing data as present in the simultaneous editing of documents or data streams merely play a secondary role in this publication. The prementioned levels of data access privileges turn out to be a key constraint in the quest for a possible prototypical application. Established constraints on data access (such as the need-to-know principle) must remain fulfilled.

Communication solutions belong to a broad field that includes audio- and video streams, message exchange services (such as instant messaging), and mere asynchronous messaging (such as mailing). Applications in this field often create continuous data streams and, from this, possibly lead to performance bottlenecks with insufficient network access. The contemplated, universally working prototype in this essay does not mitigate such capacity issues [8]. A proposal also needs to inspect all data of such a continuous data stream as per Subsect. 3.1. This demand behooves since classified data must not to be stored outside of classified security domains and leads to viewing restrictions based on the need-to-know principle [3].

2.6   Core Research Questions

The following itemization outlines research questions derived from the previous subsections.

- How can an open-source communication platform satisfy the strict constraints of a military domain to be securely deployed there?
- How can disaster recovery be assisted with digital technologies?
- How can the handling of classified data in a partially unclassified environment be achieved without violating security-based restrictions?

While these questions guide the research throughout this document, a master thesis currently written by the first author of this paper contains substantial answers. Both this publication and the impending thesis only consider a real-time communication solution (like an instant messenger) as an appropriate use case. Based on the three research questions, a fitting prototype enables digital collaboration before, during, and after disaster recovery operations. Usability and security ordinarily countervail each other. For this reason, the thesis also describes related training exercises for the involved units to achieve a usable communication product. This implies the impartation of usage restrictions.

3   Challenges and Core Requirements

After discussing the relevant existing work, this section focuses on the findings and their interpretation according to the scenario at hand. Some of the considered networks process federally classified data that require security measurements above most implementations. If prevailing information security requirements do not suffice, stricter standards (such as those introduced by the German Federal Office for Information Security) supersede them for the development of a prototype [1, 6].

3.1   General Security Requirements

As the protection of transmitted data is essential for mission success, it is necessary to provide an overview of the necessary general goals respectively their importance for a sufficient security standard. To fulfill these requirements, various aspects of data processing during the collaboration with different recipients must be considered. The CIA-triad allegorizes a threesome of general security targets.

– Confidentiality (C)
– Integrity (I)
– Availability (A)

All pursued approaches must obey the CIA-triad as clearly stated in [10]. Moreover, a more sophisticated solution has to comply with credibility, reliability, and authenticity as further security objectives. The CIA-triad represents the most basic approach of maintaining data protection. To fulfill the requirements in Subsect. 3.2, technical measures must also maintain the CIA-goals. Such safeguards directly affect IT systems and can be more easily enforced than organizational measures. However, organizational measures may complement technical solutions that do not suffice [16].

Confidentiality means the protection of data from the disclosure of sensitive information to unauthorized parties. On the one hand, securing confidentiality includes processes that thwart unauthorized access by encrypting data flows and stored data. On the other hand, it incorporates the authentication of users assuring the need-to-know principle. The processing, displaying, and transmission of login credentials deserve the same standard of protection as payload. A possible solution prototype ensures confidentiality by preventing unintended data access, not transmitting sensitive data in plain-text, and shielding against possible data breaches. This happens by dint of security gateways at security domain borders and with the aid of hardening the server-side and endpoint devices [2,9,19]. Losing the confidentiality of federally classified data can lead to substantial damage to public safety or violation of public interests [3].

Integrity secures data against unwanted modification or alteration. The prototype must at least recognize undesired alterations and use mechanisms that ensure the distribution of original data. Unauthorized parties shall not be able to tamper with any stored or processed data in the system [19]. Mission-relevant information (such as coordinates) incurs during disaster operations. A wrong alteration of these data delays rescue units or, much worse, impedes their arrival at required locations [7].

Availability as the third and last vertex of the CIA-triad implies uninterruptible access to authorized parties when necessary during a mission [19]. As operation data can be time-critical, the storage and transfer of some information can have high-availability goals. Some other data might not be time-critical. The parties in recovery operations are well advised to define an adequate criticality. A solution prototype is supposed to deal with different availability requirements for the various types of data.

3.2   Special Requirements for the Security Domain

This paper cannot expose a detailed view on the internal security requirements of federated networks and information systems. A more general approach shall therefore abstract the publicly available documentation. General requirements ensure the protection of classified data and prevent data leakage to either the general public or possibly malicious third parties. As classified documents and information must not be exposed to any uninvolved party, several general requirements apply [3]. Vacca's Computer and Information Security Handbook itemizes the subsequently mentioned nine general security principles [19].

- Need-to-know
- Least privilege
- Economy of mechanism
- Separation of privilege
- Psychological acceptance
- Fail-safe defaults
- Complete mediation
- Open design
- Least common mechanism

Among all nine general security principles, in military environments the need-to-know principle poses the most essential pillar in data protection. Confidential information may neither be disclosed to third parties nor to any party that does not contribute to the fulfillment of the mission goals. This leads to the necessity of border protection gateways and end-to-end-encryption. Federal classified data have high confidentiality restrictions. Aside from guarding data against unauthorized access, the prevention of data leakage and corruption of any kind as well matters [2,3]. These restrictions lead to the requirement of authenticating any communication partner and inspecting every inbound packet before importing (unknown) data.

The principles *fail-safe-defaults* and *complete mediation* claim not to allow any traffic that has not been explicitly trusted and monitored. This also applies to encrypted packets. Thus, a solution prototype communicating with internal (restricted) systems must enable security gateways at the boundaries between external and internal networks to inspect possibly malicious data.

Furthermore, the classification of data must be transparent and explicit. Classification notes label to which (external) units data can be released. Security gateways check such classification notes when classified data outflow to external networks. Incorrectly marked data get dropped and logged as failed transmission attempts.

3.3   Communication Support Issues

The consideration of communication at different dimensions opens up possible challenges during implementation. The exchange of documents at least requires reading privileges for the involved parties. Once the latter can collaborate, their probably different mission objectives might necessitate restricted access to resources. The levels of operations as per Subsect. 2.3 play a crucial role in this consideration. Different stakeholders do not always need to communicate with each other since they could assume different roles on the three layers. With this in mind, it leads to the conclusion that fully meshed communication (i.e. everybody communicates with everybody) becomes redundant.

3.4 Deployment Challenges

Significant problems with collaboration can arise during the mission process when fulfilling security requirements. This is why deployment options play an important role. Depending on the level of units, a monolithic deployment (one instance for all participants) can suffice. In the case of collaboration between layers, the deployment of a distributed system with restricted views on the data can turn out to be more efficient. This architectural decision commits itself to the doability determination of such deployments. This enfolds their extent (e.g. hybrid deployment) to maximize the usability across stakeholders and mission layers.

4 Proof-of-Concept Prototype

This section presents a proof-of-concept implementation that elaborates important deployment alternatives for disaster recovery operations. Its focus lies on the identified architectural requirements. Figure 3 showcases three different constellations of collaboration solutions and resulting security gateways. All of them fulfill the discussed architectural requirements. While they are all based on communicating through the Demilitarized Zone (DMZ), they vary as far as the collaboration solution itself is concerned. Figure 3(a) depicts an architecture consisting of an internal collaboration solution (that is controlled by a military unit) and an external one, which is placed in the DMZ. Figure 3(b) introduces a collaboration solution positioned in the DMZ and connected via respective security gateways to military units and external partners. In Fig. 3(c), the concept of connecting an internal collaboration solution with an external one via a secure gateway is introduced.

The prototype implementation and the validation were focused on the alternative in Fig. 3(b). This is estimated to be the most practical architecture. All functionality checks (e.g. document updates, editing, etc.) and penetration tests (such as bypass attempts of security mechanisms) imposed on the prototype were passed successfully. The penetration tests on both the collaboration environment and the reverse proxy utilized a Nessus[3] setup with provided login credentials (root and application administrator) and all plugins enabled. Additionally, the functionality tests were conducted using a requirements catalog of the Austrian Armed Forces.

---

[3] https://www.nessus.at/.

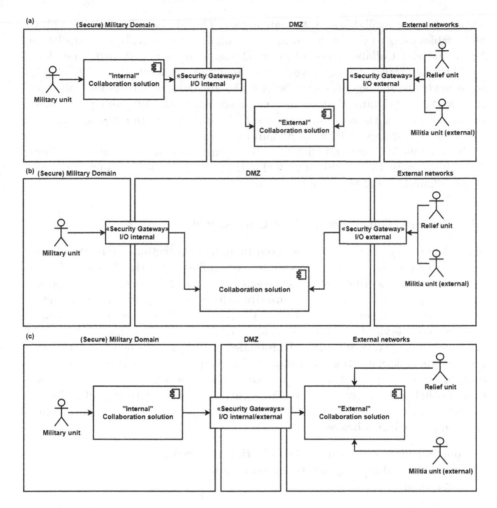

Fig. 3. Model guiding the prototype development, (a) Military dual hosting, (b) Military single hosting, (c) Civil hosting

4.1 Collaboration Environment Setup

The implementation started with a cooperation solution based upon Nextcloud[4]. During tests of this initial environment, no severe vulnerabilities were detected. However, it has turned out that a mere Nextcloud instance lacks in the functionality of (simultaneous) document editing and, hence, calls for an enhancement. For that purpose, a Nextcloud environment permits the embedding of apps. Collabora[5] as one of these apps proffers the desired (simultaneous) document

---

[4] https://nextcloud.com/.
[5] https://www.collaboraoffice.com/.

editing. It is not available as a standalone tool. The add-on relies on LibreOffice[6] and enables users to view and edit files in a collaborative way. Upon installation, Nextcloud with Collabora was subject to the same test series as Nextcloud alone.

The retests also did not reveal any dangerous vulnerabilities of Collabora since Nextcloud manages the permissions, file- and data-structures for Collabora. It is worth mentioning that an internal installation of Collabora presupposes the deployment of the additional service *Collabora Online Development Edition (CODE)*. Access to CODE must remain minimal.

In a nutshell, Nextcloud with Collabora emerges as a convenient collaboration environment that complies with the defined requirements, restrictions, and existing knowledge of the Austrian Armed Forces.

4.2   Security Gateways as Core Components

Since the prototype cannot cope without boundary protection, security gateways are used to directly protect services by decoupling networks, blocking invalid requests, and inspecting traffic for possible attacks. To this end, the proof-of-concept implementation in this manuscript utilizes reverse proxies. This architecture enables (if implemented accordingly) analysis of traffic and further control over exposed services. All related traffic must reach the proxies for Transport Layer Security (TLS) offloading. Unintended traffic gets dropped in terms of a firewall. As Nextcloud takes advantage of the Apache web server[7], the reverse proxies necessitate an alternative vendor. This hinders the concurrent infestation of collaboration environments and security gateways with exploits. Thence, nginx[8] became the latter's web service. A security-related reverse proxy offers the itemized features below.

– Functionality (connecting and conducting sessions)
– Traffic restrictions (e.g. additional host firewall)
– Traffic analysis

A reverse proxy must spring into action as a valid network participant for users and Nextcloud instances. Nextcloud acknowledges a reverse proxy as trustworthy once it appears in the field *trusted_proxies* of the configuration file `config.php`. Furthermore, the utilized TLS certificates need to be integrated into a Public Key Infrastructure (PKI) that holds all stakeholders' confidence. This ensures solely confidential connections between valid stakeholders. For the sake of TLS offloading, a reverse proxy has to look like a Nextcloud deployment for users. It displays Nextcloud's Graphical User Interface (GUI) to them when they try to connect. This is why a reverse proxy has plaintext at its disposal and can conduct the necessary traffic analysis and monitoring.

---

[6] https://www.libreoffice.org/.
[7] https://www.apache.org/.
[8] https://www.nginx.com/.

5   Summary and Conclusion

This paper is focused on discussing possibilities for the support of disaster recovery operations through collaboration management systems. The major findings include lessons learned about the core role of security features in an environment where military personnel needs to be side by side with militia and first responders. Challenges regarding the issues of digitalization in the context of disaster recovery were first addressed. The use of open-source communication platforms and how they can satisfy the strict constraints of a military domain were discussed next. How the handling of classified data in a partially classified environment can be achieved without violating security-based restrictions was identified as a core question. The answers and experimental results presented in this paper enable the deployment of a collaborative environment in a secure and cost-efficient way. As the promising output of the first experiments carried out indicates, it is worth further pursuing the suggested solutions.

Therefore, the first author of this paper continues to work on this topic in the context of a master thesis at the University of Vienna. The results he can build on comprise a first model, a prototype implementation, and an initial evaluation. The master thesis refines the prototype of Sect. 4 for the support of credibility, reliability, and authenticity. As a major outcome, the thesis provides a more advanced prototype and extended answers to the raised research questions. For further development on this topic, mathematical models of communication might be of interest.

Acknowledgments. Many thanks to Bettina Baumgartner from the University of Vienna for proofreading this paper.

References

1. Anderson, R.J.: Security Engineering - A Guide to Building Dependable Distributed Systems, 2nd edn. Wiley, Indianapolis (2008). ISBN: 978-0-470-06852-6
2. Bundesamt für Sicherheit in der Informationstechnik: NET.1.1 Netzarchitektur und -design, January 2021
3. Bundesministerium für Landesverteidigung und Sport: Geheimschutzvorschrift, April 2011
4. Bundesministerium für Landesverteidigung und Sport: Stabsdienst im kleinen Verband, February 2017
5. Cronstedt, M.: Prevention, preparedness, response, recovery - an outdated concept? Aust. J. Emerg. Manage. **17**(2), 10–13 (2002)
6. Fahrnberger, G.: Contemporary IT security for military online collaboration platforms. In: Proceedings of the 18th International Conference on Distributed Computing and Networking, ICDCN 2017, pp. 33:1–33:10. ACM, New York, January 2017
7. Hohenberger, G.: Behördliches Katastrophenmanagement im Spannungsfeld zunehmend digital geprägter Führungssysteme. Master's thesis, University of Vienna, October 2017

8. Kotevski, Z., Mitrevski, P.: A modeling framework for performance analysis of p2p live video streaming systems. In: Gusev, M., Mitrevski, P. (eds.) ICT Innovations 2010. CCIS, vol. 83, pp. 215–225. Springer, Heidelberg (2011). https://doi.org/10.1007/978-3-642-19325-5_22

9. National Institute of Standards and Technology (NIST): Framework for Improving Critical Infrastructure Cybersecurity. National Institute of Standards and Technology (NIST), April 2018

10. National Institute of Standards and Technology (NIST): Security and Privacy Controls for Information Systems and Organizations. National Institute of Standards and Technology (NIST), September 2020

11. Otto, G.A.: The end of operational phases at last. InterAgency J. 8(3), 78–86 (2017)

12. Pfundner, P.: Naturkatastropheneinsätze des Österreichischen Bundesheeres im Ausland – vom Beginn einer Naturkatastrophe bis zum Eintreffen des Kontingentes des Österreichischen Bundesheeres im Krisengebiet. Master's thesis, University of Vienna, November 2013

13. Roitzheim, C.: CSCW – Gruppenarbeit 4.0, January 2017

14. Sukman, D.: The Institutional Level of War, May 2016

15. Teufel, S., Sauter, C., Mühlherr, T., Bauknecht, K.: Computerunterstützung für die Gruppenarbeit. Addison-Wesley, Bonn (1997). ISBN: 3486243705

16. The Federal Data Protection and Information Commissioner (FDPIC): A Guide for technical and organizational measures, August 2015

17. United States Armed Forces: Joint Operations, October 2018

18. United States Army: Operations Security, September 2014

19. Vacca, J.R.: Computer and Information Security Handbook. Morgan Kaufmann, Cambridge (2017)

20. Williams, J.M.: Disaster Response Staff Officer's Handbook, December 2010

Network Architectures for Communities

LIENE: Lifetime Enhancement for 6LoWPAN Network Using Clustering Approach Use Case: Smart Agriculture

Pradeepkumar Bhale[1(✉)], Santosh Biswas[2], and Sukumar Nandi[1]

[1] Department of Computer Science and Engineering, Indian Institute of Technology,
Guwahati 781039, India
{pradeepkumar,sukumar}@iitg.ac.in
[2] Department of Electrical Engineering and Computer Science,
Indian Institute of Technology, Bhilai 492015, India
santosh_biswas@iitg.ac.in

Abstract. The *Internet of Things (IoT)* is one of the largest technological evolutions of computing. With the rapid development of communication, there was a tremendous growth of IoT technology across various fields. IoT devices might be resource-constrained like sensors, actuators, and embedded devices with the IEEE 802.15.4. IoT enables widespread and ubiquitous IoT applications: transportation, logistics, safety and security, health-care, manufacturing, etc. IoT application without sensing devices is impracticable. These sensing devices are battery-powered and constrained by inadequate energy in terms of communication and computation. The optimized communication directs to a more extended network lifetime. Least hop count, enhanced scalability, and connectivity are onerous issues that can be addressed entirely by a clustering mechanism. We conduct comprehensive simulation studies for performance analysis and comparative study of IPv6 over Low-Power Wireless Personal Area Networks (6LoWPAN). with the conventional approaches in the IoT ecosystem. The experimental outcomes prove that the intended approach outperforms closely-related works.

Keywords: Internet of Things (IoT) · IPv6 over Low-Power Wireless Personal Area Networks (6LoWPAN) · Network lifetime · Smart agriculture

1 Introduction

In this digital age, we see the IoT devices penetrating every perspective of our lives. They are used in home automation equipment, IP cameras, hospitals, agriculture and lights, etc., are connected to the Internet using IPv6 protocol. Governments across the world driving towards smart cities and smart farming where most of the work is automated [1].

Experts reckon that the 25 billion IoT devices are currently utilized, and it will extend 50 billion by 2020 [2,3]. These devices, an essential and important

© Springer Nature Switzerland AG 2021
U. R. Krieger et al. (Eds.): I4CS 2021, CCIS 1404, pp. 59–75, 2021.
https://doi.org/10.1007/978-3-030-75004-6_5

component like wireless sensing and monitoring mechanisms. They are limited power resources due to which the power dissipation grows a decisive aspect for *Network Life (NL)*. Moreover, if these power-constrained devices are implemented with IP, it will quickly drain out their battery and reduce the NL [4]. Assuming, such an enormous quantity of IoT devices are continuing to collaborate and communicate with different IoT devices to achieve a given job, adequate connectivity between IoT devices and systematic communication to extend the NL of the IoT is a non-trivial and challenging task.

In this paper, we propose an energy efficient clustering mechanism with adaptive self-organization for the three-tier architecture of IoT [5–7]. Consequently, we approach connectivity issues among the sensing layer and the IoT layer by using a clustering mechanism based on different criteria:

- Geographical parameters such as node distance from the base station and its density.
- Energy parameters like current (residual) energy of node, initial energy of node, the average of network and the total energy of network for efficient routing in the IoT networks.

The clustering approach is implemented amid the IoT devices in the sensing layer to have the least hop communications. Additionally, clustering supports to address additional challenging issues like scalability, maximal network longevity, minimal energy, increased connectivity and reduced delay. Moreover, we implemented our approach using the Contiki operating system [8] and cooja simulator [9].

The rest of the research paper is composed as follows. Section 2 provides background information on the 6LoWPAN architecture. Section 3 discusses the existing solutions for optimized hop communications. Section 4 describes the proposed approach with the system model. In Sect. 5, we discuss the experimental setup and the performance analysis with the help of Contiki OS and the cooja simulator. Conclusion and future work are described in Sect. 6.

2   Background

2.1   Network IoT Architecture

To provide IP addresses to 50 billion objects is not easy, and IPv4 is not sufficient to facilitate such a sheer volume of things. The addressing space of IPv6 is adequate to provide unique addresses to each object currently connected or will be connecting to the Internet in the future. The embedded sensor in each object may be powered by an 8-bit, 16-bit, or 32-bit microcontroller with 64 Kbytes or more flash memory. The sensor nodes use the IEEE 802.15.4 standard, which supports only 127 bytes of packet size [10]. Therefore, each IPv6 packet needs to be in a simple format, i.e., removing its high-level complexity and redundancy, makes it usable for physical objects.

The main philosophy behind the 6LoWPAN design was that IP addresses could and should be applied even to the tiniest devices. The low-power objects with inadequate storage, processing abilities, battery power, and other available resources should participate in the IoT. The 6LoWPAN working group has defined various encapsulation and header compression techniques so that IPv6 packets can be transmitted and received over low-power networks such as IEEE 802.15.4.

2.2 6LoWPAN Protocol Stack

The 6LoWPAN protocol stack incorporates seven layers is exhibited in Fig. 1. Layer 1, 2 incorporate IEEE 802.15.4 media access control (MAC), and the physical layer (PHY), respectively. Layer 2.5, also called the 6LoWPAN adaption layer, takes care of compression and fragmentation of the IPv6 packets. In layer 3, perform Routing Protocol for Low-Power and Lossy Networks (RPL) and neighbor discovery module. Constrained Application Protocol (CoAP) is based on UDP, and it incorporates in layer 7.

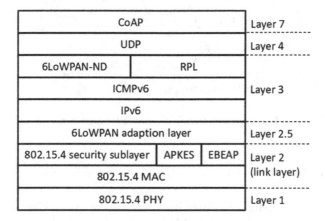

Fig. 1. 6LoWPAN protocol stack

2.3 Smart Agriculture

Nowadays, agriculture industry is growing by adopting information and communication technologies (ICT). In the specific automatic agriculture industry, developed with different radio sensor and actuators. This type of devices collect sensed data (e.g., wind, temperature, humidity, rainfall) through IoT Network. IoT enables technologies to develop new monitoring and *decision support system (DSS)* giving improved real-time techniques over existing solutions.

   We deployed the IoT network with sky mote, this mote is available in *Contiki Cooja* simulator. The sensed data, like light intensity and temperature values from the perception layer, are transferred to the IoT access network layer as exhibited in Fig. 2. In this IoT network, the perception layer comprises of sensor devices and IoT access network layer consists of four IP devices. By providing the IoT device address to the web browser, and examine sensed data over the distributed IoT network from communicating sensor nodes.

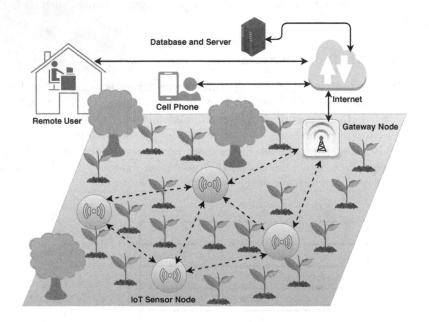

Fig. 2. A IoT sensor network deployed for smart agriculture

3   Related Work

A plethora of exciting research articles covering energy-efficient clustering in WSNs Domains exist, as shown in Table 1. There are multiple extending investigations with minor improvements in results. Many of them scarcity of profound study and general introduction. These nine chosen review papers are presented in Table 1 [5, 11–18] are great to begin with when research personnel is about to study in WSN clustering mechanism. There are some recent research paper in the last couple of years on clustering methods for resource constraint IoT ecosystem, Like *EAKDE* [18] in this paper proposed energy efficient kernel density-based mechanism which is helpful to adjust the energy distribution between the *cluster heads (CHs)*. *EAKDE* uses the fuzzy logic system to select CH. This paper betters the other conventional approach in terms of network stability. However, the drawbacks of this method are energy overhead.

The *low-energy adaptive clustering hierarchy (LEACH)* algorithm has been proposed by Heinzelman et al. [19]. This is a well-known clustering protocols. In this article, every node estimates a likelihood value to select CH. Elected CH nodes transmit their individual information to various nodes to connect their equivalent clusters. However, the protocol provides a *One-hop model* and it is proper for a smaller network, consequently, the *LEACH* can step up the breakdown of the network.

Manjeshwar et al. [20] proposed *"Threshold sensitive energy efficient sensor network protocol" (TEEN)*. It is an energy efficiency hierarchical clustering protocol. In this protocol, sensor nodes report their sensed data to the CH. The CH node transmits accumulated information to the next upper-level CH until the data arrives at the base station. TEEN is intended for reactive networks, where the sensor nodes act instantly to an abrupt change in sensed data. The sensing of the environment is performed regularly by the sensor nodes, but information sending is executed occasionally. The demerit of TEEN is that if the *threshold* is not achieved, the nodes may not interact and we do not understand if a sensor node is dead.

Agarwal et al. [21] proposed *"Adaptive threshold sensitive energy efficient sensor network protocol" (APTEEN)*. This protocol is the expansion of TEEN which targets to acquire data at both the critical timings as well as periodically. The network system of APTEEN is the same as TEEN. In accordance to energy dispersion and lifetime of the network, TEEN provides good execution as compared to LEACH as well as APTEEN. This is due to the reduced quantity of transmissions. The primary flaws of TEEN, as well as APTEEN, are operating expense and difficulty in the formation of clusters at multiple levels.

The *"Stable election protocol" (SEP)* has been suggested by Smaragdakis et al. [22]. In this paper, clustering is based on the weighted election probability of every node for turning into a CH in the cluster with the help of individual energy. This method ensures that the election of CH is not done uniformly and the distribution of CH is on the basis of particular node energy, which assures a consistent usage of the given energy.

The *"Enhanced stable election protocol" (E-SEP)* has been proposed by Aderohunmu et al. [23]. It is the expansion of SEP and takes into consideration three categories of nodes called normal, intermediate and advanced nodes. Where a portion of nodes are advanced nodes having some extra amount of energy (as in SEP), a portion of nodes are intermediate nodes having some additional amount of energy in comparison to the normal nodes and less as compared to nodes that are advanced, while the remaining nodes are normal.

Table 1. LIST OF LAST SIX YEAR REVIEW PAPERS

Year	Publish survey research papers
2014	Popat et al. [11], Kamesh et al. [16]
2015	Mukhopadhyay et al. [12], Izakian et al. [18]
2016	Cooper et al. [13],
2017	Saxena et al. [14], Xu. L et al. [5],
2018	Wazarkar et al. [17],
2019	Dubey et al. [15]

4 Proposed Works

In this section, the proposed approaches describes the selection of CH from randomly distributed nodes in the IoT ecosystem. This section also explains the formation of the cluster, based on elected CH for energy efficient communication and reliability. The notation used in the proposed approach is given in Table 2. The overall workflow and procedural steps of the proposed approach are exhibited below:

In the IoT network, one round of communication consists of two stages: the first is the setup stage and the second is the data transmission stage. In the set-up stage selection of the CH and formation of cluster take place. While in the data transmission stage, transmission of data from the member node to the CH of the cluster and from the CH to the base station take place.

The principal idea is to make the best node as a CH from all the available nodes. This will depend upon current network conditions and resource status. The optimum probability of a node to become a CH will decide through routing metric, lossy nature, and energy parameters. Also, the formation of the cluster is adaptive and self-organizing.

During the set-up phase, we have to decide the network parameters, like field area, number of devices, device parameters. A field is created and nodes are randomly placed. The routing is based on rank, means we are using the RPL routing protocol [24]. Node to node and node to CH communication is also based on rank. For this, first of all, we have to calculate the rank from *Destination Oriented Directed Acyclic Graph (DODAG)* [25]. In this phase selection of a CH and formation of the cluster also takes place.

During the data transmission stage, the CH forward sensed data to the base station. After that, we calculate and update the residual energy of every node and it will update at every transmission round. The priority in CH nodes is dynamically renewed to improve the workload of the IoT ecosystem.

After the selection of the CH, a cluster region is built around the particular CH, and nodes belonging to that region are termed as cluster members (CMs) of that cluster. In the transmission phase, the CMs transmit their sensed data to the CH and then CH of cluster transmits the collected information to the destination directly. The clustering and RPL routing procedure continue until the network devices are alive, the devices with proper residual energy and lossy condition of the network are selected as CH at every transmission round. Since new CH are elected in every round, therefore, the energy load is properly balanced among the dispersed nodes in the network. Also, every CMs transmits only to the nearest elected CH and only the CH has to transmit to the base station.

4.1 Cluster Head Selection

In order to improve the IoT network lifetime, the proposed method selects the best CH in a distributed way. The selection of CH and excellent transmission range (TX) for all other nodes has a couple of critical problems addressed in our approach: 1) choose the best CH to reduce energy dissipation. 2) how to choose an excellent TX to adjust the trade-off as mentioned earlier. We will present our methods to solve the aforementioned problems in detail.

Table 2. Notation used for CH node selection

Notation	Description
$P(u)$	Optimal probability of a CH node
$\beta_{rand}(U)$	Random number assigned to a node in the network
N_S	Sensor nodes distributed in the IoT network
$E_{int}(u)$	Initially supplied energy of the node
$E_t(n)$	Total energy of all nodes in the network
$E_{curr}(u)$	Current energy of the node
$E_{avg}(n)$	Average energy of all nodes in the network
$\psi_{density}(u)$	Density of the node
$D_{bs}(U)$	Distance of uth node from base station

In the proposed method, calculate the optimum probability for CH in a distributed manner given as follows.

$$P(u) = \beta_{rand}(U) \times N_S \times \frac{E_{int}(u)}{E_t(n)} \times \frac{E_{curr}(u)}{E_{avg}(n)} \times \frac{\psi_{density}(u)}{D_{bs}(U)} \qquad (1)$$

Average energy is calculated as:

$$E_{avg}(n) = E_t(n) \times \left(\frac{1 - \frac{r_{current}}{r_{max}}}{n_s} \right) \qquad (2)$$

$D_{bs}(U)$ is the distance of uth node from base station. This distance is calculated on the basis of distance vector formula.

Let assume that the position of a node i in the network is (x_n, y_n) and the other node j is (x_c, y_c), then the distance between them can be calculated as with help of distance vector formula as:

$$D[i, j] = \sqrt{(x_c - x_n)^2 + (y_c - y_n)^2} \qquad (3)$$

So in this way the optimum probability value $P(u)$ of every active node is calculated.

For making the global decision, the current energy of a node is compared with the average energy of nodes in the network. The initially supplied energy of a sensor is compared with the total energy of every sensor nodes in the IoT network. The total energy of IoT network $E_t(n)$ is estimated by summing energies of all sensors and the average energy of IoT network $E_{avg}(n)$ is measured by [26] given in Eq. (2).

The best sensor node is elected within the network whose $\frac{E_{int}(u)}{E_t(n)}$, $\frac{\psi_{density}(u)}{D_{bs}(U)}$ and $\frac{E_{curr}(u)}{E_{avg}(n)}$ ratios are high. The estimated value of the maximum probability of each node for the head selection is then utilized in the threshold formula or probability structure [27] given in Eq. (4).

$$
Th(u) = \begin{cases} \dfrac{P(u)}{1-P(u)\left(r \times mod \frac{1}{P(u)}\right)}, & \text{if } u \in G. \\ 0, & \text{otherwise.} \end{cases} \tag{4}
$$

Here, $P(u)$ is the optimum probability. as given in Eq. (1). Here G is the group of nodes that are active and can become a CH. After a greater probability node becomes a cluster head, as described energy models are applied to calculate the amount of energy spent by it on that particular round to transmit and receive data as stated in [28,29]. As shown in Fig. 3. To accomplish an adequate signal

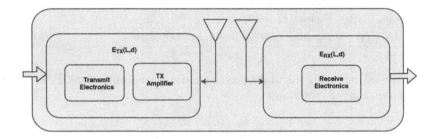

Fig. 3. Radio energy depletion model for IoT network

to noise ratio (SNR) for transmitting a message of K-bit for a distance s, as stated in [29] the energy dissipated by the radio is given by Eq. (5):

$$
E_{DTX}(K,s) = \begin{cases} K \times E_{ckt} + K \times A_{fs} \times s^2, & \text{if } s < s_0. \\ K \times E_{ckt} + K \times A_{mp} \times s^4, & \text{if } s \geq s_0. \end{cases} \tag{5}
$$

$E_{DTX}(K,s)$ is the energy spent for transmitting data. Here E_{ckt} is energy dissipated each bit for functioning the transmitter or the receiver circuit, A_{fs} and A_{mp} rest on the employed model of transmitter amplifier, and s is the distance between the sending and receiving end. We have $s_0 = \sqrt{\dfrac{A_{fs}}{A_{mp}}}$. Here s_0 is the threshold distance. For receiving the message of $K - bit$ for a distance of the energy dissipated by radio as stated in [30] is given by Eq. (6).

$$
E_{DTX}(K,s) = K \times E_{ckt} \tag{6}
$$

In the initialization stage, the root begins to build the network topology. We create a *Cluster Generation Request Message (CGRM)*. This message propagates node to node in the IoT ecosystem. The *CGRM* packet composition is exhibited in Fig. 4. Each field of *CGRM* is two bytes in size. The CGRM message takes nodes energy cost, rank, and associated Node ID. The transmitting the CGRM

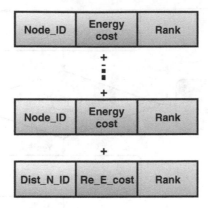

Fig. 4. CGRM message format.

using trickle algorithm [31], therefore swiftly create the network topology with minimum overhead.

In an IoT network, a node gets CGRM message to compute CH. Figure 5 shows the best CH election at node k. When a node gets CGRM from the neighbor, it leads to subsequent operations: 1) In the first-time node gets the energy cost of this neighbor nodes that value compare with *Average Network Energy (ANE)* cost if node energy cost is greater than ANE cost that nodes are the candidate for CH, in added candidate CH node with minimum rank is the best CH for IoT ecosystem.

4.2 Cluster Formation

In the clustering method, the number of clusters will be equal to the number of CH nodes elected. In the proposed approach, the formation of clusters is adaptive and self-organized. Cluster members are determined on the basis of the distance between normal nodes and CH nodes. This distance is calculated through distance vector formula. Here all nodes in the network compares their distance to the selected CH nodes based on distance vector calculation and decides the CH node or cluster to join on the basis of the minimum distance from it to transmit its data.

5   Experiments and Results Analysis

In order to illustrate the proposed approach, some assumptions are made for the IoT network. Our approach assumes that the network consists of a *Tmotes Sky* CC2420 IEEE 802.15.4-compatible radio chip [32], and it can be achieved in *Contiki cooja* [8, 9] emulator environments. IoT network is fixed and runs at the radio frequency of 2.4 GHz. The simulation parameters of *Contiki cooja* are presented in Table 3.

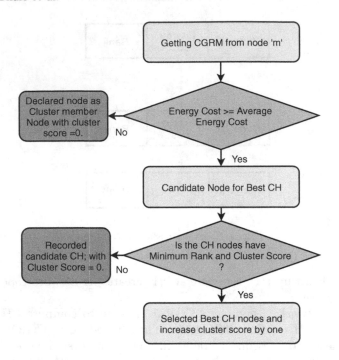

Fig. 5. Best CH election at node k.

Table 3. Cooja simulator parameters.

Radio model parameters	Value
Antenna	Omni directional
Radio model	MRM
Transmitter output power	(dBm) 0 to -25
Receiver sensitivity	(dBm) -94
Path loss exponent	1.5 to 6
Shadowing parameters (attenuation in dBm)	7
Radio frequency	2.4 GHz

5.1   Simulation Setup

The proposed approach of cluster formation and communication analysis, a model network, as is exhibited in Fig. 6. In the simulation, nodes are installed randomly in an 100 m × 100 m area. Cooja simulates and emulates various motes. Outcomes generated by cooja are more reasonable, as it expects the comparable constraints as actual hardware. We deployed the network with the random distribution of the nodes and 10 m background greed is exhibited in Fig. 7.

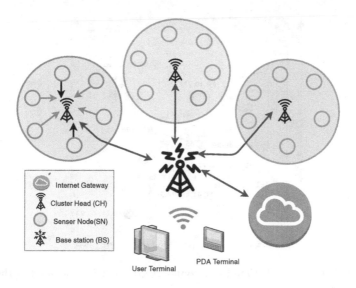

Fig. 6. Clustered IoT network

5.2 Performance Analysis

For evaluating the performance of the intended method, we employ four metrics to assess the performance: power consumption, the total quantity of successfully transmitted packets, number of live nodes, average residual energy of a node. Based on the live nodes, we can measure the lifetime of the 6LoWPAN network. Based on the packet received rate at the sink node depicts the throughput of the 6LoWPAN network. Based on the residual energy of a node signifies the energy-efficient 6LoWPAN network. A couple of experiments have been carried out on the *Contiki OS* [8] and *Cooja simulator* [9]. The complete explanation of individual experiments with result analysis is described below:

5.3 Experiment 1: Sink Node/Base Station Located in the Center of the Covered Field

In this experiment, the pink-colored nodes' air temperature sensors are continuously sensing and sending the information to the green-colored sink node, positioned in the center of the covered area as shown in Fig. 7. We have measured the average energy consumption and the radioactivity duty cycle periods of the sensor nodes during the network simulation runtime within the simulation scenario. Moreover, we have simulated two popular asynchronous MAC protocols available in Contiki OS that aim at energy saving, CX-MAC, Contiki MAC, and compared their results, whereas all the other network elements and operating conditions remain identical.

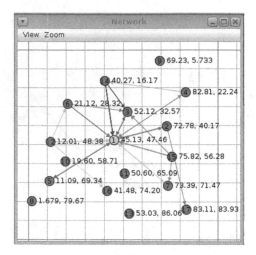

Fig. 7. Simulated N/W with 10 m background greed (Sink node located in the center) (Color figure online)

5.4 Experiment 2: Sink Node/Base Station Located in the Corner of the Covered Field

In this experiment, the pink-colored nodes are temperature sensors and continuously sensing and sending the information to the green-colored sink node. The position of the sink node is the corner of the area as shown in Fig. 8. Moreover, other configurations are the same as in the previous experiment.

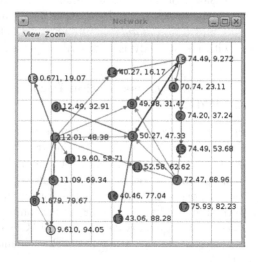

Fig. 8. Simulated N/W with 10 m background greed (Sink node located in the corner) (Color figure online)

BR serves as 6LoWPAN border router (6BR) which propagates IPv6 prefix. Sensor nodes $S_1, S_2, S_3, \ldots\ldots S_n$, which send messages to CHs. Simulator parameter for cooja is shown in Table 3.

Clustering in an IoT network is simulated in *Contiki cooja* [8,9] of 50 nodes whose format is presented in Table 3. The cluster count directly depends upon the number of elected CHs in the network. A cluster holds a single cluster head which serves as a sub-destination and route data from other cluster member nodes to the destination (Sink or Base Station). The 50 nodes are deployed by random dispersion (shown with red circle). The position of the BS is in the center of the field area (shown in green square). However, the location of the base station can be modified to compare the robustness of the proposed approach.

We compare proposed cluster-based hierarchical IoT architecture with the generic IoT architecture. For this purpose, we adopt LEACH [33] clustering strategy. The simulation outcomes of the proposed approach with the skywebsence example are carried out in Cooja simulator [8,9]. The sensing data, like light intensity and temperature values from the sensing layer, are transferred to the IoT layer as shown in Fig. 6.

5.5 After Implementing Clustering in 6LoWPAN

We evaluate our intended approach based on four metrics as mention above. A couple of cluster routing algorithm (i.e., LEACH [33] and EC [34]) are adopted for comparative analysis. Figure 9 shows all node power consumption, and our intended approach utilizes more limited power than LEACH and EC.

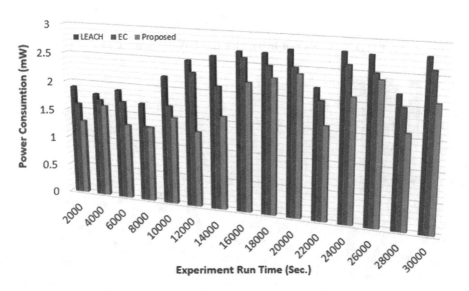

Fig. 9. Power consumption analysis of 6LoWPAN with closely related work.

Figure 10 exhibits the number of live nodes during the *43200* s simulation period. During this period, the *first node dies (FND)* to assess the 6LoWPAN network lifetime. Figure 10 confirms that the FND of our intended approach is 7285 s, while the comparative approach like LEACH and EC are 3287 s. and 4750 s respectively. LEACH gives the worst outcome because they are not considered residual energy factor during the CH node selection and communication process. Our intended approach takes residual energy and rank to build clusters to support better energy consumption. LEACH and EC approach practices the likelihood paradigm to determine CH nodes. Hence they cannot ensure CH distribution and count. Residual energy, rank, dynamic relay, and different cluster assist our intended approach to exceed various methods in the case of 6LoWPAN network lifetime. Figure 10 also exhibit the proposed solution live node count is higher with the respective run time of experiments.

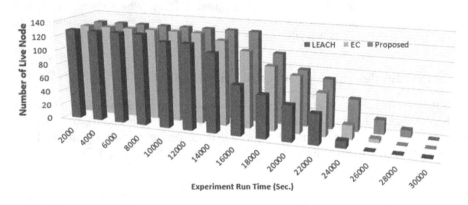

Fig. 10. Number of live nodes in 6LoWPAN network

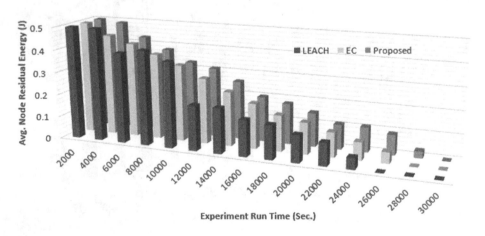

Fig. 11. Average of 6LoWPAN network residual energy.

Figure 11 exhibits the average residual energy of the 6LoWPAN network in simulation time. As per the experimental outcome, our intended solution conserves more energy than closely related work LEACH and EC. Our solution builds balanced clusters using residual energy and rank. It helps to reduce energy dissipation. Hence lifetime of the 6LoWPAN is increased as compared to LEACH and EC.

Figure 12 shows residual energy variation during the experiment run time. Maximum energy variation is observed when some nodes already have less residual energy. The intended approach has minimum variation, which means all node's energy depletion at the same ratio. Our intended approach incorporates residual energy and rank in CH node selection. It also rotates CH during simulation time. This solution not only preserves energy, it also balances traffic load toward the sink node. Hence, our approach achieves better outcomes with respect to energy efficiency and increasing 6LoWPAN network lifetime.

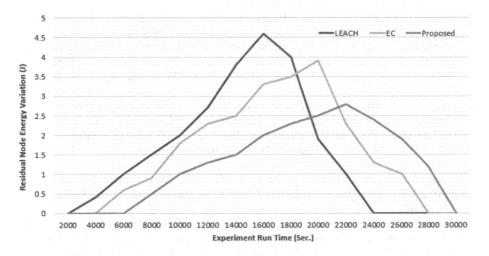

Fig. 12. Variation of 6LoWPAN node residual energy.

6 Conclusion and Future Work

In the 6LoWPAN network, efficient energy consumption is a vital issue. To deal with this issue, we enhance the 6LoWPAN lifetime. This research paper exhibited residual energy and a rank-based dynamic clustering approach, which can be applied in smart agriculture. The cluster structure of our intended approach balances the 6LoWPAN traffic load and improves the energy depletion. It incorporates uneven cluster, node rotation, and rank analysis to enhance 6LoWPAN network lifetime. The simulation outcome showed that our intended approach outperforms a closely related solution in terms of power consumption, throughput, energy efficiency, and network lifetime.

The intelligent clustering mechanism caters to various scenarios with diverse user preferences, like lifetime improvement, node classification, etc. We execute the clustering methods in non-attack IoT ecosystems and the difficulties when considering attack scenarios in IoT ecosystems. Future research objectives considering attacks like blackhole attack, selective forwarding, rank attack, and distributed denial of service (DDoS) attack to profit IoT ecosystem.

Acknowledgments. We thank the anonymous reviewers for their helpful feedback that served to improve this paper. The research work has been conducted under Information Security Education and Awareness (ISEA) Project Phase - II. The authors would like to thank MeitY and IIT Guwahati India, for the support.

References

1. Yang, Y., Wu, L., Yin, G., Li, L., Zhao, H.: A survey on security and privacy issues in IoT. IEEE IoT J. **4**(5), 1250–1258 (2017)
2. Symantec Security Center: Internet Security Threat Report. https://www.symantec.com/security-center/threat-report. Accessed 26 Jan 2021
3. Information and Technology Market Research Report: Global Internet of Things (IoT) Market. https://www.forbes.com/sites/louiscolumbus/2017/12/10/2017-roundup-of-internet-of-things-forecasts/#391d26e21480. Accessed 26 Jan 2021
4. Wang, C.F., Shih, J.D.: Pan: a network lifetime enhancement method for sink relocation and its analysis in WSNs. IEEE Sens. J. **14**(6), 1932–1943 (2014)
5. Xu, L., Collier, R.: A survey of clustering techniques in WSNs and consideration of the challenges of applying such to 5G IoT scenarios. IEEE IoT J. **4**(5), 1229–1249 (2017)
6. Zhang, Q., Zhu, C., Yang, L.T., Chen, Z., Zhao, L., Li, P.: An incremental CFS algorithm for clustering large data in IoTs. IEEE Trans. Industr. Inf. **13**(3), 1193–1201 (2017)
7. Bhale, P., Dey, S., Biswas, S., Nandi, S.: Energy efficient approach to detect sinkhole attack using roving IDS in 6LoWPAN network. In: Rautaray, S.S., Eichler, G., Erfurth, C., Fahrnberger, G. (eds.) I4CS 2020. CCIS, vol. 1139, pp. 187–207. Springer, Cham (2020). https://doi.org/10.1007/978-3-030-37484-6_11
8. Contiki: The Open Source Operating System for the Internet of Things: Instant Contiki. http://www.contiki-os.org/start.html. Accessed 26 Jan 2021
9. COOJA: Network Simulator: Cooja Simulator. http://anrg.usc.edu/contiki/index.php/Cooja_Simulator. Accessed 26 Jan 2021
10. Bhale, P., Prakash, S., Biswas, S., Nandi, S.: BRAIN: buffer reservation attack PreventIoN using legitimacy score in 6LoWPAN network. In: Rautaray, S.S., Eichler, G., Erfurth, C., Fahrnberger, G. (eds.) I4CS 2020. CCIS, vol. 1139, pp. 208–223. Springer, Cham (2020). https://doi.org/10.1007/978-3-030-37484-6_12
11. Popat, S.K., Emmanuel, M.: Review and comparative study of clustering techniques. Int. J. Comput. Sci. Inf. Technol. **5**(1), 805–812 (2014)
12. Mukhopadhyay, A.: Maulik: a survey of multiobjective evolutionary clustering. ACM Comput. Sur. (CSUR) **47**(4), 1–46 (2015)
13. Cooper, C., Franklin, D., Ros, M.: A comparative survey of VANET clustering techniques. IEEE Commun. Surv. Tutor. **19**(1), 657–681 (2016)
14. Saxena, A., Prasad, M., Gupta, A., Bharill, N.: A review of clustering techniques and developments. Neurocomputing **267**, 664–681 (2017)

15. Dubey, P., Veenadhar, S., Gupta, S.: Survey on energy efficient clustering and routing protocols of WSN. Int. J. Sci. Res. **5**(1) (2019)
16. Kameshwaran, K., Malarvizhi, K.: Survey on clustering techniques in data mining. Int. J. Comput. Sci. **5**(2), 2272–2276 (2014)
17. Wazarkar, S., Keshavamurthy, B.N.: A survey on image data analysis through clustering techniques for real world applications. J. Vis. Commun. Image Represent. **55**, 596–626 (2018)
18. Izakian, H., Pedrycz, W.: Fuzzy clustering of time series data using dynamic time warping distance. Eng. Appl. AI **39**, 235–244 (2015)
19. Al-Shalabi, M., Anbar, M., Wan, T.C.: Fuzzy clustering of time series data using dynamic time warping distance. Electronics **7**(8), 136 (2018)
20. Manjeshwar, A., Agrawal, D.P.: TEEN: a routing protocol for enhanced efficiency in WSNs. In: IPDPS, vol. 1, p. 189 (2001)
21. Manjeshwar, A., Agrawal, D.P.: APTEEN: a hybrid protocol for efficient routing and comprehensive information retrieval in WSNs. In: Parallel and Distributed Processing Symposium, vol. 3, pp. 0195b–0195b. Citeseer (2002)
22. Smaragdakis, G., Matta, I., Bestavros, A.: SEP: a stable election protocol for clustered heterogeneous WSNs. Technical report, Boston University (2004)
23. Islam, M., Matin, M., Mondol, T.: Extended Stable Election Protocol (SEP) for three-level hierarchical clustered heterogeneous WSN, pp. 43–43 (2012)
24. Tripathi, J., de Oliveira, J.C., Vasseur, J.P.: A performance evaluation study of RPL: routing protocol for low power and lossy networks. In: 2010 44th Annual Conference on Information Sciences and Systems (CISS), pp. 1–6. IEEE (2010)
25. Accettura, N., Grieco, L.A., Boggia, G., Camarda, P.: Performance analysis of the RPL routing protocol. In: 2011 IEEE International Conference on Mechatronics, pp. 767–772. IEEE (2011)
26. Xie, B., Wang, C.: An improved distributed energy efficient clustering algorithm for heterogeneous WSNs. In: Wireless Communications and Networking Conference (WCNC), pp. 1–6. IEEE (2017)
27. Heinzelman, W.R., Chandrakasan, A.: Energy-efficient communication protocol for WSNs. In: 33rd Annual Hawaii international Conference, pp. 10–22. IEEE (2000)
28. Pradeepkumar, B., Talukdar, K., Choudhury, B., Singh, P.K.: Predicting external rogue access point in IEEE 802.11 b/g WLAN using RF signal strength. In: 2017 International Conference on Advances in Computing, Communications and Informatics (ICACCI), pp. 1981–1986. IEEE (2017)
29. Cheng, L., Niu, J., Luo, C., Shu, L.: Towards minimum-delay and energy-efficient flooding in low-duty-cycle WSNs. Comput. Netw. **134**, 66–77 (2018)
30. Kumar, V., Yadav, S., Kumar, V., Sengupta, J., Tripathi, R., Tiwari, S.: Optimal clustering in Weibull distributed WSNs based on realistic energy dissipation model. In: Pattnaik, P.K., Rautaray, S.S., Das, H., Nayak, J. (eds.) Progress in Computing, Analytics and Networking. AISC, vol. 710, pp. 61–73. Springer, Singapore (2018). https://doi.org/10.1007/978-981-10-7871-2_7
31. Levis, P., Patel, N., Culler, D.: Trickle: a self-regulating algorithm for code propagation and maintenance in WSNs. In: USENIX/ACM Symposium, vol. 25 (2004)
32. Wireless Sensor Networks: Tmote-Sky. https://wirelesssensornetworks.weebly.com/blog/tmote-sky. Accessed 26 Jan 2021
33. Singh, S.K., Kumar, P.: A survey on successors of LEACH protocol. IEEE Access **5**, 4298–4328 (2017)
34. Wei, D., Jin, Y., Vural, S., Moessner, K., Tafazolli, R.: An energy-efficient clustering solution for wireless sensor networks. IEEE Trans. Wirel. Commun. **10**(11), 3973–3983 (2011)

Intermediate Pseudonym Certificate Generation for C-ITS

Hacène Fouchal[✉]

Université de Reims Champagne-Ardenne, CReSTIC, Campus Moulin de la Housse,
BP1029, Reims, France
`hacene.fouchal@univ-reims.fr`

Abstract. One of the most known mechanism to ensure privacy is the use of anonymity which means that drivers have to change their identity as much as possible. In the meantime, each message has to be authenticated when it is sent. To do so, each driver should sign its messages using its private key and has to send its certificate along with the message. The use of one certificate per driver will not ensure privacy since a certificate is easily correlated to the driver identity. For this reason, each driver will use a set of certificates denoted pseudonyms certificates (PC) Each vehicle has a set of PCs which will be used to sign sent messages and will be used as a part of the driver id. A PC is used for a limited period of time. In this paper we allow to a vehicle to generate additional PCs to its neighbors when they are close together for a period of time. It will allow to these neighbors to have more PCs. The neighbors will be able to change their PCs more frequently. Our choice is to allow a pseudonym derivation when a minimum number of vehicles are driving close to each other. The disadvantage of such a method is the network overhead which will increase due to sending of the driver vehicle certificate in each sent message.

Keywords: C-ITS · Privacy · Security · VANETs

1 Introduction

Connecting vehicles is a hot topic either for researchers and for car industry. These actors work on various issues (autonomy, safety, security, connectivity, etc,...). The connectivity issue is considered at different levels: architecture, protocols, coverage, etc,... The well known ITS-G5 (IEEE 802.11p) is a dedicated WIFI for connected vehicles working in a short range radio. In such networks, each vehicle sends continuously Awareness Messages (CAM) to its neighborhood. When a vehicle needs to notify an event, it will send another type of message denoted DENM (Decentralized Event Notification Message) which will be forwarded to all relevant vehicles. We need to consider the authenticity of senders in order to avoid untrustworthy drivers to notify non real events. Privacy is also required in order to avoid driver tracking. These two issues are solved by using

© Springer Nature Switzerland AG 2021
U. R. Krieger et al. (Eds.): I4CS 2021, CCIS 1404, pp. 76–83, 2021.
https://doi.org/10.1007/978-3-030-75004-6_6

a PKI in charge of distributing pseudonyms certificates (PC) to all trusted vehicles in the ecosystem. All messages are sent with their signature computed using their actual PCs. The used PC is also sent within the payload message.

In usual solutions, all PCs are provided by the PKI servers, in this paper we allow to vehicle to derive additional PCs to neighbors when they are close together for a period of time. It will allow to these neighbors to have more PCs. The consequence is twofold: the neighbors will be able to change their PCs more frequently and they will have lower costs. In fact our mechanism will allow to enhance the trust domain of C-ITS ecosystem. Our choice is to allow a pseudonym derivation when a minimum number of vehicles are deriving close to each other. The disadvantage of such a method is the network overhead which will increase due to sending of the driver vehicle certificate in each sent message.

This paper is composed as follows. Section 2 describes some works dedicated to vehicular networks. In Sect. 3, we present our model. Section 4 is dedicated to detailed processes used in this solution. Section 5 gives some conclusions and ideas about future enhancements of the study.

2   Related Works

The following works are dedicated to security issues on vehicular networks. In [5] a study about performances of the selection of web services in a secure environment is proposed. This scheme could be combined with a vehicular cloud solution which manages pseudonym distribution over vehicles.

[6] tackles one crucial issue about C-ITS: detecting misbehavior drivers. The authors propose a solution based on learning the behaviors of normal drivers and preventing the abnormal ones considered as misbehavior. This work have been extended in [7] in order to target malicious nodes over vehicular networks.

In [8], the authors have applied a game-based approach to specify security troubles on vehicular networks. A closer study is presented in [9] where the authors propose a simple mechanism to preserve privacy on mobile applications. They use recommender systems guided by an evaluation of the trust system.

[9] has worked on two privacy-preserving mobile application recommendation schemes based on a trust evaluation. They have proposed recommendations on mobile applications which are generated from trust behaviors of mobile application usage. In these two schemes, user private data can be preserved by applying the proposed security protocols and using homomorphic encryption.

[10] proposes a classification of different protocols which could be used on such networks for security issues. Many key performance indicators have been measured for various scenarios.

[11] has worked on a high level trust management system for VANETs. The purpose is to propose a scheme accepted by all involved nodes in the system. [12] has proposed a scheme to secure planning of electric vehicle routes within smart grids. They mainly show how to guarantee to electric vehicles to drive through secured routes. [13] is dedicated to about pseudonyms switching mechanisms. It proposes a survey on pseudonym certificate changes for vehicles. Most of these

mechanisms focus on choosing the adequate location or instant to switch to another pseudonym for a vehicle in order to ensure privacy preservation.

[14] has proposed an efficient pseudonym authentication scheme with strong privacy preservation for vehicular communications. Compared to traditional pseudonym authentication schemes, they mainly make the size of Certificate Revocation List (CRL) linear with the number of revoked vehicles. [15] presents an effective pseudonym changing strategy at social spots (PCS) to achieve the provable location privacy. The aim of the paper is to find the relevant location to change the pseudonym since these locations are known as crowded and are able to guarantee confusion.

In [16], the authors have developed a framework for changing pseudonyms when vehicles meet some other vehicles. [17] presents the preservation of privacy based on differential privacy which is applied for urban areas. It is dedicated to Unmanned Aerial Vehicles, [18] has worked on integrating security schemes for vehicles communications within various types of vehicular networks mainly on WiFi or cellular channels.

[20] has proposed an original security mechanism for vehicular networks using a cloud approach and implementing a specific blockchain.

[21] has proposed a hybrid recommender algorithm that combines users' location and preferences and the content of the items located close to such users. The locations of users are tacked and the scenarios proposed, the privacy has been investigated with low efficiency. [22] focuses on clustering algorithms which are able to detect driver profiles on trajectories collected from various vehicles. They prove that the anonymity could be broken. Then drivers could be tracked even if they use different PCs.

Our recent works [18,19] have been dedicated to integrate simple security schemes for vehicles communications.

On studies we see that privacy and cost efficiency need to be considered together. These two issues have not been studied. As far as we know, there is no study which has considered dynamic PC generation. All PCs are provided by PKI servers. Since a vehicle is equipped which a Hardware Security Module (HSM), it is able to generate a new certificate. Int the paper we detail all different scenarios of our proposal.

3   Security Architecture

3.1   Preliminaries

In C-ITS (Cooperative Intelligent Transportation System), a specific communication stack has been standardized by the ETSI standardization institute in Europe [1] and similar ones have also been proposed in the US and in Japan. Upon the *Transport-Networking* layer (composed of the geo-networking layer and the BTP layer), the *Facilities* layer has been defined to ensure an interface between the application layer (close to the driver and vehicle sensors) and the *Transport-Networking* layer. A set of protocols have been proposed at this layer.

In this paper, we will handle only on 2 message protocols: Cooperative Awareness Message (CAM) [3] and Decentralized Environmental Notification Message (DENM) [2]. The aim behind sending CAM messages is to give dynamic information about the vehicle (i.e. position, speed, heading, etc.). A vehicle sends CAMs to its neighborhood using Vehicle-to-Vehicle (V2V) or V2I communications. Depending on the vehicle speed, the frequency of CAM messages varies 1 Hz 10 Hz. A vehicle sends DENM messages in order to inform any event (i.e. accident, traffic jam, etc.). The event could be triggered automatically thanks to the connection to the vehicle CAN Bus. In fact, some smart rules are run on the OBU and generate appropriate messages or manually for sensitive cases as animal on the road.

3.2 Privacy and Authenticity

C-ITS security considers two main aspects:

- Authenticity: this aspect allows to consider only messages coming from trusted drivers.
- Privacy: this aspect allows to protect drivers data and avoid driver tracking.

Public Key Infrastructure (PKI is the usual solution considered. Each involved vehicle in the ecosystem has to be registered on the PKI server. The registration is achieved by providing a long term certificate (LTC) this vehicle (signed by a root PKI).

A vehicle could sign its messages using this LTC by means of a Trusted Platform Module (TPM) which embed cryptographic processes and private keys with safety. Authenticity is very well ensured. But with such but privacy is not considered at all. Indeed, from LTC we could extract private information which gives the opportunity to external observers to track drivers. The usual solution to solve privacy is the use of pseudonym certificates (PC) for small period. A node should have a pool of PCs which should be up to date in order to be able to switch to another PC accordingly.

In this paper, we propose to upload a set of pseudonyms certificates for a long period. This period should the maximum required delay for a car manufacturer to maintain a vehicle. That means that after this period, another set of certificates should be uploaded again in a trusted repairing garage of the car manufacturer. The set of certificates is a list of sorted pools. A pool is expected to be valid for a week. A detailed of this process is defined in [4].

4   Dynamic Pseudonym Certificate Generation

In this section we present our contribution about dynamic PC generation done by any trusted vehicle to its neighbors. We present the main ideas of our contribution, then we present the algorithm of PC derivation.

4.1   Principle

We consider a set V of N vehicles such as $V = v_1, v_2, ..., v_N$. Each vehicle v_i has a current set of M_j pseudonym certificates denoted PC_i such as $P_i = PC_{i1}, PC_{i2}, ..., PC_{iM_j}$. We recall that a PC is a certificate which is signed by the PKI. When a vehicle V_i meets another vehicle V_j for a period of time (in fact V_j is in the neighbor list of V_i since a threshold period TS, V_i will propose to V_j a new PC signed by V_i). This new PC will have higher size than any PC signed by the original PKI server since it contains the signature of the issuer (V_i) together with PKI server. Figure 1 gives the procedure run by both the issuer and the requester.

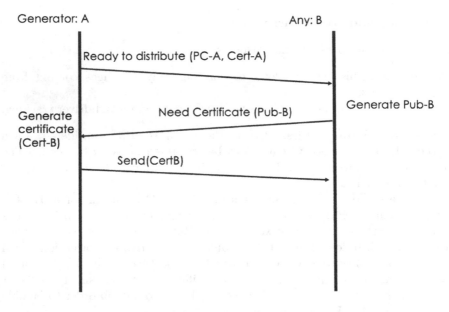

Fig. 1. Example of a dynamic PC generation

This procedure can be integrated in a large set of scenarios for enhancing the privacy protection. In the following, we describe some scenarios.

4.2   Generation from a Current PC

If a vehicle v_A is using a PC since a long period and if a neighbor v_B is asking for a PC generation. The generated PC for v_B will be related to v_A. v_B will use the new PC instead of its former one. In this case a tracker may easily rebuilt the trajectory of v_B and will be able recognize this vehicle. For this reason, v_A will not generate a new PC for only one vehicle but for more that 2 in the same time in order to not be able to recognize the original vehicles which have received new PCs. Of course, if the generation could be done for all neighbors; 10 for instance, the confusion between vehicles is higher which means that trackers will not be able to follow vehicles.

All neighbors which have received new PCs (sometimes more than one for a vehicle) will switch to new PCs without using their own PCs in the initial pool.

4.3   Generation from a New PC

When a vehicle v_A has switched its current PC to another PC, it will take a profit to ask all its neighbors to ask for a PC generation. All responders will get a new generated PC. This scenario will let all vehicles to get new PCs in the same time. This situation is very confusing for a tracker since it will be hard to detect who is who. Compared to one of the well known PC switch strategies, which allows to all nodes to change their PCs, this procedure will be done with a lower certificate cost.

4.4   Cross Generation

This last method allows to v_A and v_B to ask each other to generate a new PC for each other. In such a situation, both vehicles will have new PCs without using their own PC pools. This issue generates more confusion than the previous one since all vehicles will change in the same time.

5   Conclusion

In this paper we have proposed a simple solution to generate a new pseudonym certificates for C-ITS. We have shown that this proposal has two main features:

- Cost reduction In C-ITS, current solutions use a PC pool for a period of time (days or weeks) and need to ask PKI servers for a new PC pool.
- Privacy enhancement: This solution allows change PCs many times when neighbors are met. That provides more PCs (different Ids) for vehicles. This principle will allow to add a high level confusion which will protect much more drivers against trackers.

As a disadvantage, the messages contains larger certificates (the signature of the issuer is added to the PKI certificate) which generates a network overhead/As a future works, we intend to test better the scalability of our system by launching simulations. on OMNET++.

Acknowledgments. This work was made possible by EC Grant No. 2018-FR-TM-0097-S from the INEA Agency for Indid project. The statements made herein are solely the responsibility of the authors.

References

1. European Telecommunications Standards Institute (ETSI). http://www.etsi.org
2. Intelligent Transport Systems (ITS); Vehicular Communications; Basic Set of Applications; Part 3: Specifications of Decentralized Environmental Notification Basic Service. ETSI EN 302 637-3 V1.2.2, November 2014
3. Intelligent Transport Systems (ITS); Vehicular Communications; Basic Set of Applications; Part 2: Specification of Cooperative Awareness Basic Service. ETSI EN 302 637-2 vol. 1.3.2, November 2014
4. Eric R. Verheul, Issue First Activate Later Certificates for V2X. Presentation Inter-Cor project, June 2017
5. Serrai, W., Abdelli, A., Mokdad, L., Hammal, Y.: Towards an efficient and a more accurate web service selection using MCDM methods. J. Comput. Sci. **22**, 253–267 (2017)
6. Sedjelmaci, H., Senouci, S.M., Bouali, T.: Predict and prevent from misbehaving intruders in heterogeneous vehicular networks. Veh. Commun. J. **10**, 74–83 (2017). https://doi.org/10.1016/j.vehcom.2016.12.005. Elsevier
7. Bouali, T., Senouci, S.M., Sedjelmaci, H.: A distributed detection and prevention scheme from malicious nodes in vehicular networks. Int. J. Commun. Syst. (2016). https://doi.org/10.1002/dac.3106. Wiley
8. Mabrouk, A., Kobbane, A., Koutbi, M.E.: Signaling game-based approach to improve security in vehicular networks. In: Proceedings of the 4th International Conference on Vehicle Technology and Intelligent Transport Systems (VEHITS 2018), pp. 495–500 (2018). ISBN: 978-989-758-293-6
9. Xua, K., Zhangb, W., Yan, Z.: A privacy-preserving mobile application recommender system based on trust evaluation. J. Comput. Sci. **26**, 87–107 (2018)
10. Ramassamy, C., Fouchal, H., Hunel, P.: Classification of usual protocols over wireless sensor networks. In: 2012 IEEE International Conference on Communications (ICC), pp. 622–626 (2016)
11. Haddadou, N., Rachedi, A., Ghamri-Doudane, Y.: A job market signaling scheme for incentive and trust management in vehicular ad hoc networks. IEEE Trans. Veh. Technol. **64**(8), 3657–3674 (2015)
12. Bourass, A., Cherkaoui, S., Khoukhi, L.: Secure optimal itinerary planning for electric vehicles in the smart grid. IEEE Trans. Industr. Inf. **13**(6), 3236–3245 (2017)
13. Boualouache, A., Senouci, S.M., Moussaoui, S.: A survey on pseudonym changing strategies for vehicular ad-hoc networks. IEEE Commun. Surv. Tutor. **20**(1), 770–790 (2018)
14. Sun, Y., Lu, R., Lin, X., Shen, X., Su, J.: An efficient pseudonymous authentication scheme with strong privacy preservation for vehicular communications. IEEE Trans. Veh. Technol. **59**(7), 3589–3603 (2010)
15. Lu, R., Lin, X., Luan, T.H., Liang, X., Shen, X.: Pseudonym changing at social spots: an effective strategy for location privacy in VANETs. IEEE Trans. Veh. Technol. **61**(1), 86–96 (2012)
16. Boualouache, A., Senouci, S.M., Moussaoui, S.: PRIVANET: an efficient pseudonym changing and management framework for vehicular ad-hoc networks, IEEE Trans. Intell. Transp. Syst. (T-ITS), 1–10 (2019) https://doi.org/10.1109/TITS.2019.2924856
17. Kim, H., Ben-Othman, J., Mokdad, L.: UDiPP: a framework for differential privacy preserving movements of unmanned aerial vehicles in smart cities. IEEE Trans. Veh. Technol. **68**, 3933–3943 (2019)

18. Fouchal, H., Bourdy, E., Wilhelm, G., Ayaida, M.: Secured communications on vehicular networks over cellular networks. In: Fahrnberger, G., Gopinathan, S., Parida, L. (eds.) ICDCIT 2019. LNCS, vol. 11319, pp. 31–41. Springer, Cham (2019). https://doi.org/10.1007/978-3-030-05366-6_3

19. Wilhelm, G., Fouchal, H., Thomas, K., Ayaida, M.: A C-ITS central station as a communication manager. In: Hodoň, M., Eichler, G., Erfurth, C., Fahrnberger, G. (eds.) I4CS 2018. CCIS, vol. 863, pp. 33–43. Springer, Cham (2018). https://doi.org/10.1007/978-3-319-93408-2_3

20. Khelifi, H., Luo, S., Nour, B., Moungla, H., Ahmed, S.H.: Reputation-based Blockchain for secure NDN caching in vehicular networks. In: IEEE Conference on Standards for Communications and Networking (CSCN 2018), October 2018, Paris, France (2018)

21. Celdrán, A.H., Pérez, M.G., Clemente, F.J., Pérez, G.M.: Design of a recommender system based on users' behavior and collaborative location and tracking. J. Comput. Sci. **12**, 83–94 (2016)

22. Jafarnejad, S., Castignani, G., Engel, T.: Towards a real-time driver identification mechanism based on driving sensing data. In: 2017 IEEE 20th International Conference on Intelligent Transportation Systems (ITSC), pp. 1–7. IEEE (2017)

FttX Deployment Using Available Networks and Existing Infrastructures

Niels M. P. Neumann[1,2(✉)] and Frank Phillipson[1]

[1] The Netherlands Organisation for Applied Scientific Research,
The Hague, The Netherlands
`frank.phillipson@tno.nl`
[2] Radboud University, Nijmegen, The Netherlands
`niels.neumann@tno.nl`

Abstract. In Fibre-to-the-X, fibre is used to connect new active optic equipment at a certain location. In most cases, a connection to an existing network is required. Costs can be saved by using existing infrastructure, like empty ducts and spare fibres. Often, restrictions are given by municipalities to only use certain tracks or to only follow street patterns. This means that planners have to work with the combination of several networks to design the new network. In this article we propose a new algorithm that finds a low cost-path between two points, using multiple available networks. The given points do not have to be connected to one of the networks from the start. We split the problem in three sub-problems: connecting the points with the network, find the transition points between the networks, and finally find the low cost-path between the given points. For each sub-problems an algorithm is proposed and the combination of those is tuned for optimal performance. The algorithm is applied to a problem in telecommunication: it quickly finds low-cost paths in complex urban environments.

Keywords: Network · Algorithms · Intersections · Routing · Optimization

1 Introduction

Fibre-to-the-X (FttX) is the general name for fibre architectures, bringing the fibre to active optical equipment on a certain location in the network. This equipment can be placed within a street cabinet (Fibre-to-the-Cabinet) [12], a small active node for, e.g., VDSL+ or G.Fast (Fibre-to-the-Curb) [11], in buildings (Fibre-to-the-Building/Home) [10], at mobile access points (Fibre-to-the-Cell) or even at lamp posts or bus stops in a smart city environment [7,13].

In the design or planning phase of such a FttX network, a planner starts at the new active location and has to route to the existing fibre network, following and combining empty ducts, streets, trench patterns and existing available fibre. This can be done from a cost perspective (existing fibres, empty ducts), from

© Springer Nature Switzerland AG 2021
U. R. Krieger et al. (Eds.): I4CS 2021, CCIS 1404, pp. 84–99, 2021.
https://doi.org/10.1007/978-3-030-75004-6_7

a complexity perspective (only allowing for the use of street patterns) or from regulatory or authorities for the use of specific trenches or trajectories. In Fig. 1 a simple example is shown: The blue lines represent streets, the black lines trenches and the red lines the empty ducts. Now the planner has to connect S and T. Two possible routes are shown, A might be the cheapest solution, reusing empty ducts, and B might be the shortest route. For this, the planner has to decide where to dig, which tracks to use and where to switch between the three available networks.

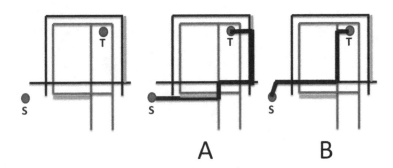

Fig. 1. Example of planning with multiple networks between source S and target T.

In this paper a new, total, approach is described for solving the problem of finding a connection between two points, using one or more available networks. In Sect. 2 the problem is introduced in more detail. In Sect. 3 three algorithms are discussed, each of which solves one of the sub-problems. These three algorithms are combined in Sect. 4, where we apply it to a Fibre-to-the-X problem, using street networks and trench patterns of different Dutch regions. The results are compared both on the running times and the lowest-cost paths found for various parameter-settings.

2   Problem Definition

In the problem two points and one or more networks are given. Each of these available networks consists of line segments and every line segment has two endpoints. The two points have to be connected with the lowest possible cost. This cost results from both creating new connections (e.g. by digging) and from routing through already available connections. When more than one network is used, routing requires knowledge on when to use which network and consequently where transitions between different networks are possible. This gives rise to three sub-problems:

1. Connect the given points with a network;
2. Determine where the given networks intersect;
3. Find a low cost-path between the two connection points using the connected networks.

An illustrative example is given in Fig. 2, where the points cab and fib have to be connected. The connection which requires the least amount of digging is shown in solid red and requires 1.6070 units of digging. The dotted line to point b however requires digging over a distance of 1.6076 units, while requiring less routing through the network.

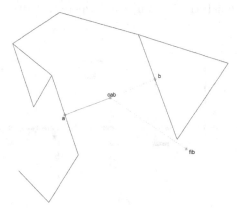

Fig. 2. A network (blue), with the shortest connection to the network (solid red) and two other possible connections (dotted red). (Color figure online)

In the following we consider the following definitions: A line segment is a line with a begin point and an endpoint. A *connection* is a connected set of multiple piece-wise linear line segments. A *network* is collection of connections. The points that have to be connected with either the network or other points are referred to as *active points*. The cost for digging and routing through the network depend on the length. Both are taken to be non-negative. All points are assumed to be in $\mathbb{R}^2$.

3   Approach

In this section we consider each of the three sub-problems defined in the previous section. Next, the three solutions are combined, giving the proposed algorithm. We also consider the limitations of the algorithm and its complexity.

3.1   Sub-problem 1: Connecting with a Network

The first sub-problem focuses on connecting active points with an available network. There have been numerous algorithms which solve finding the shortest path between two points or, given a set of points, finding the two points closest to each other to optimality, for instance Dijkstra's Algorithm [5] and the approach by Shamos and Hoey to some closest-point problems [14]. However, an algorithm which checks for the shortest distances between a set of points and a set of line segments has not been constructed yet. For each connection and for each line segment we distinguish three cases, as shown in Fig. 3. Here, z represents the active point and x and y are the endpoints of the line segment.

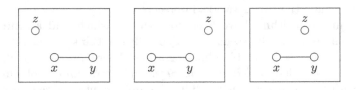

Fig. 3. From left to right Case 1, 2 and 3

We use inner products to determine to which case an active point corresponds: point z is in Case 1 if $(z - x) \cdot (y - x) < 0$, and the point is in Case 2 if $(z - y) \cdot (x - y) < 0$. Otherwise, it is in Case 3.

For Case 1 the distance between z and the line segment is given by the Euclidean distance between z and x, and similarly, for Case 2 and endpoint y. For Case 3 the distance between the line xy and the active point z is given by

$$d(xy, z) = \frac{|(y - x) \cdot (z_2, z_1) + y_1 x_2 - y_2 x_1|}{\sqrt{(x_1 - y_1)^2 + (x_2 - y_2)^2}}. \tag{1}$$

Note that we do not have to compute the distance between an active point and all line segments within a connection. We only have to consider Case 2 if the line segment xy is the last line segment in the connection. Otherwise, there is a next line segment yw and one of the three situations in Fig. 4 holds. In all cases, $d(y, z)$ is either computed again or sub-optimal.

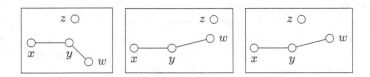

Fig. 4. The three scenarios for Case 2

Once the distance is calculated, it is compared with the shortest distance found for that active point up until then. If it is shorter, it is saved and otherwise it is discarded. The closest line segment for each active point is determined. The point on the line segment xy closest to the active point z is given by

$$x + \lambda(y - x) \quad \text{with} \quad \lambda = \frac{(z - x) \cdot (y - x)}{(y - x) \cdot (y - x)}. \tag{2}$$

3.2   Sub-problem 2: Determine Where the Networks Intersect

We may use different networks to find a low cost-path between two points. However, if more than one network is used, it has to be known at which points a transition between two networks is possible. These points correspond exactly to the points where the two networks intersect[1].

In literature, algorithms have been constructed which find all intersection points between two sets of line segments. Typically one thinks of the sets as being a set with red and a set with blue line segments. There are already algorithms that solve this so-called *Red-Blue Line Segment Intersection*-problem [1,2,8]. These algorithms do however not fulfill all requirements, as self-intersections are typically ignored. In 1976 Shamos and Hoey published an algorithm which, given a set of n line segments, determines if any two intersect [15]. This was later extended by Bently and Ottmann in 1979 to an algorithm which could find and return all the intersection points of a set of n line segments [4].

The algorithm by Bentley and Ottmann (BO) is a line-sweep algorithm, meaning that a line sweeps through the plan from left to right, identifying intersections. We consider a modified version of the BO-algorithm, where we consider each line segment of each connection separately. Line segments are ordered based on their first coordinate.

We use two data structures: the sweep line L, storing active line segments, and the event queue E with all events that are not yet processed. Only line segments which currently intersect the sweep line are called active and thus stored in L. The line segments are sorted according the their second coordinate. We also identify three events:

Event: starting point The line segment is inserted in the sweep line L.

Event: intersection The intersection is reported and deleted from E. The order of the corresponding line segments in L is reversed.

Event: endpoint The corresponding line segment is removed from L.

Line segments for which the right endpoint is to the left of L are said to be *dead* line segments. Once a line segment is recognized as dead, it is removed from the sweep line, and it is of no interest anymore. After every event, a constant number of possible new intersections have to be checked. This follows as only neighbouring line segments in L can intersect. When a line segment is inserted, only the immediate neighbours in L are considered for possible intersections. Similarly, if two line segments intersect, after swapping there are at most two new pairs of line segments which may intersect. Finally, if a line segment is removed, the new neighbours in L have to be checked for a possible intersection. If the new neighbours intersect and the intersection point is to the right of L, the intersection point is inserted as an event in E.

Cross products are used to determine if two line segments intersect. We embed all line segments in $\mathbb{R}^3$, with the third component being zero, i.e., $(x_1, x_2) \mapsto (x_1, x_2, 0)$. This gives the following theorem. The proof and more details are given in [9].

---

[1] Note that two networks intersect if the networks intersect when projected on the two dimensional plane.

Theorem 1. *Given two line segments with endpoints A, B and C, D. The line segments intersect if and only if both*

$$((A - B) \times (B - C))_3 \cdot ((A - B) \times (B - D))_3 < 0 \qquad (3)$$

$$(C - D) \times (D - A))_3 \cdot ((C - D) \times (D - B))_3 < 0. \qquad (4)$$

Here $((A - B) \times (B - C))_3$ is the third component of the cross product of the vectors $A - B$ and $B - C$.

In the original algorithm, constraints are imposed on the data to make sure that each event has distinct first coordinates. These constrains are:

1. No line segment is vertical;
2. No two line segments partially overlap;
3. An endpoint of a line segment does not lie on another line segment;
4. At most two line segments intersect in a point;
5. Every event has a different x-coordinate.

To use the algorithm in a practical setting, we relax these constraints. Under these relaxations, all intersection points are still found:

1. For vertical line segments, define the data point with the larger x_2-coordinate to be the starting point and with the smaller x_2-coordinate to be the endpoint;
2. Overlapping line segments are considered simultaneously;
3. We consider both proper intersections and intersections of a line segment and an endpoint;
4. Multiple line segments may intersect in a single point. The order of all corresponding line segments in reversed in the sweep line L;
5. Events with the same x_1-coordinate are sorted according to the x_2-coordinate.

A single network is obtained from two networks and the intersection points by subdividing intersecting line segments and noting that two intersecting line segments result in four non-intersecting line segments.

3.3   Sub-problem 3: Finding a Low Cost-Path

A 1959 algorithm by Dijkstra finds the shortest between between any two vertices in a weighted graph with non-negative weights [5]. An extension of Dijkstra's algorithm is the Bellman-Ford algorithm, which only requires the non-existence of cycles with negative weight [3,6]. We use Dijkstra's algorithm to find the shortest path between two points.

Given a weighted connected graph $G = (V, E, W)$, with vertices $v \in V$, edges $e \in E$ and weights $w(e) \in W$, Dijkstra's algorithm distinguishes two sets: a partial spanning tree X and nodes not yet in the tree Y. The output of the algorithm is a spanning tree with minimum weight. For vertices $v_1, v_2 \in V$, the weight of the edge $v_1 - v_2$ is given by $w(v_1, v_2)$. The pseudo-code of Dijkstra's algorithm is given in Algorithm 1.

Algorithm 1. Dijkstra's algorithm

   Input: Weighted connected graph $G = (V, E, W)$ and a source node s.
   Output: d a vector with distances from s to the other nodes, p a vector with for
   every node its predecessor.

   Initialization: Initialize the distance $d(v)$ to every node v at infinity and the
   distance to the source node $d(s)$ at zero. Set $X = \emptyset, Y = V$.

1: **while** $Y \neq \emptyset$ **do**
2:     Choose vertex $u \in Y$ such that $d(u) = \min_{z \in Y} d(z)$
3:     $Y = Y - \{u\}, X = X + \{u\}$
4:     **for all** neighbours $v \in Y$ of u **do**
5:         $d(v) = \min(d(v), d(u) + w(v, u))$
6:     **end for**
7:     Update the predecessor of u in p
8: **end while**

Note that the spanning tree can be reconstructed from this output. As the graph is connected, there is a minimum cost-path between every pair of nodes and hence the algorithm finishes. By replacing "$Y \neq \emptyset$" by "$t \notin X$" in the *while*-loop, the algorithm returns once a low cost-path between source s and target t is found. For disconnected sets, the condition should be replace by **while** *not all neighbours of points in X are in X*.

3.4   Combination of the Sub-problems

The three sub-problems can be combined to solve the main problem: connecting two points using available networks. In the following, the locations of the active points are fixed, as well as the available networks.

First, a single network is created from the given networks using the algorithm described in Sect. 3.2. Afterwards, multiple possible connection points to the network are determined for all active points considered, using a modified version of the algorithm presented in Sect. 3.1. In the following, k refers to the number of potential connection points between the network and an active point.

For the k potential connection points, the endpoints of the corresponding connections are determined together with the associated cost to get there. This cost includes digging to the network and routing to the endpoint.

Dijkstra's algorithm is now used to find a low cost-path. By adding the active points together with the k found links to the network, Dijkstra's algorithm only has to be run once, instead of $\mathcal{O}(k^2)$ times. The resulting path consists of both a routing part in the network and digging from the network to one or both of the active points. In disconnected graphs, more digging might be needed.

The pseudo-code of the algorithm is given in Algorithm 2.

In the following section we consider two restrictions of the algorithm in case of disconnected networks.

Algorithm 2. Find the least-cost path between two points using a network

---

Input: A network, the points to connect and the costs of digging and routing, k the number of best connection points.
Output: The least cost-path between the two points

1: Compute cost of direct digging between the two points
2: Find the k best connection points for both points with the network
3: Determine the endpoints of the corresponding connections
4: Determine the costs corresponding to the endpoints
5: Deal with possibly isolated connections
6: Apply Dijkstra's algorithm on the network together with the points that have to be connected
7: Compute the path with the least cost

3.5 Restrictions of the Algorithm

There are two restrictions, as networks do not have to be connected. Whereas graphically, the problem can be solved in most cases, letting a computer solve the problem for disconnected graphs is in general harder. Note that it is possible that the algorithm finds a shortest connection to a small isolated component in the network. This can be overcome by allowing for extra digging between two components of the network. Another restriction that is hard to overcome is that a least-cost path might require digging, even if the network is connected.

An example of this sub-optimal situation is given in Fig. 5 taken from the street network and trench pattern of the Dutch city of Venray. For simplicity only the situation is considered where the point cab has to be connected with the intermediate point 6. The costs to dig and route are c_{dig} and c_{route} respectively. Point 1 yields the shortest connection point to the network and point 3 is the connection point given by the algorithm. The total cost of connecting with point 3 and routing to point 6 is $11.76 \cdot c_{dig} + 20.33 \cdot c_{route}$, whereas digging to point 2, routing to point 4, digging to point 5 and routing to point 6 presents a path with lower cost: $11.71 \cdot c_{dig} + 19.46 \cdot c_{route}$.

We considered two options to overcome the first restriction: Either we neglect small isolated components, or we allow for extra digging from isolated parts to the rest of the network, if needed for a low-cost path. Another option of connecting all components before running the algorithm is both computationally expensive and might result in sub-optimal connections with respect to the active points considered. In Sect. 4.1 we consider the effects on both the running time and the costs of the found paths when neglecting small isolated components and when allowing for extra digging. Furthermore, we consider the effect of deleting small isolated components from the network before running the algorithm.

Solving the second restriction, digging instead of routing, is hard. To determine if digging is cheaper than routing, we should first calculate the cost of routing and the cost of digging between it the endpoints of each connection. If the associated cost of digging is smaller than the cost of routing, it is better to dig between the endpoints, instead of route between them. This analysis of

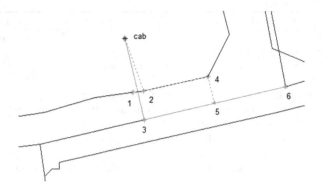

Fig. 5. In solid red the least cost-path found by the algorithm: $cab \to 3 \to 6$. The dotted red line shows a path of lower cost: $cab \to 2 \to 4 \to 5 \to 6$. (Color figure online)

considering whether extra digging is better than routing should then also be extended to groups of two or more connections. This can be extended even further to the endpoints of the piece-wise linear parts instead of the endpoints of the connection and finally even the intermediate points on the line segments and connections can be considered. This problem becomes extremely complex extremely fast. Therefore solutions for this problem are not considered. Only paths with digging at the start and end near the active points are considered.

3.6   Complexity of the Algorithm

To determine the complexity of the algorithm, we consider the complexity of each individual part. Let n be the number of connections, m a bound on the number of line segments per connection and let k be the number of shortest connection points under consideration. This gives complexity $\mathcal{O}(nmk)$ for the first part. For every point found, the endpoints of the corresponding connection have to be determined.

As there are k connection points, at most $2k$ endpoints and a maximum of m line segments, this adds a term $\mathcal{O}(mk)$ to the complexity. Note that even if all line segments are isolated, this only adds a constant factor to the complexity.

The complexity of Dijkstra's original algorithm is $\mathcal{O}(n^2)$, however, when using different data structures, this can be reduced to $\mathcal{O}(n \log n)$. As keeping track of the least total cost and finding the shortest path between the two points can all be done in $\mathcal{O}(n)$ time, the total complexity is given by

$$\mathcal{O}(nmk + nm + n \log n + n) = \mathcal{O}(nmk + n \log n). \tag{5}$$

Note that typically $m \ll n$ for the data sets of cities considered. Also note that only consider connections within certain bounds may improve the computations in practical settings, as less connections have to be considered.

4 Results

In the following different data sets are considered and the algorithm is run for each of them. First, the best configuration is determined based on the running times. Also data sets larger than that of expected practical use are considered, e.g. the entire southwest of the Netherlands. In each case fifty pairs of points are randomly generated and the median running times of the algorithm and the average costs for these pairs are computed.

Again k denotes the number of 'shortest distances' for each active point. The costs are denoted by c_{dig} and c_{route} for digging and routing respectively. We consider different values of k. The active points are chosen randomly within the bounds of the data set. For the costs we assume $c_{dig} = 25$ euro per meter for digging and $c_{route} = 3$ euro per meter for routing through the network.

We will first consider different configurations of the algorithm, before evaluating the performance. In total fifty pairs of active points are considered for each data-set and results are evaluated based on the median running times and the average costs among these fifty pairs.

4.1 Configurations of the Algorithm

First we consider the best approach to deal with small isolated components in the network. Afterwards we consider the effect of restricting the network to one of smaller size. The running times might improve for this smaller network as less connections are considered. We restrict the network to an enlarged bounded rectangle, meaning a bounding rectangle on the active points is taken and all sides are extended by some constant. We add another option here to include or remove leaves with which no connection is made in the analysis.

For the first configuration we consider k-values of 5, 10 and 15 and we distinguish between three situations:

- Deleting small isolated components from the network;
- Neglecting small isolated components from the network;
- Allow extra digging from isolated component to the rest of the network.

For the second configuration we consider:

- Not restricting the network and considering all endpoints;
- Not restricting the network and not considering leaves;
- Restricting the network and considering all endpoints within the restriction;
- Restricting the network and not considering the leaves within the restriction.

The First Configuration: Isolated Components. To determine the best option for the first configuration we consider two data sets: The city of Venray, with 23,628 connections and the city of Tilburg, with 96,851. The median running times and average costs for Venray can be found in Table 1 and those for Tilburg in Table 2.

Table 1. Venray: median running times and average costs for fifty pairs in seconds.

	Running times (s)			Costs (euros)		
	$k = 5$	$k = 10$	$k = 15$	$k = 5$	$k = 10$	$k = 15$
Delete isolated comp.	6.84	6.94	6.95	6,812	6,208	6,208
Neglect isolated comp.	3.36	3.38	3.40	6,812	6,208	6,208
Digging from isolated comp.	3.42	3.47	3.57	6,238	6,200	6,200

Table 2. Tilburg: median running times and average costs for fifty pairs in seconds.

	Running times (s)			Costs (euros)		
	$k = 5$	$k = 10$	$k = 15$	$k = 5$	$k = 10$	$k = 15$
Delete isolated comp.	22.46	22.30	22.40	14,998	14,989	14,984
Neglect isolated comp.	6.93	6.95	7.23	14,998	14,989	14,984
Digging from isolated comp.	6.90	6.93	6.93	14,998	14,989	14,984

We see that the difference in costs are small and even zero for the Tilburg data-set. Therefore, we only have to consider the different k-values and the running times. We see that deleting small isolated components takes significantly longer than neglecting them or allowing for extra digging. This follows logically as we first have to determine what the small isolated components are and then remove them, while they might not be used in the least-cost path.

The running times for neglecting isolated components and allowing for extra digging are similar, whereas the cost for extra digging is at least as good as that found when neglecting components. As a result, it is best to allow for extra digging from small isolated components. The running times are comparable and the found costs are at least as good, compared to neglecting these components.

Regarding the different k-values, we see that the costs for $k = 10$ are comparable to those of $k = 15$, whereas the running times are smaller for $k = 10$. We see that for $k = 5$ the costs of the paths found are sub-optimal. Therefore, we use $k = 10$ in the following.

The Second Configuration: Restricting the Network. Here we consider whether to include leaves in the analysis or not. Note that we do not restrict the networks in this analysis. That is considered in the next section. We again consider the data-set of Venray and the data-set for the city of Utrecht, with 243,282 connections. Again fifty pairs of active points are considered and results are given as median running times in seconds and average cost of the found paths in euros. The results for Venray are given in Table 3 and for Utrecht in Table 4.

In both cases we see that the running times are comparable, though slightly smaller when ignoring the leaves. The average cost of the least-cost paths is the same for all fifty pairs of active points. In the analysis in the next section, all leaves are ignored, unless a direct connection is made with them from an active point.

Table 3. Venray: median running times and average costs for fifty pairs.

	All endpoints	No leaves
Running times (in seconds)	3.47	3.34
Costs (in euros)	6,200	6,200

Table 4. Utrecht: median running times and average costs for fifty pairs.

	All endpoints	No leaves
Running times (in seconds)	41.77	41.47
Costs (in euros)	17,583	17,583

4.2 Running Times of the Algorithm

We have now configured the algorithm and can test it with different data-sets. We allow for extra digging from small isolated components and we ignore leaves in the final analysis step, In the analysis below we also consider restrictions of the network to smaller ones, We restrict the network using an enlarged bounding rectangle, where it is enlarged with respect to the bounding rectangle of the active points to be connected. The bounding rectangle is enlarged in all directions by a distance r. Note that r is independent on the size of the bounding rectangle. We consider r-values: 500, 1,000, 1,500 and ∞, where $r = \infty$ corresponds to the whole network. We fix $k = 10$ and for every data-set sample fifty random pairs of active points. We consider four data-sets of increasing size, and each network is a combination of street networks and trench networks.

The first data-set is that of the Dutch city Zwolle, with a total of 73,066 connections. The second data-set is of the city of Rotterdam with 344,0594 connections. The third data-set is of the capital of the Netherlands, Amsterdam, together with some smaller village surrounding it. This data-set consists of 630,137 connections. The final data-set considered is of the southwestern part of the Netherlands, including the province of Zeeland and Noord-Brabant. This last data-set has 2,776,827 and is far larger than typically considered data-sets.

For each of these four data-sets we consider fifty randomly selected pairs of active points. We compare the results in both the median running times and the average cost of the found paths. The results are shown for the various r-values in Tables 5, 6, 7 and 8.

Table 5. Zwolle: median running times (in seconds) and average costs (in euros) for fifty pairs of active points.

r-values	∞	1,500	1,000	500
Running times (seconds)	17.66	4.12	3.96	3.92
Costs (euros)	8,843	8,843	8,843	8,843

Table 6. Rotterdam: median running times (in seconds) and average costs (in euros) for fifty pairs of active points.

r-values	∞	1,500	1,000	500
Running times (seconds)	34.09	15.21	14.48	14.27
Costs (euros)	16,784	16,784	16,799	16,844

Table 7. Amsterdam: median running times (in seconds) and average costs (in euros) for fifty pairs of active points.

r-values	∞	1,500	1,000	500
Running times (seconds)	136.91	30.05	29.28	28.60
Costs (euros)	35,535	35,596	40,733	40,824

Table 8. The southwest of the Netherlands: median running times (in seconds) and average costs (in euros) for fifty pairs of active points.

r-values	∞	1,500	1,000	500
Running times (seconds)	417.86	123.94	123.73	124.04
Costs (euros)	267,604	277,363	381,449	614,935

For both the data-set of Zwolle and Rotterdam, we see that the average cost of the found paths is roughly equal for each of the r-values considered. For the larger data-sets, we see that varying r-values can have a large impact on the average cost. For Amsterdam, even $r = 1{,}500$ gives sub-optimal costs with respect to the unbounded network, although the difference is small. For Amsterdam, the difference is already differs significantly among various r-values, an effect which is even stronger for the largest data-set. Note that the differences in costs follow from only a few points with sub-optimal results. In the data-set of Amsterdam for instance, there are six data points where $r = 1{,}000$ gives a higher cost than $r = \infty$. In the largest data-set, there are 26 sub-optimal paths for $r = 500$ and 18 sub-optimal paths for $r = 1{,}000$.

This would suggest that larger r-values are larger. However, if we consider the running times we see that for the three finite r-values, the running times are comparable. The running times for $r = \infty$ are more than four times longer than those for $r = 500$ for some data-sets. This suggests that it is advised to restrict the network to significantly reduce the running times. What r-values give reasonable results in terms of both average costs and running times is likely to depend on the data-set. Based on these results, $r = 1{,}500$ seems to work reasonably well.

4.3   Observations

First, we considered two configurations of the algorithm. For the first configuration we considered the effect of small isolated components. We saw that allowing for extra digging from these small isolated components had a marginal effect on the median running times, while the costs were significantly smaller in some cases. We also saw that $k = 10$ number of points to connect with is sufficient in the considered data-sets. In the second configuration considered we saw that we could neglect the leaves of the network. The cost of the found paths remains the same, however, the running time decreases.

With these configuration, we tested the algorithm using four different data-sets. Again we randomly generated fifty pairs of active points for each data-set and considered the median running times of the algorithm and the average cost of the found paths. Here we also considered the effect of restricting the network to a smaller network. The restriction considers bounding rectangles around the active points. The bounding rectangle is extended on all sides by distance r.

In all data sets we saw that restricting the network with $r = 1,500$ gives similar cost paths compared to the paths found when not restricting the network (with $r = \infty$). The running times do however increase significantly for the unrestricted network. On the other hand, if the network is restricted too much ($r = 500$ and even $r = 1,000$), the least cost-paths cannot always be found. We advise to use $r = 1,500$ as this gives least cost-paths close to optimal, while still having a small running time. With this restriction, the algorithm finished within two minutes for the entire southwest of the Netherlands. For smaller data-sets, results are found within half a minute.

5   Conclusion

This article focused on planning of FttX networks. We constructed an algorithm that finds a low cost-path between two active points, using a combination of available networks. The main problem of finding such a low cost path splits in three smaller sub-problems. For each of the sub-problems an algorithm is implemented, which together give a low cost-path, close to the optimal least cost-path. In determining this path, the network is restricted, using enlarged bounding rectangles, based on the r-value. Furthermore, the algorithm handles isolated components, while still giving an acceptable low cost-path.

It is observed that the running times are fairly similar for the different finite restriction values, or r-values. Of course, larger r-values imply larger running times, however the differences are rather small. Furthermore, it turned out that in some cases for smaller r-values (such as $r = 500$) no path is found which includes routing through the network. Even in the case of $r = 1,000$ this sometimes happened.

The algorithm was tested for different environments stemming from the Netherlands. The size of some of these environments is beyond what is typically used, such as the entire southwest of the Netherlands. The algorithm showed that even in these extreme cases low cost paths can be found. For small data sets the algorithm finds results within a few seconds, for larger data sets consisting of multiple cities within a minute and for the southwest of the Netherlands within two minutes. Given the size of the data set, this is acceptable.

We believe that the used environments do not hold any special properties, other than stemming from urban areas. We therefore also believe that the algorithm works equally well in environments with different topographies, either in Europe or elsewhere.

Note that the running time also depends on the distance between the two points. For two points close to each other, the running times are smaller than for two points further apart. Furthermore, the running times also depend on the topology of the network. If the region considered, contains many connections, the running times are most likely larger opposed to the situation were there are only a small number of connections.

The goal to construct an algorithm which finds a low cost-path was met. The constructed algorithm does so within a minute for almost all practical data sets. We advise to restrict the network using $r = 1,500$, as the found costs are similar as for the whole network, but the running times are comparable to small r-values. The smaller costs outweigh the small increase in running times. The algorithm also works for a disconnected network. A connection with an isolated component is acceptable, given that it leads to lower cost. Such a connection requires extra digging.

It is also the extra digging that complicates finding the true least-cost path, due to the degrees of freedom of this problem. If no extra digging is allowed, the presented algorithm indeed finds the true least-cost path.

Optimal values of the parameters used in the algorithm are determined heuristically. More research on optimal parameter values is needed. A possible extension to case-specific parameters is also possible. The drawback of case-specific parameters is that more information is needed on the data set. Something our algorithm does not require. Another point for further research is the second restriction as discussed in Sect. 3.5. In the algorithm it is assumed that digging during the algorithm is never favorable over routing. In specific situations this does not hold.

References

1. Agarwal, P., Sharir, M.: Red-blue intersection detection algorithms, with applications to motion planning and collision detection. Association for Computing Machinery, New York, NY, USA (1988). https://doi.org/10.1145/73393.73401. ISBN 0897912705
2. Arge, L., Mølhave, T., Zeh, N.: Cache-oblivious red-blue line segment intersection. In: Halperin, D., Mehlhorn, K. (eds.) ESA 2008. LNCS, vol. 5193, pp. 88–99. Springer, Heidelberg (2008). https://doi.org/10.1007/978-3-540-87744-8_8
3. Bellman, R.: On a routing problem. Q. Appl. Math. **16**(1), 87–90 (1958). http://www.jstor.org/stable/43634538. ISSN 0033569X
4. Bentley, J.L., Ottmann, T.A.: Algorithms for reporting and counting geometric intersections. IEEE Trans. Comput. **C−28**(9), 643–647 (1979). https://doi.org/10.1109/tc.1979.1675432

5. Dijkstra, E.: A note on two problems in connexion with graphs. Numer. Math. **1**, 269–271 (1959). https://doi.org/10.1007/BF01386390
6. Ford, L.R.: Network Flow Theory. RAND Corporation, Santa Monica (1956)
7. Khan, M., Babar, M., Ahmed, S.H., Shah, S.C., Han, K.: Smart city designing and planning based on big data analytics. Sustain. Cities Soc. **35**, 271–279 (2017). https://doi.org/10.1016/j.scs.2017.07.012
8. Mantler, A.: Intersecting red and blue line segments in optimal time and precision (2001). https://doi.org/10.14288/1.0051494
9. Neumann, N., Phillipson, F.: Finding the intersection points of networks. In: Eichler, G., Erfurth, C., Fahrnberger, G. (eds.) I4CS 2017. CCIS, vol. 717, pp. 104–118. Springer, Cham (2017). https://doi.org/10.1007/978-3-319-60447-3_8
10. Phillipson, F.: Efficient algorithms for infrastructure networks: Planning issues and economic impact (2014). https://doi.org/10.13140/2.1.3025.1844
11. Phillipson, F.: Planning of fibre to the curb using G. Fast in multiple roll-out scenarios. In: LNIT, vol. 2, issue 1, pp. 42–49 (2014). https://doi.org/10.12720/lnit.2.1.42-49
12. Phillipson, F.: Roll-out of reliable fiber to the cabinet: an interactive planning approach. J. Opt. Commun. Netw. **6**(8), 705 (2014). https://doi.org/10.1364/jocn.6.000705
13. Phillipson, F., Vos, T.: Dense multi-service planning in smart cities. In: 2018 Proceedings of International Conference on Information Society and Smart Cities, p. 11 (2018)
14. Shamos, M.I., Hoey, D.: Closest-point problems. In: Proceedings of the 16th Annual Symposium on Foundations of Computer Science, USA (1975). IEEE Computer Society. https://doi.org/10.1109/SFCS.1975.8
15. Shamos, M.I., Hoey, D.: Geometric intersection problems. In: Proceedings of the 17th Annual Symposium on Foundations of Computer Science, SFCS 1976, pp. 208–215, USA. IEEE Computer Society (1976). https://doi.org/10.1109/SFCS.1976.16

Applications and Services Supporting Work and Life

Potentials of Augmented Reality – Insights into Industrial Practice

Arlett Semm[(✉)] [ID], Christian Erfurth [ID], and Seyyid Uslu

Department of Industrial Engineering, University of Applied Sciences Jena,
Carl-Zeiss-Promenade 2, 07745 Jena, Germany
{Arlett.Semm,Christian.Erfurth,Seyyid.Uslu}@eah-jena.de

Abstract. With emerging technologies, research is increasingly focusing on the digitalization of the working world and the resulting potentials, but also risks, for employees. People and technology are beginning to grow together in industrial environments. New technologies can support skills and improve results of the daily work, but the most important factor is still the human being. Assistance systems based on Augmented Reality (AR) are increasingly attract the attention of companies. Currently, there are not many implementation reports and applications in companies. This paper discusses the findings based on observations from industrial site inspections in the areas of training, commissioning of goods, and the manual assembly process. Inspections took place at three pioneering companies in the automotive industry, online distance selling, and the energy sector. When it comes to the use of assistance systems, the main goals of these companies that are very open to innovation are to improve efficiency and quality, e.g., minimize errors and optimize speed. Qualitative content analysis was used to evaluate the interview transcripts, the collected transcripts and notes from the guided tours, and the brief participations in these industries. The results are presented in the form of user experiences with AR addressing their advantages and disadvantages in the context of use. In addition, these were categorized into a predefined classification of influencing factors and challenges.

Keywords: Augmented reality · Assistance systems · Smart glass · Best practices · Practical case study

1 Introduction

In times of pandemics, it becomes clear that the digitalization of the working world is a necessary step. Assistance systems are now being used in a wide variety of areas within companies. Reasons for this include changed requirements for companies, such as higher flexibility and efficiency. By using such assistance systems to support employees, companies hope to realize optimization. This results in potentials and risks for employees and health aspects in particular play an important role. This makes it necessary for companies to address the innovations of digitalization and identify best practices for a sustainable implementation.

© Springer Nature Switzerland AG 2021
U. R. Krieger et al. (Eds.): I4CS 2021, CCIS 1404, pp. 103–122, 2021.
https://doi.org/10.1007/978-3-030-75004-6_8

As part of the research project "Healthy work in Pioneering Industries", it was important to consider the topic of digitalization not only from the perspective of scientific research, but also from a practical perspective. The aim was to take into account real user scenarios and experiences from companies. The assumption was: There are already companies that have carried out digitalization projects. In these companies, there would be positive and negative experiences. In addition, there will be experiences in dealing with employees in such digitalization projects.

The research questions addressed included:

- What will the working world of the future look like?
- What changes must be faced?
- What is the status in leading companies?
- What practical examples already exist for augmented reality (AR)?
- Which areas of application for AR assistance systems already exist?

In the context of this research project, which focused on practical examples in the area of digitalization and Industry 4.0, the research team at the University of Applied Sciences Jena studied aspects of the introduction and application of technological innovations in companies. Insights into current technologies, the status of digitalization in pioneering companies, approaches to the introduction of technological solutions and the consequences for employees' tasks and health were considered. The method used for this was brief field observations and interviews, which were severely limited in time, because access to the field was strongly limited. The findings from the observations and interviews were extracted contextually. The results of this work are presented in a research and knowledge platform. The research project was carried out in interdisciplinary collaboration with researchers from the fields of occupational psychology, occupational medicine, social sciences and industrial engineering. The results are based on company visits, observations and guideline-based interviews. This paper focuses on exemplary areas where AR has been used: Commissioning, assembly, training, and education. Expectations and limitations, advantages and disadvantages as well as possible positive and negative consequences of AR assistance systems, especially AR smart glasses, are discussed.

2   Motivation and Related Work

With increasing technologization in industry, there is a growing need to reduce media disruption by using digital images of objects integrated in processes [17]. In such places where people are actively involved in the processes, the use of AR technologies can provide support. Exemplary reasons for the introduction are technological advancements [7], the diversity of service employees in terms of education, language, experience [15] as well as demographic change and the increasing individualization of products [17] due to an increasing customer orientation [16]. Likewise, decreasing lot sizes [1, 17] up to lot size 1 [5], an increasing number of components [12] as well as the increasing pressure to perform [7] due to a growing amount of special information and high demands on the skills of factory workers, among others, are crucial reasons.

Many contributions mention possible application areas for AR technology, such as: Design, (remote) maintenance, commissioning, assembly [4], picking [5], knowledge management, education, training, qualification and (mobile) learning [11, 17]. Already in articles more than 10 years ago [4, 14], already elaborated application areas with corresponding application scenarios and listed important prerequisites and ways to introduce AR technology. Some types of systems currently in use are assistance systems, digital documentation systems, training [10] and education systems [11]. A comprehensive overview of existing contributions on the topic of augmented reality (AR) from the field of manufacturing and assembly from 1990–2015 can be found in [18].

When introducing AR technologies, companies encounter different influencing factors, challenges and obstacles. Based on expert interviews, the authors in [8] identified 11 influencing factors and 25 associated challenges in the implementation and use of wearables. The influencing factors were grouped into three super categories: Technological, organizational and environmental (e.g., data protection and security).

Funk [5] identified 8 conditions (possible solutions) important for the success of the system regarding the development, design, and implementation of assistive systems. Many other contributions are mainly concerned with technical constraints such as: Robustness, resolution and runtime [11, 13].

The most important factor in the enterprise is still the human. S/he is creative, the most flexible element in production, has expertise and can make decisions [17]. A digital assistance system is used to support humans in the role of workers. It can provide up-to-date action- and decision-relevant information [17] as well as step-by-step instructions [15] to bridge the gap between the worker's skills and the required competencies on the job [9]. One opportunity exists here for people with cognitive disabilities of all ages. Insights into the challenges and opportunities of AR learning and training as well as direct workplace support for this target group are provided in Blattgerste's paper [3]. In particular, the multimodal possibilities such as visualization, contextualization, animations and acoustic input and output of AR play an important role. Self-learning situations can be supported by animations and storytelling. This can promote the autonomy of this target group.

In this case, the crucial success factor is employee acceptance, which can already be considered during the development and introduction of AR. The affected employees should be involved from the very beginning [16]. Usability also plays a major role [10]. The assistance system should be adaptable to the environment, the employee's cognitive abilities, user experience, and knowledge (incl. multilingualism) [5, 7, 15].

Companies are pursuing the following goals, among others, with the introduction of AR: To increase the flexibility of workers as well as to reduce costs, the number of errors, training and execution time [11, 15]. Therefore, companies are already testing smart glasses such as the Google Glass [6] or the HoloLens [15] as well as smart watches [1], projectors [7], handheld and projection displays [11]. An application comparison of paper, pick-by-light, head-up displays and cart-mounted displays in the context of order picking with their advantages and disadvantages can be found in [6].

In [5], contour visualization proved to be the best solution in terms of hardware integration, assembly time and number of errors caused. Speech recognition proved to be the most suitable input option. A practical test was not performed; a possible problem could be the environmental noise [10].

Another important issue is the requirements of data protection. Smart glasses, for example, are able to collect a lot of data. It must be ensured how this capability and the data are to be handled to guarantee the fundamental right to informational self-determination and people's data protection rights. The article [2] compiles corresponding sub-problems, meta-requirements and solution components from the research conducted, from expert interviews and from the literature.

Most of the AR research in the last 20 years has come from the scientific domain [13], with fewer reports on industrial AR applications. Moreover, most of the research deals with technical aspects of assistance systems [8]. There are not many deployment reports and applications in enterprises yet. Therefore, exploratory interviews on this topic were conducted in [8] with domain experts from manufacturing, industrial automation, automotive, and industrial wearable computing technology providers.

3   Examples of Practical Use and Findings

Since the focus in AR research is on the scientific domain [13], this paper considers findings from the industrial domain. An empirical approach was used within the case studies to collect data. The application areas investigated are order picking (commissioning) and the training of new employees using assistance systems. For this purpose, two practical studies from the online distance selling and automotive industry as well as an assistance system-supported assembly scenario in the training and education of a company from the energy sector are reported. The focus was on the consideration of opportunities and risks as well as advantages and disadvantages of wearables, in particular smart glasses, with a special attention to usability.

First, the case studies are briefly introduced and followed by a more detailed look at them in the remaining subsections. Each subsection contains three tables which summarize the results from the specific observations.

Online Distance Seller
The underlying research project examined practical examples of leading companies that are pioneers of digitalization in specific areas or projects. At the selected online distance seller, there is a permanent optimization process and experiments with new technologies, such as the test use of a variety of AR smart glasses as assistance systems in order picking.

At this company, 11 guided interviews with employees, management in the form of a product manager and technology experts from the IT department were conducted as part of the research project. Of particular importance for the results in this article were the interview with the product manager and two interviews with the technical experts. Additional information was collected in the form of minutes during investigations of the warehouse areas and the IT department at the company site.

Automotive Industry
Another company observed was an automobile manufacturer. This company mass-produces automobiles according to individual customer requirements without any noticeable loss of productivity. In order to offer this individualization, there is a large variety

of components with almost 500 constantly changing components. For this purpose, the company has set up an extra picking area in front of the assembly line with assembly employees. A portable AR-based assistance system is used to support the employees.

During the inspection of the production area and the associated commissioning at the automobile manufacturer, individual brief interviews were conducted with employees and a supervisor on the technology used. This article contains the results from the commissioning area with the high diversity of components. Three employees and one supervisor were interviewed directly on site. In addition, an author of this article went through a test commissioning process using an AR smart glass with the picking app as an assistance system. The existing smart glass has a normal eyeglass frame with a small transparent glass monitor placed in front of one eye.

Company From the Energy Sector

The third company comes from the energy sector and tests, for example, new technological innovations for the field of education and training sector. In collaboration with two external companies, assembly instructions were developed as an assistance app for an AR smart glass. The app was tested by different users from the company as part of extensive test scenarios as well as further optimized.

In this company, a detailed protocol created from the inspection and participation in a test run of the assembly app with seven commercial trainees in the area of training and advanced training as well as with two external company representatives. Three teams were formed from the trainees: one team of three and one team of two, each with an AR smart glass and the paper assembly instructions, and one team of two with only the paper assembly instructions. After the initial briefing on the subject matter and materials, as well as a 10-min introduction to the use of the AR smart glass, the apprentices were allowed into the workstation for assembly. According to the instructor, they had no prior experience in this area. An author of this paper also used an AR smart glass with this app throughout the time and traced the complete steps on it himself. In addition, short expert discussions with the trainer, the technology expert of the IT company and, following the run-through of the scenario, short questions with the three trainees of the team with the AR smart glass took place in the context of this.

The evaluations were carried out using qualitative content analysis of the interview transcripts, and notes from the inspections and short participations in this field.

3.1 Insight into Practical Case Study: Automotive Industry

The pick-by-vision solution as an assistance system in the commissioning department of the automotive manufacturer is a combination of visualization (tablet, smart watch, smart glass) and a scanner (waistband scanner, hand scanner on the back of the hand or finger scanner) for data collection. Employees choose their own tools and can switch between them at any time. The advantages and disadvantages of the devices observed as well as those identified in the interviews are summarized in Table 10 in the next section.

The aim of the assistance system is to optimize the commissioning process and minimize the number of errors in the process.

Due to the high variety of components and the constantly changing items in this area, it is no longer easy for individual employee to keep track of everything. The supervisor

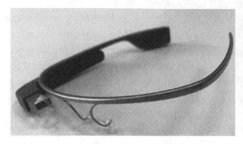

Fig. 1. Possible combination: smart glass and back-of-hand scanner.

gave the example that there used to be one sun visor for the left and one for the right. Today, however, there are many different variants of sun visors.

The training of new employees and the associated understanding of the functions and processes in commissioning now only takes between 1–2 weeks with the new assistance system. The system is linked to the ERP system and displays data in an app. The information is displayed identically on all three device types (smart watch, tablet, smart glass) so that it is possible to switch between devices at any time (device independence).

The process of commissioning with the smart glass is as follows: At the beginning of the commissioning round, the employee reads in all the data for this commissioning list on the terminal (Bluetooth). Using Bluetooth is the workaround for the too weak WLAN antenna of the smart glass, which prevents a permanent connection with the WLAN. The commissioning round then begins. The display shows all the components to be picked in the round one after the other in the corresponding order. The items are also sorted in order of the route. The employee is shown on his respective display, highlighted in color, which part is to be picked next. Once the correct material has been selected and scanned in, it is color-coded and moved out of sight to the right-hand corner. The individual items are confirmed accordingly by scanning the code. Only in the event of scanning the correct part, the system continues. The employee is forced to put away the wrong component and scan the correct so that the program continues (wrong code = error). Employees receive audible and visual feedback indicating whether the correct item has been selected or not. This avoids errors. If a component is no longer available on site, the item can be skipped via a master code. It may happen that it takes some time to get the replacement parts.

For some steps there are workarounds with paper lists on which part numbers are recorded.

The display on the smart glass contains not only the cryptic item number, as with the paper list, but detailed information about the item being searched for, making identification easier. Employees no longer have to memorize abstract item numbers for matching items and know how to read them to find the appropriate item in its storage location.

For some items, an additional confirmation of the color variant is required. This serves to check whether the supplier has delivered the correct color. In addition, the dual control principle is used: As soon as an employee has finished picking his trolley, s/he pushes it next to a trolley that has already been picked and checks it for correctness using the attached paper list before starting the next tour. This way of doing things brings this commissioning area closer to 0 errors, despite the enormous variety of items. Previously, the area had about 20 errors per shift, most of which occurred during assembly. About twice a month, the errors got through to the control station.

Effects:

- Through this implementation approach, the error rate tends towards 0 → quality improvement, improved employee environment
- Faster picking, less thinking processes
- Low demands on memorization
- Hands are free for material (except bundle scanner; no paper or pen, no physical ticking off) → more ergonomic work
- Ability to display more things on the monitor than just abbreviations as on paper → information improvement
- Employees can participate in setting up and revising the system, what they want to see in the display → increase in acceptance
- Monotonous, not self-determined,
- Dependence on technology increases → loss of transparency (knowledge about individual parts no longer present)

These monotonous areas are nevertheless experienced as a relief. Due to the variety of items, the human being is only needed as a gripping arm. Due to the demographic development in the company, such areas are necessary, for example, for people with performance compensation. The works council takes great care to ensure that no direct performance measurements take place.

In the following tables (Tables 1, 2, 3, 4, 5, 6, 7, 8 and 9), the scheme of Hobert and Schumann [8] was used to compare the results with other research results [8] and to enrich them with new results. The categories and numbering were partially adopted from [8]. Hobert and Schumann [8] introduced 11 influencing factors and 25 associated challenges in the implementation and use of wearables. The influencing factors are grouped into three main categories Technological (T), Organizational (O) and Environmental (E). For each company, a table was created for each main category. The first influencing factor of the main category Technological (T) is "Existing technical infrastructure" and gets the number T1. Various challenges are assigned to the influencing factor T1. These are also numbered as for example with Tc1.1: Which stands for the influence factor Technological 1 and there for the Challenge 1. This is always numbered continuously. Not all 11 influencing factors and 25 challenges were included in the tables for each company, since only those were included which occurred in the specific company observed. For the challenges, after the numbering, own examples from the specific company were given. In addition, solutions from the companies were assigned to the challenges. The challenges and solutions resulted in positive or negative effects for the specific area in the pioneer company. Tables 1, 2 and 3 show the results observed at the automotive industry company.

Table 1. Technological (T) results in the automotive sector; scheme according to [8]

Influencing factors	Challenges	Solutions: automotive industry company	Positive/negative effects
Existing technical infrastructure (T1)	Problem: Complete WLAN coverage (Tc 1.1)	Data read in via Bluetooth at the beginning of the picking round	WLAN independent
Lack of industrial wearables (T3)	Technical limitations of the wearables: Battery capacity, Overheating (Tc3.3) Weak WLAN antenna	Device independence: Switching between devices is possible at any time	Powered by external battery: Over 8 h of use possible
		Smart glasses are charged overnight and permanently powered by an additional battery the next day	No charging during operation, so no heat generation,
		No charging during use (no heat generation)	Additional acoustic and visual feedback possible
		Small display: Limited space	

Table 2. Organizational (O) results in the automotive sector; scheme according to [8]

Influencing factors	Challenges	Solutions: automotive industry company	Positive/negative effects
Requirement of expert knowledge (O1)	Few experienced technology provider (Oc1.2) and complete solutions on the market	Complete solution for scenario integrated by a technology provider (including smart glasses, software, consulting, setup, customization and maintenance)	
		Technology provider already implemented many such solutions	
Corporate culture (O3)	Lack of management support (Oc3.1), costs vs. benefits	Technology acquisition is expensive	Financial savings through: Training of new employees only 1–2 weeks
			Error minimization
			Technology dependency
	Lack of technology acceptance by employees (Oc3.2)	Information enhancement: Enrichment with further useful information and presentations Co-determination in software development by employees possible (e.g., what content should be displayed?)	Hands free
			Less demands on memorization despite high number of variants and high fluctuation of articles
			All information permanently in front of the eyes
			Monotonous
			Externally determined
			Technology dependency
Age structure (O4)	Skepticism of older employees towards wearables (Oc4.1)	Two employees over 50 wear the smart glass permanently	Older employees' fewer problems with ergonomics: More acceptance

Table 3. Environment (E) results in the automotive sector; scheme according to [8]

Influencing factors	Challenges	Solutions: automotive industry company	Positive/negative effects
Safety provisions (E3)	Important: Protection of employee health (Ec3.1)	Device independence (change possible)	change of view
			Headache, dizziness (use: 1–2 h)
	Enable necessary safety precautions (Ec3.2)	Wear work gloves even scanning with them possible	
	Avoid distraction (Ec3.3)		Disturbing: in field of vision

3.2 Insight into Practical Case Study: Online Distance Seller

The online distance seller under consideration uses the "chaotic warehousing". The "pick-by-paper" method with a paper picking list was not optimally manageable for the employees due to the large number of items in the warehouse, inflexible and not efficient. For the past three years, the "pick-by-scan" system has sent employees monotonously from one item to the next on an optimized route using a mobile data entry (MDE) device. Routes are planned in the system and can be changed in the middle of an operation. The display shows the storage location and the item ID. Each individual item has its own barcode (Unique Identifier UID). An employee must be able to remember all the numbers and transfer them to the right storage location and the right item.

Employees were consulted a lot at the beginning of the development and implementation process, but hardly any of their suggestions were implemented.

The MDE devices are connected to the company software via WLAN. In the warehouse, the WLAN strengths are different and depending on how many employees work with the MDEs in the same area, WLAN connection problems occur (work interruption). The MDE device guides the employee via an optimized route, but this does not always make sense. The employees have a very limited scope for decision-making. They cannot make independent decisions and differ from the specifications, as they only ever see individual items and not the complete list. Confidence and satisfaction with the technology are therefore limited.

The company has conducted tests with the use of the pick-by-vision system using the smart glass with a transparent display on one side in the warehouse area. Work orders were to be projected directly into the employees' field of vision via the display so that they could read them immediately. It was also planned to scan directly with the camera in the smart glass. The employees for these tests were selected according to various criteria: Equal distribution by gender, wearers of glasses, low, middle and high performers. Warehouse workers were assigned to their usual area. People wearing glasses wore the AR smart glass over their own without this being experienced as distracting. The results were below the performance of the previously used MDE after understanding the technology, how it works, and after a longer training period. Numerous statistics were collected and evaluated by the company for an analysis.

The smart glass had contrast-related problems when reading the barcodes as well as connection problems to the network (WLAN problems) in the form of frequent disconnections. In addition, warehouse workers are forced to constantly turn their heads when scanning with the smart glass. This resulted in physical problems. The advantages and disadvantages identified are also shown in Table 10 in the next section.

"But that's where we've had ergonomics problems so far. [...] Because you can't put the things on for a long time." [...] "Exactly. Well, not the eyes, but the neck. So, the things are just relatively heavy. You need a battery; they have to last a long time." (Quote: Technology expert).

The acceptance of smart glasses by the warehouse workers depended on the respective supervisor and view of the technology. The employees rated the freedom of movement gained as positive. However, efficiency could not be increased, so it did not add any economic value for the company. For this reason, the tests were not extended further. However, the company is planning tests in other areas, including with a smart glass, also AR-based, over both eyes and with a larger field of view. Use in the training area or for familiarization is being considered.

"So, when the employee is new, he can sort of work with the thing for the first two or three hours of the day [...]. And that's all you want him to do. And during that time, he is sort of getting told all the time, 'Now you need to put the following item here and here; Now please put it there; Watch here and there.' [You] can save yourself some mentoring by putting on the glasses of the person who chooses a language..." (Quote: Technology expert).

With the previous MDEs, the respective language can also be specified. However, this led to the problem that problem-solving and maintenance personnel could no longer read the error messages. Further physical problems arose due to the weight of the smart glass. In the following tables show the results observed at the distance seller (Tables 4, 5 and 6).

Table 4. Technological (T) results in the online distance seller sector; scheme according to [8]

Influencing factors	Challenges	Solutions: online distance seller	Positive/negative effects
Existing technical infrastructure (T1)	Problem: Complete WLAN coverage (Tc 1.1)	Not solved	
Existing system landscape (T2)	Integration of wearables into the existing system architecture (Tc2.1)	The existing system architecture is a complete in-house development	Therefore, the wearable can be integrated without any problems
Lack of industrial wearables(T3)	Technical limitations of the wearables: Battery capacity, Overheating (Tc3.3) Weak WLAN antenna Unsuitable for scanning	Powered by an additional battery Use only 1–2 h	Information available in different languages

Table 5. Organizational (O) results in the online distance seller sector; scheme according to [8]

Influencing factors	Challenges	Solutions: online distance seller	Positive/negative effects
Requirement of expert knowledge (O1)	Lack of knowledge about wearables in the company (Oc1.1)	Programmers and technology experts available in the company	Uncomplicated quick changes possible
Corporate culture (O3)	Lack of management support (Oc3.1), costs vs. benefits	Technology acquisition is expensive	No efficiency increase
			No economic added value for the company
			Further tests in the field of training with the smart glass: Savings in mentoring
	Lack of technology acceptance by employees (Oc3.2)	Employee surveys conducted	Hands free
		Few suggestions implemented	Gained mobility
			Picking with chaotic storage
			All information permanently in front of the eyes
			Monotonous
			Externally determined
			Limited margin for decision
			Technology dependency: Confidence and satisfaction with technology limited
			Acceptance of smart glass depends on the supervisor and his attitude towards smart glasses

Table 6. Environment (E) results in the online distance seller sector; scheme according to [8]

Influencing factors	Challenges	Solutions: online distance seller	Positive/negative effects
Safety provisions (E3)	Important: Protection of employee health (Ec3.1)	Using the camera in the smart glass for scanning	Constant turning of the head
			Physical problems due to the weight of the smart glass
			Headache, dizziness (after 1–2 h of use)

3.3 Insight into Practical Case Study: Energy Sector

In the company from the energy sector, an assembly instruction app on an AR smart glass was developed for education and training. The smart glass used is visualizing information over a limited field of view in front of both eyes. To ensure optimal understanding of the content of the individual instruction steps, all information is displayed together despite the lack of space in the small field of view.

For each step, up to five sub steps were presented as short instructions, in the form of simple word groups in a continuous line, separated by commas. In some cases, this type of presentation caused participants to overread individual sub steps. Once the missing of a sub step was noticed, users had to go back to that step. However, there was no way to jump to any point in the program. Learners had to click through each step individually using the available "back and forward" button. With a total of 40 steps, this was sometimes very time-consuming.

For a better representation of the current status of the workpiece to be processed, a 3D image was also displayed. In some steps this 3D representation was animated. Some information was intentionally not displayed. At these points, reference was made to the paper instructions. Certain values are subject to regular changes. These values were currently recorded in the enclosed paper manual. The application was not able to do this at the time. Creating this application on the smart glass was complex and costly, as well as dependent on the display options used. A quick and regular adaptation would have caused recurring costs with the chosen implementation variant. Therefore, a mix of program and paper manual was chosen due to cost-benefit considerations. In addition, the app should not only be applicable to a specific case but should be transferable to similar cases with other values (generalistic applicability $\rightarrow$ greater benefit). Due to the lack of space, abbreviations are used, but they were not explicitly defined. The instructor had to explain them. One statement of the apprentices was that a picture, a group of words or a short sentence cannot answer every question. Therefore, they would have liked more detailed information, possibly additional information to fold out, and more visual elements such as pictograms and other pictorial representations. Audio input and output was also not provided. However, the test users did not miss this.

Three teams of trainees participated in the test run. The instructions on the AR smart glass, its operation and control via appropriate hand signals as well as in the app control was done in 10 min, although the apprentices had no previous experience with the smart glass or such an assembly situation. After the briefing, they immediately got started and used the technology without any problems. The IT expert noted that the limitation of two hand signals makes learning easier. Once there are more options, the complexity increases, which must be taught and learned. Therefore, the introduction would take more time.

In the test run, some technical limitations of the application and the smart glass have been shown (usability):

- Instruction steps difficult to see on light backgrounds (low contrast).
- Consequence: Active search for dark backgrounds makes assembly efficiency worse
- Visibility problems/visibility is reduced (view through):

- Light refraction (rainbow) and reflection due to special light from neon tubes
- Small white navigation point in the field of view e is considered distracting
- Scenario with students at the university: When wearing a mask due to Corona pandemic, the inside of the smart glass fogged up in the field of view

- Weight of smart glass caused problems: Pressed on forehead and strained neck:

  - I get headaches.", "You can't walk around with that all day." [Apprentice]:

  Use of smart glass after 1-1.5 h by only one participant in the AR group of three, Constant moving/turning of head while viewing 3D object.

- Difficulties due to occupational safety aspects:

  - Need for occupational safety goggles
  - Or a safety helmet
  - Especially dark work gloves (body injuries) and one-way gloves (for chemicals) were not detected by smart glass,

- Collaboration limited as everyone in the group went through the steps on the smart glass at their own pace:

  - "Like there and nobody even saw it." [Trainee]
  - Smart glass allows collaborative use, but was not offered in app.

The smart glass assisted the largely independent work by the two AR teams – a team of three and a team of two. AR team three worked very safely and quickly. In between, they asked the instructor questions. This was taken off instructor's hands by the smart glass. He had the opportunity to respond to all three teams (two AR teams, one paper team) and provide additional knowledge, since he did not have to explain everything permanently.

The team of three AR users followed the instructions very closely, and the result was similar to the 3D model. They were able to view the build situations all around via the 3D display (the 3D model). After the execution, the participants with the smart glass were convinced and sure they had executed it correctly: "You knew how it should be done." and "I think we did it right." [Apprentice]

After the lunch break, all groups continued working without the smart glass, as it was too heavy in the long run. However, in the paper instructions, the three AR team often did not find the right place - frequent scrolling caused delays. In some cases, they did not understand the instructions. One of the groups of three then repeatedly took the smart glass to help.

The group of two worked only with the paper instructions, which led to frequent questions to the instructor. Identical implementation of the steps of a paper-based instruction in a digital application is almost never necessary. When creating and selecting an assistance system, it is important to consider how exactly to implement it.

One advantage of a paper manual is that user can return to any position at any time without having to go through the steps in order. Everything can be seen at a glance. Paper manuals are usually inexpensive and can be easily and regularly adapted. Such possibilities can also be implemented in an app.

In terms of accessibility, there is greater potential in digital media and consequently in the use of AR. In paper instructions, the text is very small. Many steps are explained purely text based. For some points, there are small black and white illustrations with a simple top view. It is not clear from these how exactly it has to be executed. The dimensions are not easy to see. In the group of two people with the paper instructions, this led to errors. They had to start over because of a mistake at the beginning that could not be fixed. The missing colors also made the work difficult in some places.

During the work, they held the paper instructions in their hands. However, they needed freedom of hands for the assembly. The paper was squashed in their hands. Then, however, they had to put it away again from time to time and then searched several times for the filed paper instructions as well as for the current position in the instructions.

The group of three AR members tried both variants, the smart glass app and the paper instructions. Despite the physical strain, they used the smart glass constantly until the end in order to be able to implement the steps better.

In the subsequent survey, however, the group favored the paper manual because it can be held in the hand and in the middle of it, it is possible to jump back to the beginning without effort.

The participants expressed privacy concerns about the AR smart glass. They could not imagine using it in an office environment, especially because of the gesture control.

According to the IT expert, the application was customized to refresh knowledge of existing employees, with less detail and by skipping steps. This did not work properly because each employee had knowledge deficits at different points. Therefore, the decision was also made to use the small-step guide.

In the following tables show the results observed at the energy company (Tables 7, 8 and 9).

Table 7. Technological (T) results in the energy sector; scheme according to [8]

Influencing factors	Challenges	Solutions: energy sector company	Positive/negative effects
existing system landscape (T2)	Integration of wearables into the existing system architecture (Tc2.1)	An independent training system (without connection to the existing system architecture) was developed in cooperation with external software developers	No problems
Lack of industrial wearables(T3)	Technical limitations of the wearables: (Tc3.3) Visibility problems, small display: Limited space	Lack of space all information on the small field of view	Everything always visible at a view
		3D visualizations	Visibility problems: Difficult to see on bright backgrounds (low contrast)
		Animations	Light refractions on the display (rainbow) caused by neon tubes
			Wearing masks leads to fogging of the display

Table 8. Organizational (O) results in the energy sector; scheme according to [8]

Influencing factors	Challenges	Solutions: energy sector company	Positive/negative effects
Requirement of expert knowledge (O1)	Few experienced technology provider (Oc1.2) and complete solutions on the market	Cooperation and joint development with experienced external software developers in the field of smart glass applications	Creation of an individual solution of a step by step guide
Corporate culture (O3)	Lack of management support (Oc3.1), costs vs. benefits	Technology procurement and the software development is expensive	Training improvement
		Initialized by the management: Cost-benefit consideration: Decision to mix digital and paper-based guidance, regular adjustments of the software too expensive	
	Lack of technology acceptance by employees (Oc3.2)	Information enhancement: Enrichment with further useful information and presentations	Hands free
			All information permanently in front of the eyes
			Better representation of the steps to be performed
			Gives employees more self-confidence
			Allows largely independent work
			The possibility to work at one's own tempo
			Technology dependency

Table 9. Environment (E) results in the energy sector; scheme according to [8]

Influencing factors	Challenges	Solutions: energy sector company	Positive/negative effects
Safety provisions (E3)	Important: Protection of employee health (Ec3.1)		Weight of smart glass: Forehead and neck pain
			Headache (after 2 h of use)
	Enable necessary safety precautions (Ec3.2): Dark work gloves and disposable gloves for chemicals are not recognized by smart glass	Safety glasses (helmet) required: Smart glass must be removed for this purpose	Necessity of switching between occupational safety equipment and smart glass
		Use white work gloves	
	Avoid distraction (Ec3.3)		Disturbing: Constantly in the field of vision
			Distraction by small white navigation point from actual task

4 Discussion

Within the research project "Healthy work in Pioneering Industries" empirical investigations were carried out on the basis of case studies of pioneering companies. The results obtained are not surprising and thus represent a confirmation of the existing general assumptions. The special details in the specific application context are nevertheless helpful for future AR applications and specific further developments.

The companies listed use "chaotic warehousing" or have a high diversity of parts and variability. At this point, the AR potentials of assistance systems can, for example, support warehouse workers in their work, increase their flexibility and reduce training times [13, 15], and include the diversity (such as language, age) of employees [8, 15, 16]. here are many different nationalities working in the online distance seller company. It is necessary to be able to integrate different languages.

In many warehouses, paper lists used for commissioning [6]. In the observed case companies, these are only partially used as an additional security or control option. Commissioning based on paper lists with numbers requires workers to memorize and then interpret the information [6]. In contrast, more comprehensive information is possible on AR systems. Workers no longer have to follow pure rows of numbers that lead them to storage racks, storage locations, and items.

In the energy sector company, step-by-step instructions with 3D object representation directly in the field of view were used for better communication and understanding of the assembly scenario by the apprentices. Providing this form of knowledge sharing and support during the assembly process increased the participants' self-confidence in this situation. They leave the training situation with the feeling that they can handle such a scenario again next time.

However, the possibilities of the AR assistance systems have not yet been fully exploited in the practical examples. An orientation towards the paper lists, the familiar systems and possibilities is still be seen.

Further Possibilities with augmented reality assistance systems, for example:

- The contour visualization [5],
- The automatic image recognition,
- The use of multimodal AR with integration of audio and video, of pictograms and other pictorial representations,
- As well as the use and integration of the entire environment.

In Table 10, the advantages and disadvantages of pick-by-vision devices from the two case studies in the field of commissioning are compared again and briefly summarized to give a short overview. The devices are divided into data visualization devices: Smart glass, tablet, smart watch and devices for scanning: Trouser waistband scanner, back of the hand scanner, finger scanner.

Table 10. Advantages and disadvantages of pick-by-vision devices.

Data visualization/scanning	Advantages	Disadvantages
Smart glass (Fig. 1) (small transparent display in front of one eye, existing camera is not used)	Continuously wearable	Short battery life (max. 3 h with new glasses)
	Information can be constantly displayed in the field of vision	Heat development during charging
		Weak antenna for WLAN connection
	Bluetooth connection available for feedback to the system	Stationary PC necessary due to WLAN problem
	Older employees have fewer problems with ergonomics	Unsuitable for scanning (bad posture: Permanent physically straining rotation of the head necessary)
	Hands free	Constantly in field of vision (disturbing)
		Constant change of view: Display → environment necessary
		Headache, dizziness (after 1–2 h use)
Tablet	Does not need to be worn	Must be replaced when the trolley is changed (for each new picking run)
	Size of the display	
	WLAN connection	
Smart watch (no use)	Light	Arm must be rotated for optimal viewing angle on the display
	Wearable throughout	
	Hands free	
Trouser waistband scanner	Well tangible	Heavy
		Hand not free
Back of the hand scanner (Fig. 1)	Light, small	Can get caught with it
	Buttons for operation directly in the glove (function keys)	Gloves more expensive than normal work gloves
	Good grip	
	Hands free	
Finger scanner	Small, light	Slips easily
	Hands free	

In Fig. 2, a summarized overview of all positive and negative impacts on technology, companies and employees of all three pioneer company case studies is presented. For each category, the impacts are shown using tag clouds. The classification follows the already mentioned scheme of Hobert and Schumann [8] with the main category Technological (T) and the Company based on the main category Organizational (O). Deviating from the scheme, the perspective of the third category was changed from Environment to Employees, as this is the most important factor in the company behind it. Therefore, more focus was placed on these effects in the underlying research. Significantly more effects were recorded for the impact on people. Based on the investigations, the effects on employees were divided into positive and negative effects. In the Technology category, only positive effects were recorded, with the exception of "visibility problems" and "low contrast". The Company category also had only positive effects, with the exception of "expensive technology". Effects that only occurred in one of the companies were shown as smaller than those that occurred in all three companies.

Fig. 2. Positive and negative effects on the technology, company and employees

5 Conclusion and Future Work

With digitalization, the type of work in which employees in certain areas only perform monotonous, mindless tasks is steadily increasing. This has been shown by the practical studies highlighted in the article. An important principle should be: You cannot and should not take all decisions away from employees.

To counteract monotony, new concepts for rotating work environments should be created, among other things, in which the employee is exposed to a change between cognitive performance demands and relief several times a day. This can also be a form of flexibilization of work, in which digital assistance systems can provide support.

An important success factor alongside the design of the technology is acceptance. There are employees everywhere who have a positive or negative attitude toward digitalization. It is important to involve employees in the development right from the start and to bring appropriately accepted employees on board as "lead users". Appropriate transparency helps to manage sensitive issues such as performance measurement and data protection.

It is important to explore the possibilities for people with cognitive disabilities. These are not the focus of digitalization efforts of companies, which tend to focus on the profitability or attractiveness of their business. The argument behind this is: However, this technology in particular (AR assistance systems) could support or even enable the inclusion of more people in their first job. This needs to be investigated in more detail in the future. One of the authors of this article is working on a thesis that will investigate this in more detail in the future.

Acknowledgement. The research project "Healthy work in Pioneering Industries" was supported by the German Federal Ministry of Education and Research (BMBF) under the grant number 02L14A073.

References

1. Bauer, D., Wutzke, R., Bauernhansl, T.: Wear@Work – a new approach for data acquisition using wearables. Procedia CIRP **50**, 529–534 (2016). https://doi.org/10.1016/j.procir.2016.04.121
2. Berkemeier, L., McGuire, M.-R., Steinmann, S., Niemöller, C., Thomas, O.: Datenschutzrechtliche anforderungen an smart glasses-basierende informationssysteme in der logistik. In: Eibl, M., Gaedke, M. (eds.) INFORMATIK 2017, vol. P-275, pp. 1037–1048. Gesellschaft für Informatik, Bonn (2017)
3. Blattgerste, J., Renner, P., Pfeiffer, T.: Augmented reality action assistance and learning for cognitively impaired people: a systematic literature review. In: Proceedings of the 12th ACM International Conference on PErvasive Technologies Related to Assistive Environments, pp. 270–279. ACM, New York (2019)
4. Friedrich, W.: ARVIKA - augmented reality for development, production and service. Zeitschrift für interaktive und kooperative Medien – ICOM **2**(2), 3–4 (2002)
5. Funk, M.: Augmented reality at the workplace: a context-aware assistive system using in-situ projection (Dissertation). Universität Stuttgart (2016). https://pdfs.semanticscholar.org/a7d8/f8c5543716e889b1c7ce5643df6a9d09ab24.pdf. Accessed 13 Apr 2018

6. Guo, A., Wu, X., Shen, Z., Starner, T., Baumann, H., Gilliland, S.: Order picking with head-up displays. Computer **6**(48), 16–24 (2015). https://doi.org/10.1109/MC.2015.166

7. Hinrichsen, S., Riediger, D., Unrau, A.: Development of a projection-based assistance system for maintaining injection molding tools. In: 2017 IEEE International Conference on Industrial Engineering and Engineering Management (IEEM 2017), pp. 1571–1575. IEEE, Singapore (2017). https://doi.org/10.1109/ieem.2017.8290157

8. Hobert, S., Schumann, M.: Enabling the adoption of wearable computers in enterprises – results of analyzing influencing factors and challenges in the industrial sector. In: Proceedings of the 50th Hawaii International Conference on System Sciences, pp. 4276–4285 (2017). https://doi.org/10.24251/hicss.2017.518

9. Hold, P., Erol, S., Reisinger, G., Sihn, W.: Planning and evaluation of digital assistance systems. Procedia Manuf. **12**(9), 143–150 (2017). https://doi.org/10.1016/j.promfg.2017.04.024

10. Huck-Fries, V., Wiegand, F., Klinker, K., Wiesche, M., Krcmar, H.: Datenbrillen in der Wartung. In: Eibl, M., Gaedke, M. (eds.) INFORMATIK 2017, pp. 1413–1424. Gesellschaft für Informatik, Bonn (2017)

11. Liu, H., Wang, L.: An AR-based worker support system for human-robot collaboration. Procedia Manufact. **9**(11), 22–30 (2017). https://doi.org/10.1016/j.promfg.2017.07.124

12. Liu, Y., Li, S., Wang, J., Zeng, H., Lu, J.: A computer vision-based assistant system for the assembly of narrow cabin products. Int. J. Adv. Manufact. Technol. **8**(76), 281–293 (2015). https://doi.org/10.1007/s00170-014-6274-9

13. Nee, A., Ong, S.K., Chryssolouris, G., Mourtzis, D.: Augmented reality applications in design and manufacturing. CIRP Ann. Manufact. Technol. **12**(61), 657–679 (2012). https://doi.org/10.1016/j.cirp.2012.05.010

14. Regenbrecht, H., Baratoff, G., Wilke, W.: Augmented reality projects in the automotive and aerospace industries. IEEE Comput. Graph. Appl. **11**(25), 48–56 (2005). https://doi.org/10.1109/MCG.2005.124

15. Schlagowski, R., Merkel, L., Meitinger, C.: Design of an assistant system for industrial maintenance tasks and implementation of a prototype using augmented reality. In: 2017 IEEE International Conference on Industrial Engineering and Engineering Management (IEEM), pp. 294–298. IEEE, Singapore (2017). https://doi.org/10.1109/ieem.2017.8289899

16. Spath, D., Ganschar, O., Gerlach, S., Hämmerle, M., Krause, T., Schlund, S.: Produktionsarbeit der Zukunft – Industrie 4.0. Fraunhofer-Verlag, Stuttgart (2013)

17. Stocker, A., Brandl, P., Michalczuk, R., Rosenberger, M.: Mensch-zentrierte IKT-Lösungen in einer Smart Factory. Elektrotechnik & Informationstechnik **10**(131), 207–211 (2014)

18. Wang, X., Ong, S.K., Nee, A.: A comprehensive survey of augmented reality assembly research. Adv. Manufact. **1**(4), 1–22 (2016). https://doi.org/10.1007/s40436-015-0131-4

A Conference Goes Virtual: Lessons from Creating a Social Event in the Virtual Reality

Kathrin Kirchner[1]([✉]) [iD] and Britta Nordin Forsberg[2] [iD]

[1] Technical University of Denmark, Akademivej, 2800 Kgs. Lyngby, Denmark
kakir@dtu.dk
[2] KTH Royal Institute of Technology, Lindstedtsvägen 30, 111 28 Stockholm, Sweden
britta.forsberg@indek.kth.se

Abstract. Conferences and workshops are important activities in organizations for communication and collaboration, and in academia specifically to criticize and develop new research ideas. In order to enable social interactions during the pandemic situation, organizations use online solutions like video conference systems. A huge number of virtual conferences has been offered, and attracted more participants as the cost and participation effort were lower. However, socializing and informal exchange between conference participants during coffee breaks and conference dinners is nearly impossible in a virtual conference setting. Conferences are important to meet other researchers, to build a network and collaborate in the future, which is critical to society - to create frontier knowledge. Virtual reality could be an alternative to usual video conferences as they could allow social interaction between different participants and thus support to get in direct contact with future collaborators. Our paper explains how we created and executed a social event in virtual reality at an online conference in academia that included 22 participants in three Nordic countries. Based on 17 interviews with Swedish and Danish participants, we analyze perceived advantages and challenges that the event participants faced. Our results provide interesting insights and recommendations for organizers of virtual conferences to enable socializing in virtual reality.

Keywords: Virtual collaboration · Virtual reality · Socializing · Conference organization

1 Introduction

Conferences fulfil a variety of purposes: communication, collaboration, networking, sharing, information, and marketing, etc. The purpose of workshops are many: idea generation, planning, teambuilding, etc. In academia, which constitutes the case for this study, conferences are incorporated in the core research process in order to communicate, criticize and develop new research ideas. Recently, the pandemic situation hit hard on these practices, as it became inappropriate to meet in real life due to the risk of transmitting the infection. Then, in order to maintain this kind of social processes to some

© Springer Nature Switzerland AG 2021
U. R. Krieger et al. (Eds.): I4CS 2021, CCIS 1404, pp. 123–134, 2021.
https://doi.org/10.1007/978-3-030-75004-6_9

extent, organizations switched to online solutions supported by already existing technological tools for video conference systems [9], and the number of virtual conferences exploded [11]. As socializing and informal exchange between conference participants during coffee breaks and conference dinners is nearly impossible in a virtual conference setting, the current pandemic situation has social consequences on organizations and its people. There is also a positive environmental side effect though; less travelling reduced the carbon footprint [11].

Many conference organizers are turning their conferences to online platforms to share and discuss scientific ideas in the pandemic and thus moving at least a part of the physical meeting experience to the online world. This could also be a shift to more online conferences in the future in order to respond to health issues, travel restrictions, difficulties with childcare or inaccessibility of physical conference places for disabled researchers [20]. Although video conferences have shown that they are easy to set up and used, they also have a downside: a lack of spontaneity, so people have less chances to generate ideas in causal interactions with unexpected people [7] as it would be the case in spontaneous face-to-face meetings at the coffee machine or the lunch table in the company.

Virtual reality could serve an alternative to video conferencing systems for online meetings, as, since it has the power to create a more realistic setting of the space or room where we meet and can provide the potential to nurture the collaborative and social climate. In this paper, we describe how we created and executed a social event in virtual reality at an online conference, where the participants could mingle and talk at the end of the conference. We further analyze perceived advantages and challenges of a virtual reality event based on 17 interviews with Swedish and Danish conference participants. With our paper, we contribute to answer the question how virtual reality can support and successfully facilitate virtual conferences or other types of virtual business meetings.

Our paper is structured as follows. Section 2 provides an overview about related work. Section 3 provides our case study – the virtual event that we organized for an online conference. Section 4 explains shortly the methodology and data collection. In Sect. 5, we present the results from the interviews with the event participants. Section 6 summarizes our findings and gives recommendations for future similar events.

2 Literature Review

The central topic for this paper is the creation of a social arena in virtual reality (VR) and the specific case for this study is the preparation and execution of a conference that gathered participants from different countries in a science community in academic organizations. This conference has a tradition of being executed in-person and a main objective, besides sharing information, is to maintain and expand the professional personal network of the conference participants. Our literature review focuses on two points: how technology can support virtual collaboration in general, and how virtual reality can facilitate virtual collaboration in particular.

2.1 Supporting Virtual Collaboration with Technology

The point of departure for this literature review is the virtual kind of collaboration that has exploded during the pandemic situation where predominantly video conferences have become a substitute for in-person conferences, which have established as a norm for meetings [21]. This change has brought several advantages that contribute to both environmental and social sustainability including equality. Less traveling to conferences is a clear advantage for the environment. Both environmental and social aspects contribute to an equality perspective where disabled people can participate more easily. Furthermore, participants that cannot afford travelling can be included. An additional advantage is related to private life; an easier access to childcare. Virtual conferences also bring financial benefits: the cost to organize a conference can be cut down to half the sum for an in-person conference while at the same time an increased amount of registered participants can be included. So the question arises which tool can support a virtual conference (or more general, a business meeting) in an effective way.

Some authors used a quantitative approach by relying on the task-technology-fit theory. This theory discusses that effectiveness in collaboration and communication is influenced by a match between the requirements for the specific communication task and the characteristics of the tool that is used for communication [4]. Business meetings can have several objectives, like exchanging information, communicating sentiments, making decisions, or building relationships [17] which correspond to the tasks in the technology-fit theory. The capabilities of software systems can support these different types of business meeting objectives in several ways. A video conference (supported, e.g., by MS Teams or Zoom) allows to hear and see the videos, experience mimics and gestures and to use shared screens. Other types of online meetings like telepresence robots or virtual reality allow additionally feeling co-located and observing what other participants are looking at (like in face-to-face meetings) [18]. VR conferencing allows also more social interactions than a typical video conference as participants can organically meet in small groups (instead of using breakout rooms in video conferences where people get assigned to rooms) or interact with virtual objects in the virtual room [12].

2.2 Virtual Reality as a Social Arena in Organizations

Compared with other digital solutions for communication within organizations, such as video conferences, a substitute concept named Virtual Reality (VR) is emerging. "VR is a communication medium that provides users with a 3-dimentional (3D), 360-degree computer-generated virtual environment" [5]. The authors conclude that 2D is established as the media for communication and entertainment. Even though 2D mediums have been the dominant technology in this field, the role for VR is expanding into different industries and sectors like tourism, education, retail and public relations domains. VR is recognized for its ability to give the user a more immersive experience than just 'captivates and holds our attention because it feels expansive, detailed and complete' [10], p. 101–102. Slater [16] predicted a new age of communication based on the usage of VR in a broader sense. The immersive environment has the capacity to provide alternative perspectives [19]. This paper pays attention to avatars as a representation or proxy of the players (users) that can intentionally be controlled by the user to move in the virtual space. The author describes further that the avatars are gaming-informed. Avatars are important for the social dynamics in virtual environments like online gaming or collaborative systems [2]. Thomas [19] emphasizes the interactivity that is enabled in the virtual environment. Also [14] states that immersiveness and also realism have been the ambition already from the naissance of VR, but claims that it still does not have reached that capacity to provide experiences similar to real life in several regards. However, they discuss whether a real copy of the real world is desirable. Roth et al. [14] highlight the importance of matching what the technology can offer in relation to the dynamics of communication between people. They focus on synchronization in social signals like eye contact, gestures, and facial expressions - and how empathy is embedded, enabled and expressed. Another social aspect in VR that has been investigated by [1] is anxiety, like phobias or social anxiety to get a negative evaluation by others in social or performance situations. Grand online games with multiplayer features such as Second Life have already enabled people for almost two decades to create and share virtual worlds and objects and to create their avatars [3], also without head-mounted displays (HMD).

3   Designing a Virtual Reality Event

The case reported in this paper is the annual conference of the Scandinavian Academy of Industrial Engineering and Management (ScAIEM) 2020. The conference brought together around 160 participants from technical universities of five Nordic countries. The event is not a classic conference focusing on paper presentation. It is rather organized in sessions where attendants from Nordic universities exchange ideas and experiences, and identify new opportunities for collaboration.

Due to the pandemic situation, the conference was conducted virtually in 2020 (scaiem.dtu.dk) by the Technical University of Denmark. Participation was free of charge, so more people registered for the conference than in previous years. Virtual sessions were conducted in parallel via Zoom. All Zoom sessions had between 10 and 80 participants. The social conference event was transferred to the virtual world.

This specific VR-event was co-hosted by Playitfair (which is an organization that has been funded by the Swedish Innovation Agency, Vinnova) and the KTH Royal Institute of Technology in Stockholm. Together with the conference organizers from the Technical University of Denmark, we decided three months prior to the conference to introduce the idea of using VR for the social activity. Some aspects emerged as important in the preparation: deadline for registration, choice of VR-platform, check availability and choice of type of head-mounted-devices (HMD), designing the event, on-boarding of participants, reducing anxiety especially for first time users, preparation for both facilitation and guidance during the event and also calculation of the cost (versus value).

Deadline for Registration
As the conference was going to be executed as a video conference, the deadline for registration could be pushed closer to the activity since there was no need for booking of locations, food, coffee, etc. However, as the VR-activity required allocation or purchase of headsets, it put demands on registration in good time before the execution of the

conference. The organizing committee encouraged all participants to investigate if there were any HMDs for VR available at their respective university.

Choice of VR-Platform

The choice of the VR-platform to use for the event was based on a number of parameters:

- what kind of HMD the platform supported in combination with what types we had access or found most relevant to invest in,
- the expectation of the graphical quality and variation of the virtual room(s) to visit
- which features were available for designing the virtual event.

We decided to go for a platform that was regarded as one of the most exclusive and well-developed environments in order to give an immersive experience to the audience.

Availability of Head-Mounted-Devices (HMD)

The selected platform supported most types of headsets that were identified and could be borrowed for the event in the different universities by the participants. If the participant owned or could borrow only platform-unsupported HMDs, then we had to replace them by another model that we send via post. Other universities bought HMDs from a supplier. The logistics pushed to the timetable since the HMDs had to arrive well before the conference day. One of the HMDs was out of function, but the supplier quickly dealt with it.

Designing the Event

A face-to-face social event can be more or less pre-designed and the same goes for a virtual version. We decided to have a free agenda for the event where the participants could focus on the experience itself, since it can be quite overwhelming to participate for the first time in a virtual reality event. In order to support people during the event we allocated a VR-experienced guide and facilitator that was in charge of a master-keyboard to control the event in terms of teleporting the participants to different worlds and help with other activities.

On-Boarding of Participants and Reducing Anxiety for First-Time Users

Several days prior to the conference we organized a 60 min on-boarding session so that the participants could try their equipment, check that they can access the VR-platform, create an avatar (Fig. 1a) and ask any questions to the organizers and the guide in the VR-space. We also recorded a movie showing when a person they knew, at least by name, using VR (Fig. 1b). The purpose was to reduce anxiety.

Calculation of the Cost

The calculation of the cost was based on the fee for the platform, purchase or hiring cost for head mounted devices (HMD), and the time for designing the event in terms of creating an agenda, number of needed VR-rooms, etc. We used pre-designed VR-rooms, but other conferences may also have costs for developing new and specific VR-rooms.

Fig. 1. An avatar of a participant created with a real face photo (a) and a participant with VR headset and remote controls (b)

4   Method and Data

4.1   Virtual Reception Setting

The virtual reception started as the last event of the conference sessions. From the 50 participants that registered for the VR event, 22 showed up at the reception. Reasons for non-participation were different, e.g., some had other obligations within their work or their family, and others became ill. The conference started in the first virtual room with mingling of the participants. Our guide introduced the participants to the platform and explained some fun features like the creation of fantasy animals by using the VR remote controls or taking pictures in the virtual reality rooms. The guide furthermore helped participants that had questions how to use the platform. He later transferred all participants to a second room for mingling and social events like basketball or playing an instrument. The virtual journey continued with socializing in the Oval Office (Fig. 2a), and sightseeing in Copenhagen (Fig. 2b), the place of the virtual conference. The guide placed all participants for a group photo (Fig. 2b) that was later sent to all. The reception closed by a goodbye of the organizers in the auditorium (Fig. 2c). The virtual event lasted approximately one hour.

Fig. 2. Impressions from the virtual reception (names are covered with black bars): a) socializing in the Oval Office b) Sightseeing in Copenhagen c) Talk in the auditorium

4.2 Qualitative Interview Setting

The conference included 160 registered online participants, and 50 of them registered for the virtual reality event. Twenty-two of them participated – including the authors of this paper. Because of the explorative nature of our research question, whether VR can support and successfully facilitate virtual conferences, and the relatively small amount of participants, we decided for interviews instead of conducting a survey. Thus, 20 participants were contacted, but three did not answer or did not want to be interviewed.

We developed an interview guideline with eight main questions: (1) the motivation to participate in the virtual reception, (2) previous experiences with virtual reality, (3) previous experiences with virtual conferences, (4) what they did participate in during the event, (5) positive experiences with the event, (6) perceived challenges, (7) experiences in comparison with other ways of socializing, e.g., in Zoom, and (8) ideas for further improvements. The interviews were semi-structured to give the chance to ask additional clarifying questions or dive deeper into a topic.

Interview data was collected from 17 event participants. Each interview lasted 20 to 30 min and was recorded and transcribed. Five interviewees were from Denmark, 12 came from different Swedish universities, and all were on different professional levels - from master students to full professors.

5 Results

5.1 Motivation to Participate

Most participants of the virtual reception did not have previous experiences with virtual reality, and they had rarely used VR headsets already in computer games. Most of them had participated in online conferences before, but the socializing was rarely offered or only limited (like in a common Zoom meeting for all). A motivation to participate was therefore to experience something new, as one participant pointed out:

I1: *"So just experiencing and seeing what it's like was one motivation. And then the second motivation was that in Corona times I miss networking with my colleagues, so any chance of mingling with colleagues was appreciated."*

In addition, the pandemic situation played a role in deciding to participate, as pure Zoom meetings started to become boring:

I1: *"With Zoom it's always the same physical environment, I'm always sitting in a chair, I'm always looking at the Zoom interface with a black frame around it, looking at moving heads."*

Another interviewee was open minded to all experiences that could happen in the VR:

I3: *"I was not really sure what to expect, especially in regards to interacting with other people in the networking as part of the reception. So, I was quite open minded in terms of what was going to happen. I was positively surprised."*

5.2   Experiences with the Virtual Reception

At the beginning of the virtual reception, when the guide explained how the virtual reality world works and which features it has, nearly everyone tried these features out. Especially participants that did not experience the virtual reality before were more excited to try out the features than to meet other participants in the virtual reception, as an interviewee pointed out:

I2: *"How does this work and which button do I press now and we were exploring this new thing rather than socializing. I think if you do it for two more times, we would actually be more confident to pull and relax and actually start socializing."*

One of the features was to press a button and create fancy animals, like a dinosaur, a lion or a goat, which was also a way to interact with others or to talk with others about. Furthermore, the virtual reality room allowed playing games and interacting with the environment:

I4: *"We were able to explore all these animals and figures; I think it was also a bit of a distraction. But in the main meeting room where you were able to go and interact with your hands in basketball or playing an instrument. It was pretty fun to be able to interact with the environment using VR."*

Besides of the fun, the VR allowed to meet other people:

I1: *"You can walk around freely and you can organically come up with groups of people, you can chat with. That's quite nice, it's more dynamic than having these breakout rooms on zoom."*

The virtual reality gave the feeling of closeness and to get to know people a bit better, as an interviewee mentioned:

I5: *"But here it actually felt like we were together and that people that I have been chatting with and writing emails for suddenly they are in front of me so that was quite nice."*

One participant met even a new collaborator in the in the virtual reality, which is already near a real world conference event:

I6: *"I met a couple of new people, and one at least I've arranged a meeting with afterwards. The ability to move around and bounce into people worked well."*

Interestingly, the behavior in the virtual world seems to be comparable to the behavior in the real world:

I7: *"I don't think I would ever approach a person that will stand alone in the corner and just say hi to talk - as you go to people that you've spoken with, or maybe also to people when you attended a session where this person was."*

The problem of getting in contact with unknown people in virtual reality might thus be more challenging, and it is easier to approach people that one already knows. That is especially true, when participants sat physically in the same hall while attending the virtual reality event:

I8: *"I was surprised by how much harder it felt in this virtual reality environment to talk to people I didn't know. So actually I think I ended up talking to people I knew, and most of them were physically very close to where I was."*

However, another interviewee even mentioned that the technology can make it easier to connect with others and overcome shyness:

I3: *"I think if you were in VR, you know, to have these interfaces between you and the other real person that makes it a little easier to break this ice you know. Come, go out of the bubble."*

5.3 Perceived Challenges

From the interviews, we identified two groups of challenges: issues with the behavior in the virtual world and technical issues. As the main part of the conference was conducted via Zoom, people did not see each other in real life. Especially if a conference participant visited the conference for the first time, it was not easy to get to know people before the virtual reality reception, as common coffee breaks and lunches were not possible on Zoom. In larger Zoom sessions, with over 60 participants (as for the keynote speeches), it was impossible to recognize other participants (as it would be possible in the real world). Therefore, it was not easy to recognize someone later in the virtual reality, because everyone is using an avatar:

I1: *"You just see an avatar. It can be similar to what the person looks like. It can also be something completely different. And you don't really see how old this person is; I cannot go through the room and look for the young PhD student who is similar to me."*

In addition, missing mimics can hinder to get in contact:

I1: *"I cannot detect if this person looks kind of grumpy or annoyed. Looks like maybe a person who is too shy to approach other people, you know, then it could be an easy way to approach that person, or this person is annoyed and just wants to be left alone. I think on that level that there are many barriers to approach someone."*

Furthermore, participants also perceived challenges with using the technology. One interviewee mentioned the unintuitive usage of the platform:

I1: *"I felt the controls were a bit unintuitive. I could move. No problem. But I think there was no real interface like there were no middle controls for,.., making gestures or how to change the audio settings or to check if my microphone would be working to see if I'm displaying the right name."*

Another problem was the sound and the surrounding noise, which made it difficult to talk to others:

I3: *"So I liked that there was the audio depending on how far you were from the other persons. So, but I felt like you could always hear in the background people talking, even if they were very far from you. And that made it sometimes a little complicated to hear the person I was actually talking to, like, face to face.*"

The noise appeared as a major problem in the virtual reception:

I1: "*I felt that I heard a lot of noise. It was really difficult to hear something clearly through the many voices that were there.*"

The use of a VR headset brings people to another world, but they also reported problems when using the headset for too long or in different situations.

I3: "*...using the headset for a long time. Then you start getting very sweaty around the eyes, and it gets hot really quick, and you can get a little motion sickness. If you use it for a long time and also this experience we had - there was a video in 360 around us - and in that at some point I started feeling a lot of motion sickness.*"

6 Summary and Recommendations

The participants of our virtual reality event were curious to join and experience the virtual reality that was a new technology for most of them. Only some experienced virtual reality already in amusement gaming. Therefore, we recommend an onboarding event before the actual virtual reality event so that all participants can set up the technology and get a bit familiar with it. We also found the experienced guide useful who helped new participants with explaining the technology and helped with difficulties.

Our virtual reality event was considered as an interesting opportunity for socializing in pandemic times. However, such an event requires more time for preparation, both for the participants and for the organizers. Although the effort and the cost are higher than for video conferences, this effort will be lower to the organizer for future events, as the virtual rooms would already exist; participants already installed the necessary software and collected experiences in the virtual world.

The interviewees generally perceived the event as more lively and fun than just Zoom meetings, and they liked the possibility to interact with the virtual environment and other participants. However, as several participants did not know each other before, it was not easy to get in contact with a new person, as the person behind the avatar and the missing mimics and gestures complicated the get-to-know each other. This was partly caused by the online nature of the whole conference - as it was not easy in the large Zoom conference sessions before to recognize and memorize other participants. In the future, social games could be played in the virtual world in order to facilitate interaction between different people. Here, virtual team-building games can be played in small groups to get to know each other [6, 15] and later also exchange professional interests. Another way could be to use the option to create an avatar by using a photo of the person for creating the face of the avatar. That would make it easier to recognize other conference participants, e.g., because they gave a talk in the Zoom conference and are therefore easier recognizable in the virtual room if their avatar's face is similar to the real one. HTC recently announced a new technology that can replicate the face of the user based on several data points from tracking the face [13].

Nevertheless, the platform and virtual reality also had some disadvantages. A major problem was the sound. In general, people further away from a person could not or only softly be heard. However, most participants complained about the noise and that they could hear people speaking that they could not see (because they were maybe directly behind them) - which hindered a conversation with the person next to them. The selection of a suitable environment for the virtual meeting is therefore essential. The design of the virtual space could also help here by providing several small social rooms where people can meet in groups and thus be separated from other groups. This principle is for example used in gather.town, a 2D platform that offers social rooms where people can meet without disturbances from other social rooms [22].

Furthermore, a long stay in the virtual reality led to exhaustion and nausea, especially in an environment that is moving around a person in a 360-degree environment. VR headsets are nowadays still heavy, as they contain the powerful processing hardware. In the future, headsets will get smaller, more mobile and more powerful [8]. With heavier headsets, it is advised to plan for shorter meetings to avoid sweating and exhaustion.

In our future research, we plan to facilitate virtual reality events also in other settings, like company meetings, fairs, or teaching situations and investigate the usefulness and drawbacks of this technology for collaboration and communication in the virtual space.

References

1. Aymerich-Franch, L., et al.: The relationship between virtual self similarity and social anxiety. Front. Hum. Neurosci. **8**, 1–10 (2014). https://doi.org/10.3389/fnhum.2014.00944
2. Freeman, G., et al.: My body, my avatar: how people perceive their avatars in social virtual reality. In: Conference on Human Factors in Computing Systems, pp. 1–8 (2020). https://doi.org/10.1145/3334480.3382923.
3. Girvan, C.: What is a virtual world? Definition and classification. Educ. Technol. Res. Dev. **66**(5), 1087–1100 (2018). https://doi.org/10.1007/s11423-018-9577-y
4. Goodhue, D.L., Thompson, R.L.: Task-technology fit and individual performance. MIS Q. Manag. Inf. Syst. **19**(2), 213–233 (1995). https://doi.org/10.2307/249689
5. Kandaurova, M., Lee, S.H.M.: The effects of Virtual Reality (VR) on charitable giving: the role of empathy, guilt, responsibility, and social exclusion. J. Bus. Res. **100**, 571–580 (2019). https://doi.org/10.1016/j.jbusres.2018.10.027
6. Littlefield, C.: 75+Team Building Activities for Remote Teams: Simple Ways to Build Trust, Strengthen Communications, and Laugh Together from Afar. Independently published (2020).
7. Marks, P.: Virtual collaboration in the age of the coronavirus. Commun. ACM. **63**(9), 21–23 (2020). https://doi.org/10.1145/3409803
8. Marr, B.: The 5 Biggest Virtual and Augmented Reality Trends in 2020 Everyone Should Know About. https://www.forbes.com/sites/bernardmarr/2020/01/24/the-5-biggest-virtual-and-augmented-reality-trends-in-2020-everyone-should-know-about/?sh=40d2729c24a8
9. Misa, C., et al.: Lessons Learned Organizing the PAM 2020 Virtual Conference. ACM SIGCOMM Comput. Commun. Rev. **50**(3), 46–54 (2020)
10. Murray, J.H.: Inventing the Medium. Principles of Interaction Design as a Cultural Practice. MIT Press, Cambridge (2011)
11. Niner, H., Johri, S., Meyer, J., Wassermann, S.: The pandemic push: can COVID-19 reinvent conferences to models rooted in sustainability, equitability and inclusion? Socio-Ecol. Pract. Res. **2**(3), 253–256 (2020). https://doi.org/10.1007/s42532-020-00059-y
12. Pidel, C., Ackermann, P.: Collaboration in virtual and augmented reality: a systematic overview. In: De Paolis, L.T., Bourdot, P. (eds.) AVR 2020. LNCS, vol. 12242, pp. 141–156. Springer, Cham (2020). https://doi.org/10.1007/978-3-030-58465-8_10

13. Robertson, A.: HTC announces Vive Pro lip tracking module and new VR body trackers - The Verge. https://www.theverge.com/2021/3/10/22323093/htc-vive-pro-vr-facial-lip-tracker-third-gen-tracker-announcement-price. Accessed 15 Mar 2021

14. Roth, D., et al.: Hybrid avatar-agent technology – a conceptual step towards mediated "social" virtual reality and its respective challenges. I-Com. 14(2), 107–114 (2015). https://doi.org/10.1515/icom-2015-0030

15. Scannel, M., et al.: The Big Book of Virtual Teambuilding Games: Quick, Effective Activities To Build Communication, Trust And Collaboration From Anywhere! McGraw-Hill (2011)

16. Slater, M.: Grand challenges in virtual environments. Front. Robot. AI 1(May), 1–4 (2014). https://doi.org/10.3389/frobt.2014.00003

17. Standaert, W., Muylle, S., Basu, A.: An empirical study of the effectiveness of telepresence as a business meeting mode. Inf. Technol. Manage. 17(4), 323–339 (2015). https://doi.org/10.1007/s10799-015-0221-9

18. Standaert, W., et al.: How shall we meet? Understanding the importance of meeting mode capabilities for different meeting objectives. Inf. Manage. 103393 (2021). https://doi.org/10.1016/j.im.2020.103393

19. Thomas, S.: The star in VR. Celebr. Stud. 10(4), 453–468 (2019). https://doi.org/10.1080/19392397.2019.1672996

20. Viglione, G.: A year without conferences? How the coronavirus pandemic could change research (2020). https://doi.org/10.1038/d41586-020-00786-y

21. Viglione, G.: How conferences will survive the coronavirus shock. Nature 582, 166–167 (2020)

22. Williamson, J.R., et al.: Proxemics and social interactions in an instrumented virtual reality workshop. In: CHI 2021: ACM Computer Human Interaction, pp. 1–20 (2021). https://doi.org/10.1145/1122445.1122456

GUIDed: Assisted-Living Smart Platform and Social Communication for Older Adults

Christos Mettouris[1(✉)], Alexandros Yeratziotis[1], Charalampos Theodorou[1], Evangelia Vanezi[1], Achilleas Achilleos[2], George A. Papadopoulos[1], Sotiria Moza[3], Marina Polycarpou[3], Joanna Starosta-Sztuczka[4], Karol Pecyna[4], Terje Grimstad[5], and Strahinja Lazic[6]

[1] Department of Computer Science, University of Cyprus, 2109 Nicosia, Cyprus
{mettour,ayerat01,ctheod07,evanez01,george}@cs.ucy.ac.cy
[2] Frederick Research Center, 7 Filokyprou Street, 1036 Nicosia, Cyprus
com.aa@frederick.ac.cy
[3] MATERIA, Athalassis 41, 2221 Latsia, Nicosia, Cyprus
{sotiria,marina}@materia.com.cy
[4] Harpo Sp. z o.o, 27 Grudnia 7, 61-737 Poznan, Poland
{jstarosta,kpecyna}@harpo.com.pl
[5] Karde AS, Irisveien 14, 0870 Oslo, Norway
terje.grimstad@karde.no
[6] Kompetenznetzwerk Informationstechnologie zur Förderung Der Integration von Menschen Mit Behinderungen (KI-I), 4040 Linz, Austria
strahinja.lazic@ki-i.at

Abstract. The aging population, the increased incidence of chronic disease, the technological advances and the rapidly escalating health-care costs are driving healthcare from hospital and day care centres to home. The GUIDed AAL EU project focuses on the challenge of keeping older adults independent and functioning in their own homes for as long as possible, by facilitating important activities of daily living through ICT solutions. Through a modular and customizable smart home platform, backened system and Android application, assisted-living solutions and services are offered to facilitate seniors' daily lives in their own home and the community. The main target areas are smart home control, home safety enhancement, city navigation, nutrition and health improvement, and socialisation/communication. In this paper, we present three of the five GUIDed services and report on our findings from the evaluation of the High-Fidelity (Hi-Fi) paper prototypes for these services. The Hi-Fi prototypes were tested by older adults and their caregivers using focus groups in four European countries, namely Austria, Cyprus, Norway and Poland. The results showed that all of the users found the GUIDed system understandable and easy to use, which is an encouraging finding considering older participants' low technological literacy.

Keywords: Assisted-living · GUIDed services · Smart home · Social communication · High-fidelity prototypes · Older adults

© Springer Nature Switzerland AG 2021
U. R. Krieger et al. (Eds.): I4CS 2021, CCIS 1404, pp. 135–151, 2021.
https://doi.org/10.1007/978-3-030-75004-6_10

1 Introduction

The combination of reduced birth rates and increased life expectancy has led to a restructuring of population demographics across the developed world [1, 2]. The share of older adults (65 or over) among the total population in the EU-28 in 2016[1] was recorded to be 19.2% and more specifically, in Norway (16.4%), Poland (16%) and Cyprus (15.1%)3. Therefore, population aging together with increased incidence of chronic disease, technological advances and the rapidly escalating health-care costs are driving healthcare from hospital and day care centers to home.

Increasing healthy life expectancy requires the introduction of support in the form of technological products and services. Technological developments have increased viability of homecare due to the miniaturization and portability of diagnostic and information technologies, remote monitoring, and long-distance care [3, 4]. Although many disjoint technological solutions and services are available, the ability of older adults to find, choose and combine such services is a critical issue. While most older adults feel that technology makes a positive impact on society, almost three quarters lack confidence in their ability to use devices to complete online tasks [5]. According to a recent review [6], internet use among older adults has increased over time. Nevertheless, studies have found that fear of technology is more prevalent in older generations who did not grow up with computers [7, 8]. Social issues, such as the "digital divide" have been found to be significant, where many older adults are still perceived as being resistant to modern technologies [9]. Given the near ubiquity of internet and electronic technologies in everyday life, there is an urgent need to enable older people to embrace the digital age [9]. Technophobia can be caused by anxiety about science or mathematical problems. People who feel intimidated by these subjects are more likely to experience technology anxiety [10].

Older adults who face this phobia respond better if they are provided with consistent support from younger adults. The younger generation, often children and grandchildren, or local program officers, assume the role of good mentors and reward small steps taken by technophobic to overcome their fears. Teaching skills only addresses part of the problem, of course; the costs of devices and of Internet service also keep older people offline, and so do physical limitations or cognitive impairment. Still, learning the technology is the key to the problem [10].

The GUIDed AAL EU project addresses the challenge of keeping older adults independent and functioning in their own homes for as long as possible, by facilitating important activities of daily living through IT solutions. GUIDed uses a modular and customizable smart home platform, a backened system and an Android application, consisting of assisted-living solutions and services to facilitate seniors' daily lives in their own home and the community. The main target areas are smart home control, home safety enhancement, city navigation, nutrition and health improvement, and socialisation/communication.

In this paper, we present three of the five GUIDed services and report on our findings from the evaluation of the High-Fidelity (Hi-Fi) paper prototypes for these services with primary end-users via focus groups. The GUIDed Hi-Fi prototypes were tested by older

---

[1] https://ec.europa.eu/eurostat/cache/infographs/elderly/index.html.

adults and their caregivers in four European countries with positive results. In addition, a technical description of the system, its architecture and the services are provided. The paper is consisted of six sections. Section 2 discusses Background and Related Work. Section 3 describes the methodology, while Sect. 4 presents the GUIDed platform from a technical point of view. The results of the evaluation of the Hi-Fi paper prototypes are discussed in Sect. 5. The paper closes with Conclusions and Future Work in Sect. 6.

2 Background and Related Work

In terms of EU funded projects aiming to offer ICT solutions for enhancing and supporting the home living of older adults, the IOANNA[2] (Integration Of All stores Network & Navigation Assistant) project aims at developing ICT-based solutions for seniors for everyday facilitation in shopping management and navigation, focusing on assistive mobility and social engagement through crowdsourcing. The FrailSafe[3] project aims to better understand frailty and its relation to other health conditions. It aims to delay frailty by developing a set of measures and tools, together with recommendations to reduce its onset. To achieve these objectives, FrailSafe combines state-of-the-art information technologies and data mining techniques with high-level expertise in the field of health and ageing. In terms of enhancing the social presence of older adults, the MedGUIDE[4] project offers an approach to social networking and e-learning focused on polypharmacy management, to support informal and formal caregivers of seniors with dementia. Seniors will be supported in their medication adherence using sensor technology and smart pill-boxes. The Many-Me[5] project builds a social interactive care system using ICT and user-centred services to help people with dementia, their relatives, informal and formal carers.

According to a research in [11], older adults already use existing digital tools in the form of smartphone applications to combat the effects of isolation due to the COVID-19 pandemic. The research categorizes the apps in 6 categories: Social Networking, Medical: telemedicine, Medical: prescription management, Health & Fitness, Food & Drink, and Visual & Hearing impairment.

In [12], the + Simple platform is discussed that groups content (news, procedures, social networks and pages of interest). Older adults were trained to use the tool through a 2-h course. The aim was to promote elderly adults' social inclusion through a digital literacy process [12]. The training involved 40 Digital online Classrooms. Moreover, 106,550 tablets with the " +Simple" platform were delivered to people over 60 years of age.

Guided Access Mode [13] is an app that supports older adults in their asynchronous communication with family and friends. The technology required an adaptation period but was a feasible communication tool. Use increased perceived social interaction with ties, but increased social connectedness (meaningful social interaction) was only reported

---

[2] https://ec.europa.eu/eip/ageing/commitments-tracker/d4/integration-all-stores-network-naviga
tion-assistant-seniors_en.

[3] https://frailsafe-project.eu/.

[4] https://www.aal-europe.eu/projects/medguide/.

[5] https://many-me.eu/.

by participants with geographically distant relatives [13]. In addition, the sense of well-being and confidence with technology was also enhanced.

Social networking sites (SNS) such as Facebook (and Webcams) Twitter, can assist in creating and maintaining social relationships essential in contributing to the wellbeing of seniors [14]. Reduced mobility and geographical distance from family can cause loneliness among seniors. SNS can aid in overcoming these obstacles by allowing seniors to maintain involvement with their family and friends, despite their immobility or distance from them. In addition, technology such as video conferencing can also help older adults overcome mobility challenges that come with aging by staying connected [14].

WhatsApp is an app that can be perceived as user-friendly with a clean and simple to use design, meaning that groups that are normally excluded from using it, (e.g. older people) are able to use it [15]. In [15] it is supported that, by enhancing its usage further from just exchanging messages, it is much more likely that elderly will adhere to health advice they receive via this channel, as well as being much more likely to pay attention to any incoming messages from medical experts.

Connect2affect [16] is a new initiative that aims to create a network of resources that meets the needs of anyone who is isolated or lonely. Helps build the social connections older adults need to thrive. It requires taking an assessment quiz to establish the necessary next steps to each unique individual.

Although the abovementioned technologies contribute in enhancing the lives of older adults in areas such as healthcare, social communication, navigation, shopping and more, these are nevertheless offered in a disjoint manner. An integrated set of services under a common platform/application with a single, unique user interface (UI) is missing. Furthermore, scattered services with different UIs and different ways of user-system interaction only contribute to the older adults' lack of confidence in their ability to use them, as well as to the technophobia they may experience.

The GUIDed platform aims to reduce these effects caused by technology. It addresses the challenge of keeping older adults independent and functioning in their own homes for as long as possible by facilitating important activities of daily living through an integrated set of ICT solutions. To achieve this, GUIDed will offer a selection of smart devices and services integrated in a smart home platform based on budget options, while giving heavy emphasis on training the older users on using the service and maximizing their benefit. A common design will contribute to better adoption of the system and less abandonment of the technology. The service categories of the GUIDed solution are: Smart Nutrition and Health service (S1); Smart Home Control service (S2); Smart City Navigation service (S3); Smart Home Safety service (S4); Social Communication service (S5). In terms of addressing older adults' technology related anxiety, GUIDed offers services via which older adults may receive support from younger adults, such as relatives, on a daily basis. The support may related to daily activities related with technology, or even training in using the GUIDed services themselves. The training component will be incorporated in the GUIDed system via an innovative assistant, utilising Augmented Reality (AR) technology.

3 Methods

From a methodology perspective, a user-centred design approach is adopted, focusing heavily on a co-creation aspect. Considering this, we point out the different categories of end-users that are to be recruited in different phases of co-creation activities: **Primary end-users**: Older adults living independently in their own homes with no or moderate need for assistance; **Secondary end-users**: Family members and informal caregivers; **Tertiary end-users**: Care organisations (day-care centres, hospitals, clinics, retirement homes, nursery homes) and staff (healthcare professionals). Other: technology product vendors, telecare service providers, policy makers and the like.

To ensure that the end-users' demands are respected throughout the design and development of the GUIDed platform and its services, the following process was followed in sequence:

1. Older adults' recruitment process and an analysis of the respective demands and needs.
2. National strategies and governmental recommendations for Assistive Technologies were reviewed in Cyprus, Austria, Norway and Poland.
3. Based on 1 and 2, the GUIDed platform and its services were then defined and presented to the primary end-users via workshops in order to collect their initial impressions.
4. Based on 3, the platform and its services were defined and the specifications designed (see Sect. 4).
5. Experimental evaluation and feedback activities commenced and continue (see Sect. 5).

Focusing on the experimental evaluation and feedback activities (i.e., step 5 in the aforementioned process), in order to adequately monitor, discuss, evaluate and collect feedback based on the design and development activities, it was decided to divide the Testing phases (see Table 1).

Table 1. Testing phases for the experimental evaluation and feedback activities.

Testing phase	Evaluation tool	Method to collect feedback
1	Paper prototype	Focus groups
2	Mock-ups (semi-functioning)	Questionnaires
3	First functional prototype	Living lab

In Sect. 5 of this paper we present the results from the first Testing phase that includes the design of High-Fidelity (Hi-Fi) paper prototypes for three of the services, as well as their evaluation with primary end-users utilising focus groups. The feedback collected in Phase 1 for each service is currently under review by the GUIDed team to determine which recommendations will be implemented and how to address specific considerations pointed out for the Phase 2 testing, i.e. in the design of the mock-ups (semi-functioning).

3.1 Paper Prototype

The first selected method for testing (whether the technical developments of the GUIDed system meets the needs of the older adults) was paper prototypes. Paper prototyping is a widely used method in the user-centred design process and utilised in the early design stages in order to test the functionalities and layouts of a graphical interface before programming begins [17]. Paper prototypes (e.g. sheets of paper or in online format) consist of an easy method for the end-users to understand the functionalities of a system/platform and provide valuable feedback, insights and issues with regards to its usability [18]. More specifically, this is done by presenting the functionalities to the end-user by using paper prototypes and encouraging her/him to comment on them ("talking aloud") while the researcher takes notes. Thus, paper prototyping assisted the project team pinpoint any design issues of the GUIDed platform for the end-users such as difficulties with navigating or comprehending the services and to identify potential points for alterations. While there are several techniques for conducting the paper prototyping method, the one utilised in this phase was wireframes. A wireframe is used to demonstrate the page layout of the interface. As seen in Fig. 1, the design of the paper prototypes was based on a set of 'rules' so as to facilitate the end-users and the focus groups activities.

"Rules" (ref. editable template beside):
1. Simple, elegant colour scheme, the same one in all 5 service paper prototypes. Distribute colour codes to the project team.
2. No red against green, or the other way around.
3. Screen font Calibri or similar (i.e. sans serif – no small "feet" as e.g. in Times).
4. Large text, short expressions.
5. High contrasts between text colour and background.
6. No all-caps words, and no ordninary words with a single capitalised letter. Use first capital letter only in a sentence or a button, or names of persons, cities etc. when grammatically correct prose).
7. Left-adjusted text (no centre-adjusted except in buttons and the like).
8. No abbreviations, at least without explanation.
9. GUIDed set of navigation application specific icons – in-house design.
10. Same main basic action buttons in all 5 service paper prototypes (Start, Quit, Exit, Save, Home, Back, Reload, etc.).
11. Always a short way "home", possible to go "back" and Exit without any disaster.
12. Suitable illustration icons in "one family of expression", with transparent background to avoid ugly white square backgrounds (icons "borrowed" before final purchase).
13. Short guidance texts when assumed necessary.
14. Easy-to-read "normal" language. Short sentences
15. Error messages in clear everyday-language. No "techie phrases".

14. If possible, no horizontal scrolling, minimal vertical scrolling.
15. No unnecessary decorations or disturbing animations
16. Identical example branding in all 5 service paper prototypes (GUIDed logo).
17. No "bells and whistles", such as decoration elements, childish animations, clip art humour / cartoon style, smileys etc.
18. Avoid over-loading the app screens.
19. All text in native languages.
20. Enable for native ways of expressing time, date, day as well as order and decimal figures.

Consistency between features and functionalities.
Minimalistic clean design and functionality.
Prepare for responsive design.

Tool and format:
• PowerPoint.
• One screen pr. page (vertical), to allow printing to larger posters for co-creation.
• Page size A3 or A2 to provide group-work posters.

Fig. 1. Design guidelines adopted for the Hi-Fi prototype designs instructions for the format of the evaluation tool format.

3.2 Focus Group

The paper prototype evaluation tool was used to conduct one-hour long focus groups, with participants. However, the number of participants for each focus group was influenced by the national social distancing measures against COVID-19 (see Sect. 5). Focus groups consist of a valuable qualitative research technique in an interactive interview setting where end-users have interactive and directed discussions and can freely express their opinions, perceptions and beliefs towards a product/service/system. During this process, end-users together with other participants can freely interact and share ideas and opinions which in turn assists the researchers in data collection [19]. Due to the group setting, for many end-users focus groups constitute a more pleasant and stress-free process compared to one-to-one interviews [20]. Furthermore, the group dynamic as a process facilitates discussion and can lead to more in-depth and spontaneous conversations, debates and ideas regarding the service/system. As such, this technique assisted the GUIDed project team to acquire valuable feedback in these early design and developmental stages of the platform with regards to its services.

4   GUIDed Platform

4.1   Architecture

The GUIDed system is comprised of the smart home platform, the backend system, and the Android mobile application (see Fig. 2). In terms of the backend system, an open-source, widely used platform with good documentation was selected as the basis for our development, Drupal. The GUIDed Drupal-based hybrid CMS (Content Management System) resides on the public cloud and provides the administration web system, the Web APIs (Application Programming Interfaces) and the push notifications. The Web APIs and the push notifications provide the capability to interact with the Android mobile application using HTTP requests and event-driven push notifications that are initiated from the server. The smart home platform is based on a Raspberry Pi 3. The smart home platform, as well as the mobile app for the primary user (older adult) and the mobile app for the secondary user (healthcarer, family member) communicate with the backend system through the provided Web APIs.

The architecture components are described in the following sections.

4.2   Smart Home Control and Smart Home Safety Services

The smart home control service provides an augmented reality Android application that allows its users to control their home environment. A user can choose between a simple interface with buttons or a camera view with AR features to control devices such as lights or plugs.

The smart home safety service enables users to track the presence of smoke or carbon monoxide in their homes. As soon as dedicated sensors register smoke or carbon monoxide, a message is displayed on its user's device. This service also provides the capability to include further types of sensors such as temperature or humidity sensors. Analogue to the smart home control service, users have the option to use a simple interface or the camera view with AR features to review its sensors' status.

Technology

From the hardware perspective, the usage of the smart home and safety services is enabled by a smart platform (RPi in Fig. 2) that needs to be installed in the user's

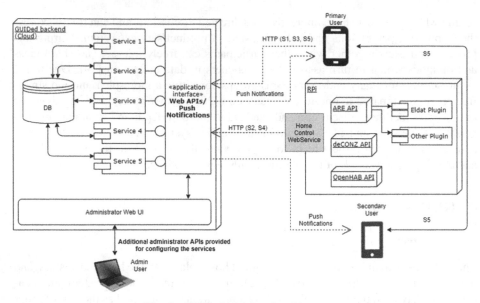

Fig. 2. GUIDed high-level architecture.

home. The platform is composed of the smart hub and a set of sensors and actuators which may be adapted to the individual user's needs. The smart hub, as the central component of the smart platform, is based on a Raspberry Pi 3 Model B + (RasPi) with the Raspberry OS and a "RaspBee II" Zigbee gateway. The Zigbee gateway serves as a bridge to communicate with Zigbee sensors and actuators. Raspberry Pi 3 was selected as it integrates well with established smart home and accessibility software, while offering an affordable price (around $40). "RaspBee II" was selected as it is a universal ZigBee Gateway, specifically made for the RasPi, that enables the integration of ZigBee smart home devices from different vendors, which usually require a proprietary gateway to control their devices.

The utilized software includes deCONZ, OpenHab, ARE, a proprietary middle-ware/backend application ("Home Control Web Service") and a proprietary front-end application ("Configuration Client"). The deCONZ software is responsible for the control of the ZigBee network and is required for the "RaspBee II" to operate.

OpenHab represents an open-source home automation software that enables efficient integrations of smart home systems or protocols such as deCONZ, KNX, MQTT, Z-Wave, etc. OpenHab was selected as it is open source with a strong community, while also facilitating the integration of different smart home systems. The ARE is an open-source system developed in the context of the EU project AsTeRICs[6] that executes plugins for smart home systems such as Hue or KNX. It is extensible and can therefore be used to support smart home systems that are not supported via OpenHab for example. The "Home Control Web Service" handles authentication, configuration, the routing for smart home operations and data exchange with ARE, OpenHab, deCONZ and the

---

[6] AsTeRICS EU FP7 Project: www.asterics.eu/.

GUIDed backend system on the cloud. The "Configuration Client" enables users to configure the installed devices so that the "Home Control Web Service" is aware of how and which devices to address. The communication between the distinct applications happens over Web APIs following REST architectural principles. An overview of the architecture is presented in Fig. 2.

Frameworks
Spring Boot is used for creating the "Home Control Web Service". After testing different frameworks such as Javalin, Spark and Spring Boot for the services' requirements, Spring Boot was chosen as it offers more features and a larger online community. VueJs with the Vue UI library Vuetify is used for creating the "Configuration Client". VueJs was chosen as it has a strong online community and the learning effort is lower compared to Angular or React. AsTeRICS (Assistive Technology Rapid Integration and Construction Set) is used for creating plugins that can be executed in the ARE.

4.3 Social Communication Service

The social communication service aims to offer a sense of real-life physical presence between the older adult and the communicating family member, healthcare provider or friend, avoiding thus social isolation and loneliness. Our objective is to provide a video calling service with a simple, easy to use UI, that is also appropriate for use by older adults. Using the service, older adults can keep in contact with family and friends while engaging in everyday activities such as eating together, drawing with the grandchildren and knitting.

Besides conducting video calls, the service offers a secondary functionality called "Meet Others". This functionality enables primary users, through the push of a (virtual) button, to conduct video calls to a random GUIDed primary user. The remote user will be randomly selected by the GUIDed system, provided that the remote user agrees to this communication and that the preferred languages of the two users match.

Architecture
The Social Communication Service was developed using the WebRTC framework. WebRTC is a free, open-source framework that enables Real-Time Communications with audio and/or video, by providing web browsers and mobile applications with the means for real-time communication via its APIs. The Social Communication Service includes two different architecture designs: a Client-Server architecture between Android devices (smartphone/tablets clients) and a signalling server, and a P2P (Peer-to-Peer) architecture between two Android devices. The Android devices and the signalling server communicate using WebSockets API. The server and client create a persistent connection between them (see Fig. 3), in order to hold an availability status at all times, to enable for reliable information exchange, when a request is made to create a Video Call connection between two Android devices. When a client-caller device (Android device) wants to initiate a Video Call with a client-receiver device, then the caller device sends a request to the server to notify the receiver device for the video call request. The server

then forwards this request to the receiver device and waits for a response. Immediately after the caller device sends the request to the server, it creates another request to the server that includes a WebRTC offer object and Ice Candidate object that the server will forward to the receiver device, after the video call request was accepted. The receiver device sends its response to the Video Call request, which is forwarded by the signalling server and waits for the server to forward the Offer and Ice Candidate information sent from the caller device. Then, the receiver device constructs an Answer and Ice Candidate object according to the Offer object received and sends the response to the server, which is then forwarded to the caller device. When both the caller and receiver devices forward through the server their Offer, Answer and Ice Candidates Objects to each other, then the communication through the signalling server ends and the P2P communication is initiated. It's important to note that the signalling server does not retain any information about the two clients during the video call: it deletes all WebRTC clients' data (Offer, Answer, IceCandidates) as soon as the signalling process is terminated. Apart from the signalling process, the server listens and handles any special case events e.g. client disconnection, client reset and client network changes.

As soon as the signalling process is completed, the two devices are connected through a process called PeerConnection (see Fig. 3 and Fig. 4) provided by the WebRTC API. The connection occurs on a private, full duplex communication channel throughout the lifetime of the video call. On this channel, each device shares its camera view (either front or rear) and receives the other device's camera view.

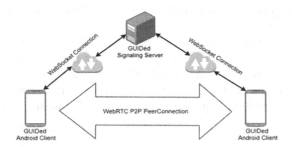

Fig. 3. Social Communication Service architecture schema.

Technologies, Frameworks and APIs

Table 2 depicts the technologies and frameworks used to implement the GUIDed signalling server and Android application.

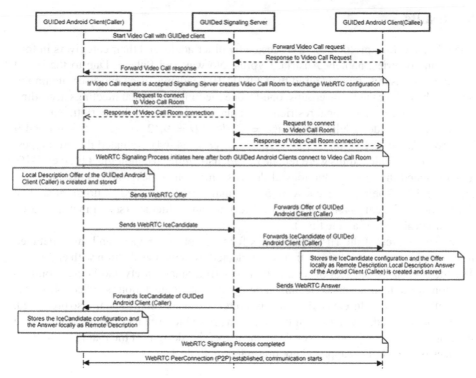

Fig. 4. Social Communication Service sequence diagram.

Table 2. Technologies & frameworks used for development of Social Communication Service.

Technology	Framework used	Version/API	Purpose in GUIDed
Node.js	Atom.io	Node version 12.13.0	Signalling server
Java	Android Studio 4	Java SDK 8	Android app
XML	Android Studio 4	Xml version 1.1	Android app
JSON	Atom.io & Android Studio 4		Signalling server & Android app
WebSocket	Atom.io & Android Studio 4	WebSockets version 1.3.2	Signalling server & Android app
Android	Android Studio 4	API 23 - API 30	Android app
Android OS	Android Studio 4	Android 6.0 - Android 11	Android app
WebRTC	Atom.io & Android Studio 4	Google-webrtc-1.0.32006	Signalling server & Android app

5 Results

The GUIDed Hi-Fi prototypes[7] were tested by older adults and their caregivers in four European countries, namely Austria, Cyprus, Norway and Poland. Due to the social distancing measures imposed amid the COVID-19 pandemic, each end-user site implemented the testing via focus groups, one-to-one meetings or virtual meetings according to their resources and national restrictions in place at the time of the recruitment.

In total, 39 older adults (*mean* age $= 72.74$, *SD* $= 9.12$, *range* $= 59$–94) and 9 caregivers (*mean* age $= 48.55$, *SD* $= 10.05$, *range* $= 34$–64) evaluated the prototypes. The majority of older adults were female (59%), had "little" technological literacy (41% as they stated that used technological devices only sometimes) and resided in urban areas (51.3%). Their caregivers were 55.6% male, 66.7% resided in urban areas and the majority of them (44.4%) had "great" technological literacy (stated that they used technological devices all the time).

Next, we present the Hi-Fi prototypes for three of the services and more detailed feedback, i.e. recommendations, that was collected from their evaluation with end-users. The focus is on the services of Smart Home Control, Smart Safety and Social Communication due to their advanced technical design and implementation (see Sect. 4) in this stage of the project. Moreover, the main user interface design of the app is also presented. Feedback collected, was based on the questions posed to primary end-users during the focus group sessions in order to evaluate the respective designs of the main UI and three services of the GUIDed app, and are presented in Table 3.

Table 3. Focus group questions on the three services and main UI.

Main UI	Social communication	Smart home control	Smart safety
Which of the two UIs you prefer and why?	Do you understand what the service does?		
What do you think about the screen brightness?	Do you think this service should be configurable on the mobile application or on the web interface?	Not applicable	Not applicable
What do you think about the screen colors?	What features are missing? (if any)		
What do you think about the font and buttons size?	Does anything seem out of place or unnecessary? Would you add or remove anything?		
Do you understand what the icons/buttons mean and their functions?	What do you think it might be difficult when using this service? (if anything)		
	What do you think will be easy when using this service? (if anything)		
	Any comments?		

---

[7] Hi-Fi User Interface Prototypes: URL.

5.1 Main UI of the GUIDed App

It is through the main UI of the GUIDed app that users can acquire access to one of its five available services, as presented in Pages[7] 3 and 4. End-users first need to register and create an account on the GUIDed web interface. Older adults can create their accounts on their own, as primary end-users, or if they require assistance, accounts can be created by secondary and tertiary end-users. Via the GUIDed main UI, the end-user journey includes the following steps: 1) User account is created initially using the web interface (CMS); 2) User types username or email and password to login the first time. The user remains logged in to the app unless he/she manually logs out; 3) The main screen of the app is loaded; 4) The user can click icon on top left corner for the extended menu to appear; 5) The user can click to logout from the application.

5.2 Social Communication Service

Once logged-in to the GUIDed app, end-users are able to access the social communication service by clicking on the "Communication" button (see Page[7] 4) of the main UI. Pages[7] 6 to 9 present screens of the UI designs for this service. Via the Social Communication service, the end-user journey includes the following steps: 1) User clicks on the Communication tile/button from the main UI of the app; 2) The service loads in contacts mode; 3) The user can use the scrollbar to navigate to one or more contact screens; 4) The user can click on a person to initiate a video call for social communication or for assistance and support; 5) The user can click the "Meet Others" button to connect with other users that are not in his/her network – connect with new people, but registered in the GUIDed system; 6) Once selected (known or unknown contact), the user to call loads up centrally in the app; 7) The user can click to make a video call, e.g., with his/her granddaughter; 8) The receiving user can click to accept/reject the video call; 9) The calling user is shown centrally in the app; 10) The calling user can see and socially interact in an augmented camera view, e.g., with granddaughter, likewise the called user can also see and socially interact in an augmented camera view, e.g., with granddad. It is the wide-angle lens that enables the augmented camera view; 11) Both users can switch camera view and terminate the call at any time.

When using the "Meet Others" option: 1) The user clicks the respective button to connect with new people; 2) A person is selected (matching or randomly) to meet new people and engage socially in the GUIDed community, 3) The user can click to call the person that was selected or click to go back to the contacts screen; 4) The user that receives the call sees the photo of the caller; 5) The user receiving the call can choose to accept or reject the call. In the case that the communication happens, it follows the same approach from hereon as with having a conversation with a person that is already a contact; 6) Any of the two users can invite the other contact to connect. A user can accept or reject the new connection.

5.3 Smart Home Control Service

Once logged-in to the GUIDed app, end-users are able to access the smart home control service by clicking on the "Home control" button (see Page[7] 4) of the main UI. Pages[7]

11 to 13 present screens of the UI designs for this service. Via the Smart Home Control service, the end-user journey includes the following steps: 1) User clicks on the Home Control tile/button from the main UI of the app; 2) The camera view opens within the GUIDed app – AR mode; 3) The user can point to a synchronised smart sensor device to control it; 4) The appropriate controls of that device are augmented in the camera view and the user can interact with the device, e.g., turn on/off, dim light, choose colour; 5) The user is able to click the "UI" mode button to receive a list of rooms and devices he/she can control; 6) The UI view opens within the GUIDed app; 7) The user can click in any room (e.g., Living Room) to access it's smart devices; 8) The user can drag the circle to control the light intensity; 9) The user can click the button to turn on/off the device (e.g. light); 10) The user can click on any colour to change the light ambience; 11) The user can click the "AR" button to return to AR mode; 12) The user can click back button on the mobile device to return to the previous screen.

5.4 Smart Home Safety Service

Once logged-in to the GUIDed app, end-users will be able to access the smart home safety service by clicking on the "Safety" button (see Fig. 2) of the main UI. Pages[7] 15 to 17 present screens of the UI designs for this service. Via the Smart Home Safety service, the end-user journey includes the following steps: 1) User clicks on the Safety tile/button from the main UI of the app; 2) The camera view opens within the GUIDed app – AR mode; 3) The user can point to a synchronised smart sensor device to retrieve its status; 4) The user can click the "UI" button to enter UI mode; 5) The UI mode of the GUIDed app is loaded; 6) The user can check the status of the sensors and act accordingly; 7) The user can click the "AR" button to return back to AR mode; 8) The user can click the back button on the phone to return to the main UI. When an emergency is detected, text and loud sound reminder/notification pops up.

5.5 Results, Recommendations and Considerations from Hi-Fi Prototype Evaluations

In overview, the results of the Hi-Fi prototype testing showed that all of the users found the GUIDed app understandable and easy to use, which is an encouraging finding considering older participants' low technological literacy. Some suggestions for improving usability included increasing the contrast of the screen colours and taking under account colour blindness when choosing the palette, changing the labels of some buttons (e.g., replacing the term 'user interface' with something more intuitive), and replacing some of the icons with more appropriate ones. Despite the fact that participants rated the app as intuitive and easy to use, most of them requested an introductory training to support them while using it. The training component has already been planned to be incorporated in the GUIDed application via an innovative assistant, utilising augmented reality technology.

In regards to appearance, most participants showed a preference towards user interface design No 2 with tiles (left design on Page 4[7]) since, according to them, it seemed cleaner with larger buttons than user interface No 1 (with typical buttons, right design on Page 4[7]). The only remark was that all tiles referring to individual services should be the same size (not underestimating the importance of any service).

Table 4. Primary end-user feedback

Main UI	Social communication	Smart home control	Smart home safety
• Both screens are easy to use with a slight preference to design No 2 (tiles based)	• Offer ability to work with normal telephones as well in case the other user does not have the app installed	• Add voice control for the service	• Add option to be able to reset or cancel the sensors in case of mistake
• Make the tiles size even	• Add names under photos	• Add option to be able check the whether the gas is on	• Add more sensor options in the service: flood sensors, opening windows, doors for burglars, water leakage and fire alarm
• Square tiles are cleaner	• Add voice commands	• Add option to be able to close the shutters in the house	
• Add high contrast for persons with visual impairments (lighter background)	• Add contacts and contact list creation in web interface is not shown and will probably be difficult for older adults	• Enlarge on/off button	• Ensure pop-ups for alerts are in large font size and have a sound notification too
• Change the colour for communication service icon as it is difficult to see	• Increase width of sidebar to make it more visible	• Change the UI button to 'rooms list' and the AR button to 'back' (or to more general labels like "Buttons mode" and "Camera mode")	• Add customisable options about the handling of an emergency alert and automatically notifying: e.g., when smoke is detected to notify the fire department via an automatic call or notify secondary user, like a son or daughter
• Make 'Welcome to" label more visible	• Add larger in size buttons		
• Provide option to increase the size of the font	• Add a favourites section	• Add option to control TV or front door	
• Add an emergency button	• Offer option to turn off camera and mute the voice	• Add option to control devices when user is not home (e.g., switch off the stove)	
• When choosing colours consider color blind people (e.g., avoid using green and red together)	• Offer ability to define some availability windows		• Make the colour bar more distinguishable as it was deemed difficult to understand by users
• Change the Health icon with a 'heart' or 'first aid kit' icon, the home icon with a 'home' and the communication icon maybe with a 'phone' icon, navigation with "pedestrian" icon	• Tap on a picture of a contact should initiate a call	• Offer option for guidance/training on what one will be able to do with this service and how to use it	• Training will be needed for end-users to
	• Offer option to transfer the contact list directly from the phone	• Slider will be difficult to move	• Change screen order: first see the UI screen when starting the service and then camera screen (if needed)
	• Provide a list of people contacted more often. Also offer the option to import a telephone contact list or manual registration of contacts on the administration web interface.	• Clarity on who will add and synchronise the devices on the service	• Change the UI button to 'sensors status' and AR button to 'back'
• To change the "Navigation" as it can be misinterpreted as the art of navigating in an application to "Moving around", the "Home control", if this is only for lights, suggested to call it "Light control" and the "Communication" can mean a lot, suggested to call it "Contact with others".		• Add option to be able check the radiators and doors	• Camera view (AR) is a bit confusing
		• The AR and UI modes are confusing and need more explanation.	• Concern in the case that the sensors provide incorrect information
	• Offer option to have more than two persons be part of the conversation (e.g., family meeting). In this case, how many can participate and must everyone have the app installed?	• Clarity on how to access devices in other rooms if the user is at home and whether there is still access to the devices from outside the home	• Add option for voice notifications
• Rename the 'exit' button to 'log out'		• Concern about cost and number of smart devices that will need to be purchased and from where. Concern whether all commercially available smart devices will be controllable by the app and how many devices can be controlled in total	• Add option for the service to provide information about maintenance of devices without asking for the status by pointing to a device
• Important for older people that the app remembers passwords	• Clarify where do the persons in the 'Meet others' option come from		
• App should be functioning in both a smartphone and a tablet (accessibility issue)	• "Meet Others" label should be "Meet others"		• Consider moving temperature and humidity to the smart home control service since they do not concern the safety
• Offer the availability of a training, maybe through a gamified component	• Web or in app registering was found to be conflicting by end-users as to why this is different or what they prefer	• AR component seems artificial. Better to control the devices from the app, not by pointing at device option.	• Add documentation of maintenance (e.g. when did you change battery last time)
• Add a fall detection service as this would be an added value (especially for people living alone)	• "Meet Others" was worrisome for many end-users. Maybe add a safety disclaimer in the app (related to Ethics and Safety)	• Add option to be able to work with different systems to reduce the number of apps one needs e.g., turn on light automatically when it gets dark, remote control for heating, check the garage door is locked, control the coffee machine and stove, manage music and see who is ringing the doorbell, also when not at home.	• Consider a backup plan or a liability strategy if sensors stop working
		• Integration of GUIDed to user's smart home system via APIs would be nice	
		• Provide a list of devices which can be operated through the service	

Participants valued all of the services included in the GUIDed app. As they stated, the GUIDed app combines "all important services in one" constituting it an "everyday life companion" and "assistant". Two of the services rated as most useful included the *Smart Home Control service* and *Smart Safety service* as they simplify everyday procedures and offer convenience and safety, respectively. Some participants valued less some of the services due to personal lifestyle preferences. For example, older adults who did not take medication stated that they would not use so much the *Health and Nutrition service*. Moreover, all participants provided the GUIDed team with recommendations for additions and improvements in order to suit their individual needs. More specifically, participants requested the addition of an emergency button in the GUIDed app home screen to provide an easy means to call for help in case of an emergency.

Regarding the Smart Nutrition and Health service, participants requested the addition of a reminder to measure their blood pressure or sugar levels and fields to insert those measurements in the app. For the Smart City Navigation service, people requested the implementation of voice guidance apart from visual notifications as it seemed easier for them to have auditory assistance while walking around. With regards to Smart Home Control service, users stated that it would be helpful for them to have the ability to control their TV or front door. Finally, for the Smart Home Safety service and Social Communication service, users requested the incorporation of anti-theft devices and the simplification of the calling process (e.g., a call should be initiated when the user touches the photo of a contact stored in the app) respectively.

Table 4 summarises the main recommendations and considerations resulting from the end-user feedback collected during the evaluation of the main UI of the GUIDed app, and the Social Communication, Smart Home Control and Smart Home Safety services.

6   Conclusions and Future Work

Three of the five GUIDed services were presented in this paper, reporting on our findings from evaluating their respective Hi-Fi paper prototypes with primary end-users via focus groups. In addition, a technical description of the GUIDed system and the three services was also provided.

In conclusion, the results from the first end-user testing phase of the GUIDed Hi-Fi prototypes were very promising and insightful. The GUIDed system was rated as easy, intuitive and valuable, which will provide a great level of self-confidence, independence and convenience to older adults with some modifications, additions and adjustments required. For three services per se, Smart Home Control, Smart Safety and Social Communication, the recommendations and considerations collected from the end-users were specifically reported.

The feedback collected in Phase 1 for all of the five services, including that for the services of Smart Nutrition and Health, and Smart City Navigation, are currently under review by the GUIDed team to determine which recommendations will be implemented and how to address specific considerations pointed out. This process will lead to preparing for the second Phase of testing. For this, we will improve the designs of the services accordingly, and the evaluation tool will be mock-ups (semi-functioning), that will be evaluated by the end-users, using questionnaires.

Acknowledgements. This work is supported by the European Commission as part of the GUIDed EU project funded by the Active Assisted Living (AAL) Programme Call 2019 – under grant agreement no aal-2019-6-190-CP.

References

1. Coleman, R., Pullinger, D.J.: Designing for our future selves. Appl. Ergon. **24**(1), 3–4 (1993)
2. Coleman, R.: Living longer: The new context for design. Design Council Publication, p. 1–55 (2001)
3. Landers, S.: Why health care is going home. N Engl. J. Med. **363**(18), 1690–1 (2010)
4. Patel, M.S., Asch, D.A., Volpp, K.G.: Wearable devices as facilitators, not drivers, of health behavior change. JAMA **313**(5), 459–460 (2015). https://doi.org/10.1001/jama.2014.14781
5. Becker, S.A.: A study of Web usability for older adults seeking online health resources. ACM Trans. Comput. Hum. Interact. **11**(4), 387–406 (2004). https://doi.org/10.1145/1035575.1035578
6. Hunsaker, A., Hargittai, E.: A review of Internet use among older adults. New Media Soc. **20**(10), 3937–3954 (2018)
7. Wang, C.C., Chen, J.J.: Overcoming technophobia in poorly-educated elderly–the HELPS-seniors service learning program. Int. J. Autom. Smart Technol. **5**(3), 173–182 (2015)
8. Rosen, L.D., Weil, M.M.: The psychological impact of technology. Comput. Soc. **24**, 3–9 (1994)
9. Span, P.: Helping seniors learn new technology. New York Times (2013). https://newoldage.blogs.nytimes.com/2013/05/03/helping-seniors-learn-new-technology/?_r=0
10. Hogan, M.: Age differences in technophobia: an Irish study. In: Wojtkowski, W., Wojtkowski, G., Lang, M., Conboy, K., Barry, C. (eds.) Information Systems Development, pp. 117–130. Springer, Boston (2009)
11. Banskota, S., Healy, M., Goldberg, E.M.: 15 smartphone apps for older adults to use while in isolation during the COVID-19 pandemic. West. J. Emerg. Med. **21**(3), 514 (2020)
12. Blasco, B.: World Health Organisation. +Simple, digital inclusion for older people. https://extranet.who.int/agefriendlyworld/afp/simple-digital-inclusion-older-people/. Accessed 19 Jan 2021
13. Barbosa Neves, B., Franz, R., Judges, R., Beermann, C., Baecker, R.: Can digital technology enhance social connectedness among older adults? A feasibility study. J. Appl. Gerontol. **38**(1), 49–72 (2019)
14. Alibhai, K.: Social Isolation and Technology: How Technology can be Used to Reduce Social Isolation Among Older Adults in British Columbia (2017). https://www.socialconnectedness.org/wp-content/uploads/2019/10/Social-Isolation-and-Technology-How-Technology-Can-be-Used-to-Reduce-Social-Isolation-Among-Older-Adults-in-British-Columbia.pdf. Accessed 20 Jan /2021
15. Duque, M.: Learning from WhatsApp Best Practices for Health: Communication Protocols for Hospitals and Medical Clinics (2020)
16. AARP Foundation. Connect2Affect. https://connect2affect.org/. Accessed 19 Jan 2021
17. AAL website. Toolbox. Methods of User Integration for AAL Innovations (2013). https://www.aal-europe.eu//wp-content/uploads/2015/02/AALA_ToolboxA5_online.pdf. Accessed 16 Jan 2021
18. Nedopil, C., Schauber, C.,Glende, S.: Guideline-The art and joy of user integration in AAL projects. Brussles: Ambient Assisted Living Association (2013). https://www.aal-europe.eu/wp-content/uploads/2015/02/AALA_Guideline_YOUSE_online.pdf. Accessed 25 Jan 2021
19. Morgan, D.L.: Focus groups. Annu. Rev. Sociol.. **22**(1), 129–152 (1996)
20. Ennis, C. D., Chen, S.: 17 Interviews and focus groups. Research methods in physical education and youth sport, p. 217 (2012)

Community Data and Visualization

Abusive Use of Distance Indicators on Dating Platforms Through Trilateration
Creating Movement Profiles with Publicly Available Data

Marius Bäsler[1]($\boxtimes$) and Manuel Bäsler[2]($\boxtimes$)

[1] FOM, Bismarckstraße 107, 10625 Berlin, Germany
mariusbaesler@gmail.com
[2] DUOUNO, Kreuzstraße 4, 13187 Berlin, Germany
manuelbaesler@gmail.com

Abstract. Numerous social media platforms expose their user's location data to the public. This study was conducted to show how easily this data can be collected and visualized. Using basic a basic PC, trilateration and a database, 104 million data points from over 23 thousand unique users were collected over the course of nine days. Visualization with the help of Leaflet showed that the daily commute of randomly selected users was easily visualized and critical information like his or her home address, habits and work place could get extracted. Website operators need to implement measures to mitigate lateration attacks. Otherwise, their user's privacy can be violated by everyone with basic scripting skills.

Keywords: Dating · GPS · Mobile app · Movement profile · Range indicator · Social media · Tracking · Trilateration

1 Usage of Location Data

Starting in 2013 the popular dating website Tinder exposed its users to a critical security threat [1]. Every person with rudimentary programming skills was able to track any user of the service including their precise location and in addition, their Facebook profile ID. This made it very easy to get the victims exact names, since Tinder is only publishing the first name but through the Facebook profile the user's whole identity was public. Tinder's not publicly available API was reverse engineered and a programmer found out, that you can query for any identifier (ID) of a Tinder user and receive its current exact longitude and latitude. The flaw was fixed shortly after. But nevertheless, tracking was still possible using True Range Multilateration because services like these are indicating the distance to the matched person and therefor it's possible to calculate locations. A blog post from 2014 [2] shows the general approach without going into the exact details or showing any code.

In general, lateration is known for its use to locate cell-phones, when they are in range of at least three radio-towers. In march 2020 the chairman of the German federal government agency for health care called Robert Koch Institute, announced they want to use tracking of cell-phones via trilateration to create tracking data for the Corona tracing

© Springer Nature Switzerland AG 2021
U. R. Krieger et al. (Eds.): I4CS 2021, CCIS 1404, pp. 155–166, 2021.
https://doi.org/10.1007/978-3-030-75004-6_11

app. The Deutsche Telekom AG argued several hours later, that this data cannot be used, since it's not precise enough and you had to warn hundreds of people in big cities, when the tracking radius is around 100 m [3]. Therefor this idea was depraved and the later released "Corona Warnapp" uses Bluetooth low energy to trace the distance to other smartphones and warns the user, when he had contact with an infected person.

Other possible use cases for mobile localization services could be the automated ticketing of public transport passengers. This was researched in 2012 in a project called "Ring&Ride" [4]. The results showed that the combined use of wireless LAN technologies, Global Positioning Systems (GPS) and the cell-data could be utilized to automatically calculate routes and charge the passenger for the usage of public transport vehicles.

On the other hand, a study showed that the extrapolated estimation of people in a specific area with the help of location tracking revealed numerous challenges [5]. Not every person is only carrying one mobile and specific population groups don't carry one at all. These demographic factors will complicate the meaningful interpretation of location data.

Despite the possibilities of exploiting range indicators on dating websites many popular services, liker Tinder or even instant messengers like Telegram [6], still include them, which makes them vulnerable to trilateration attacks. This paper will describe in detail on how to conduct those attacks and how power and harmful the results can be. All code is written in JavaScript and will roughly consist of three portions: the data-collection, position calculation and visualization. Data is saved in a high-performance multi-model graph database to make queries and saving the data, easy and direct.

2   Methodology

2.1   Target Website and Its Application Programming Interface

The name of the targeted service will not be disclosed to eliminate any possibility of seriously harming a person's personal data. To collect the data a dummy account is needed, which was created with randomly generated profile details. After logging into the website, a specific application programming interface (API) request was searched which contains geological surrounding community members in its answer. The search was conducted using Firefox and its development tools which lists all requests. Sorting the request-results by size can help to quickly identify the searched request. The request path is the following:

```
/api/v23/profiles?lang=de&length=600&sort_criteria=NEARBY
_ASC&filter%5Blocation%5D%5Blat%5D=52.527&filter%5Blocati
on%5D%5Blong%5D=13.387
```

Which filters all profiles for the given geo location, which is in this case the center of Berlin. Additionally, filters are added to only get profiles which are online. Figure 1 shows the attached request header. The API-key is generic and always the same per login session, the X-Session-Id is extracted after login, also the login cookie. The cookie

```
Host: WEBSITE
User-Agent: Mozilla/5.0
Accept:  application/json,  text/javascript,
*/*; q=0.01
Accept-Language: en-US,en;q=0.5
Accept-Encoding: gzip, deflate, br
Referer: WEBSITE
X-Api-Key: KEY
X-Site: WEBSITE
X-Session-Id: KEY
X-Requested-With: XMLHttpRequest
DNT: 1
Connection: keep-alive
Cookie:    __cfduid=COOKIE;    __ssid=COOKIE;
cookies_accepted=true
Pragma: no-cache
Cache-Control: no-cache
```

Fig. 1. HTTP request headers which can be extracted through a web-browser and its development tools.

lasts as long as the specific tab in which the user logged in is active and is never getting unvalidated automatically.

The acquired response consists of a JSON file which lists all users who fit the mentioned filter criteria. The only limitation is that the location is precise only up to 50 m because it's getting jittered automatically by the platform.

2.2 Data Collection

A loop is running web requests which are yielding user-IDs and their distances to the base station. The user-ID, timestamp, the three different GPS locations of the stations and the distance from the station to the user are saved to the database with the JavaScript fastango3 library. Figure 2 shows a data-entry which can later be used to calculate the position of the user at the specific timestamp. Detailed program flow is described in Sect. 2.4. The script produced around 12 million entries per day. Collection was done nine days which resulted in a 7.6 GB big database with 104 million entries. The collection script and database are running on a privately-owned Debian server with a four-core Intel Xeon CPU (E3-1225 v5).

ArangoDB as a database was chosen, amongst other facts, due to its easy and fast setup procedure. Since its multi-model and document based, the user doesn't have to specify columns, any type of keys or relations. Users can just dump any JSON file into it and obtain the data fast.

Additionally, ArangoDB features the Arango Query Language (AQL), an easy and accessible language to get data out of the database [7].

```
{
        "i": 8765456,
        "t": 1593527486011,
        "s": "ONLINE",
        "l": {
            "0": {
                "0": 52.43891050,
                "1": 13.1
            },
            "1": {
                "0": 52.43891050,
                "1": 13.17352941
            },
            "2": {
                "0": 52.4,
                "1": 13.13676470
            },
            "3": 2750,
            "4": 6950,
            "5": 4550
        }
}
```

Fig. 2. Entry inside the database, which consists of one measure-point for a user at a specific point in time and the three positions of the corresponding stations.

2.3 True Range Multilateration

The required mathematical groundwork is at least 1000 years old and was used in the past for navigation and construction [8]. It can be utilized when the exact location of a moving object is unknown but locations of two, three or more statically or moving base stations and their distance to the target are known. When three circles are drawn around the base station according to their distance to the target like visualized in Fig. 3, the result are different intersection points. The target is located at the point where all three circles meet.

In mathematical terms the location can be calculated with the following two equations (based on only two stations):

$$x = \frac{r_1^2 - r_2^2 + d^2}{2d} \tag{1}$$

$$y = \pm\sqrt{r_1^2 - x^2} \tag{2}$$

where x is the latitude of the target and y the longitude. d describes the distance between the two stations, r_1 the distance from station 1 to the target and r_2 the distance from station 2 to the target. When using only two stations the longitude will be ambiguous because a square root is taken and the result can be either negative or positive. This ambiguity can be eliminated by utilizing a third station.

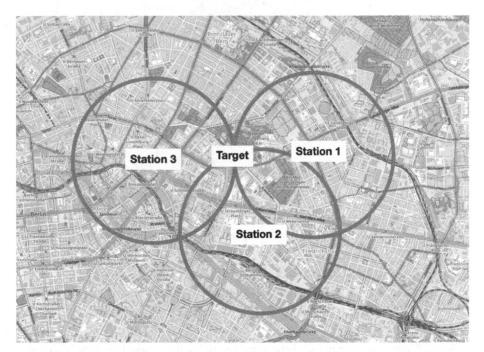

Fig. 3. Visualisation of multilateration with three stations and one target. Distance between target and the stations is known. Map data provided by OpenStreetMaps.

2.4 Program Flow

The script is starting off with creating a grid of base stations which have a radius of five kilometer. Then a request is made to get all users around a specific GPS location. This request is normally used by the dating website to show a list of users which are closest to your current position and can be scrolled indefinitely. The circles widen as long as new users appear in the request which are closer than five km to the corresponding station. Figure 4 shows a common pattern which is used for trilateration in urban areas. The 120° beam angles will cover large areas very effective with a small amount of base station. However, this paper didn't utilize physical station or radio waves, no effort was made to arrange the base stations in a more efficient way.

Requests for each base station are started simultaneously, to get the most precise distances possible. The collected data is then matched against each other and users getting extracted which are present in the data of all three stations. The position of these users is known at this point. Their user-ID, a timestamp, the location of all involved stations and the corresponding distances are then saved to the database. This concludes one iteration. After choosing three different base stations the loop is starting again and finishes with saving new user data.

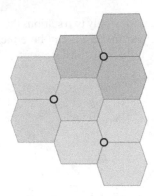

Fig. 4. Bee hive structure to cover huge areas with a low amount of base stations.

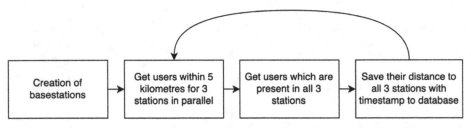

Fig. 5. Abstracted program flow of the data collection pipeline. First step is only conducted once, while the rest of the code is looped.

Figure 5 shows the summarized program flow of the data collection. Until that point no lateration was done. The trilateration follows in the visualization part. For that a HTML webpage was constructed with the help of Leaflet [9] which makes map-based visualization straight forward. Supporting that a small node.js based web-backend was written which retrieves the data from the database and transmits the collected data to the web-frontend.

Figure 6 describes the visualization process. In the first step a map is drawn and buttons for all days for which data is found inside the database are created. When clicking a button, the frontend is sending a request to the backend for the corresponding data. The retrieved data is then parsed and processed which involves the trilateration of the distance values to create a list of GPS locations.

JavaScript on the frontend is executing the trilateration and is drawing a polyline on all data-points. The user-ID cannot be selected interactively and is hard coded into the HTML. A web-server is then started on the client machine with the Python-command:

```
python3 -m http.server
```

which will serve all files which are inside of the current working directory. To get more performance while serving the files, a web-server like nginx would be advisable.

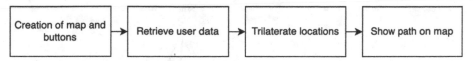

Fig. 6. Abstracted program flow of the visualization through the web front- and backend. Result is a map with the tracked location-path of a specific user.

3   Collected Data

Data was collected over the course of almost nine days starting on June 30, 2020 until the July 8, 2020. Over 104 million datasets were collected from 23,335 unique users which had GPS enabled when logged in. One specific user contributed 129,063 location points to the collection. No serious problems were encountered during the data collection, not a single disconnect or timeout was recorded, even-though the script worked without any throttle or waiting.

The only downtime while gathering occured due to a memory upgrade of the server from four to twelve GB of memory which resulted in a 15-min gap. This was needed since a Windows 10 virtual machine was running which kept the websites tab open at all times to keep the login cookie valid. The database reached a size of 7.6 gigabyte on a PCIe NVMe SSD which enables much faster input-output operation than a traditional hard disk drive. Database indices were manually created over the user-ID, the timestamp and a combined one, to accelerate, the database queries which are executed inside the visualization.

3.1   User Location Profiles

Figure 7 shows the finished visualization website. At the top are buttons for each day for which data was gathered, the number in parenthesis indicates the count of datasets for that day. Even when 50-m jitter are applied one can guess that this person is living in the Marschnerstraße 10 to 18, most likely in the house-number 14 or 16. The location data of the user with the most data points could not get visualized in time since the browser was not able to draw these many lines with the current approach.

Figure 8 describes the traveled path of a random user. On the fifth of July he travelled from Friedrichshain to Baumschulenweg over Berlin Hauptbahnhof. With additional tweaking the timestamps of the travelled path could be added to the map so detailed following of his daily commute would be possible. But this would take a lot of time and that's why it was ditched in this project paper.

In Fig. 9, 10 and 11 all days of the data collection period are visualized in the form of differently colored paths. Colors were selected randomly with a simple JavaScript function which shuffles the RGB value. Especially, Fig. 9 shows very clearly how the person moved daily to the same locations and sometimes took a different path. He always moved to a specific building at the Nollendorfplatz. Very straight lines indicate missing GPS data, which could either indicate a temporarily closed app or a lost connection to the GPS satellites. The latter one is more likely and so one can see five to six very straight paths which signals a travel by the Berlin underground train and one mat blue path with

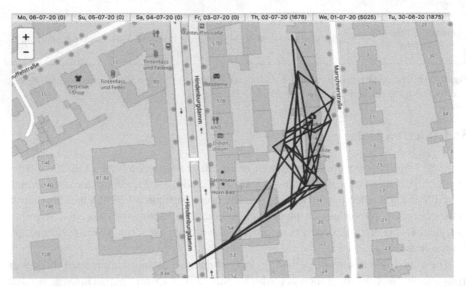

Fig. 7. Movement profile of a randomly selected user on the first of July. Map data was obtained with OpenStreetMaps.

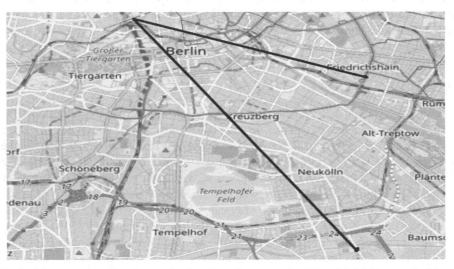

Fig. 8. Movement profile of a randomly selected user on the fifth of July. He travelled from Friedrichshain over Berlin Hauptbahnhof to Baumschulenweg. Map data is obtained with OpenStreetMaps.

detailed GPS points, which could be a sign for the travel by Stadtbahn and therefore the GPS signal was not lost.

Figure 10 on the other hand shows one single trip of a user in the monitored nine days to the so called "Museumsinsel" in Berlin. All manually checked users travelled by train. A user who stayed mostly inside of his apartment is pictured in Fig. 11. He

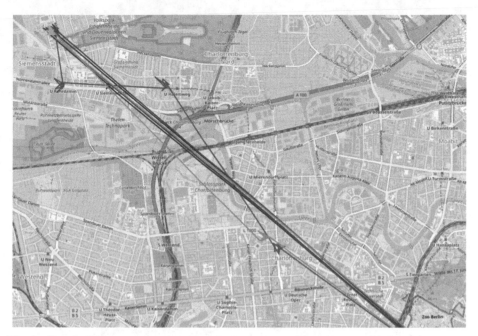

Fig. 9. Traveled distances over nine days of a random user. The daily, most likely work commute is clearly visible. Picture is cropped due to the limited zoom levels on OpenStreetMaps. Map data was obtained with OpenStreetMaps.

Fig. 10. User committed only to one bigger trip across the city from Western Berlin to its center. Map data was obtained with OpenStreetMaps.

potentially visited the park and graveyard on the other side of the road and shops that are in the same street, but did never commute into another city district while the app was running.

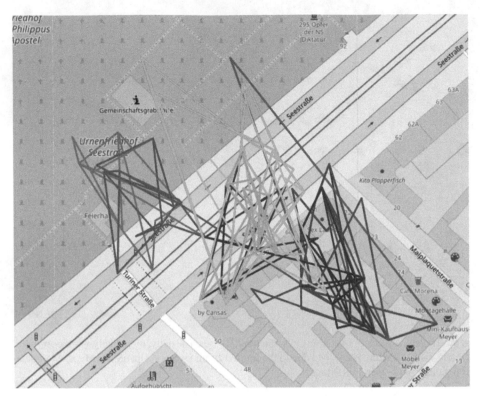

Fig. 11. Movement profile of a user who stayed at home, most of the time. Different gray scales indicate different days. Map data was obtained with OpenStreetMaps.

4   Discussion and Design of a Secure Approach

Data collection and agglomeration was shockingly easy. Anyone with basic understanding of REST-APIs and databases can collect location data of any member of common dating services. The surveyed websites didn't include any kind of effective countermeasures.

4.1   Effective Mitigation

A first measure against automated location data collection could be the conversion of the distance indicator from a text string to a png image file. This way automatic parsing of the distance as integer is a more complicated, since an Optical character recognition software needs to get introduced. But since nowadays powerful free and opensource tools like Tesseract exist, it's easy to circumvent implementations like these [10]. Nonetheless, they could act as a first layer of security.

Furthermore, the platform could introduce machine learning and train a model on the types of requests a user sends. The script outlined in this paper is always sending the same request. Machine learning could easily detect this behavior and as a result the user could be forced to enter a captcha via the frontend in a specific timeframe or he is logged out and the cookie is invalidated.

Another approach could be the abstraction of the place the user is at. For example, "near the Fernsehturm". To programmatically exploit this text string the attacker has to run it through the API of for example Google Maps to obtain the GPS coordinates, which is not free. In addition, the jitter would be a lot bigger and the search radius wider than for example the 50 m which are implemented by the platform on which this research took place.

A lot of security algorithms are annulled by Google Chrome's headless mode [11] which enables developers to control a non-graphical instance of the browser via the command-line. This feature makes it easy, to click simple captchas or collect rotating cookies.

4.2 Precision

The automatically added jittering of the GPS location, which makes the coordinates less precise can be partially bypassed with some effort. Starting with the creation of a grid with a mesh-size of 1 m and a test-user the exact jitter algorithm could be analyzed. Since the platform is jittering to a precision of 50 m the exact thresholds could be examined. At which points will the 50-m steps jump? Is it fully randomized? With the help of the previously created grid an exact measurement and analysis could be performed to get these threshold values to reverse engineer the jittering algorithm.

4.3 Outlook

The awareness for these types of security breaches is low while at the same time the risk for abuse is high. A distance indicator alone can be very dangerous since it enables attackers to stalk any member of a given community. The results of this paper recommend, that any platform that is offering the aforementioned feature should implement security measures as soon as possible.

Dating websites like these could also be used to easily verify the observance of Corona-virus related measures. Are people really staying at home or are they still mobile? These kind of data collections are violating several EU privacy laws and should only be conducted inside a scientific frame with anonymized data. Because of the delicate nature of this paper and its potential for abuse, no code can be published.

Noteworthy is also that the approach described in this paper is scalable indefinitely across the whole world and is only limited by the capacity of the request answering servers and their DDoS-protection.

References

1. Seward, Z.M.: Dating app Tinder briefly exposed the physical location of its users. https://qz.com/106731/tinder-exposed-users-locations/. Accessed 10 July 2020
2. Veytsman, M.: How I was able to track the location of any Tinder user. https://blog.includesecurity.com/2014/02/how-i-was-able-to-track-location-of-any.html. Accessed 10 July 2020

3. Greis, F.: Telekom hält Handytracking von Infizierten für "Unfug". https://www.golem. de/news/coronavirus-telekom-haelt-auswertung-von-handydaten-fuer-unfug-2003-147073. html. Accessed 10 July 2020
4. Eichler, G., Schwaiger, R.: From single device localization towards mobile network-based route calculation. In: Proceedings of 9. GI/ITG KuVS-Fachgespräch Ortsbezogene Anwendungen und Dienste. (LBAS) Universitätsverlag Chemnitz (2012)
5. Eichler, G., Fadler, M.: Location and movement analytics – methods to exploit signaling data. In: Proceedings of 13. GI/ITG KuVS-Fachgespräch Ortsbezogene Anwendungen und Dienste (LBAS). Logos Verlag, Berlin (2016)
6. Weiß, E.-M.: Telegrams Nearby-Funktion lässt genauen Standort ermitteln (2021). https:// www.heise.de/news/Telegrams-Nearby-Funktion-laesst-genauen-Standort-ermitteln-500 4687.html. Accessed 10 Jan 2021
7. ArangoDB, Inc.: Graph and Beyond. https://www.arangodb.com/. Accessed 10 July 2020
8. Geyer, M.: Earth-referenced aircraft navigation and surveillance analysis. https://rosap.ntl. bts.gov/view/dot/12301. Accessed 10 July 2020
9. Agafonkin, V.: https://leafletjs.com/. Accessed 10 July 2020
10. Smith, R.: Tesseract OCR. https://github.com/tesseract-ocr/tesseract. Accessed 10 July 2020
11. Bidelman, E.: Getting started with headless chrome. https://developers.google.com/web/upd ates/2017/04/headless-chrome. Accessed 10 July 2020

Visualizing Customer Journeys: How to Illustrate the Entire Customer Interaction Universe of a Commercial Website in Real Time

Niklas Scheidthauer[1] , Julian Knoll[2]([⊠]), and Rainer Gross[1]

[1] Nuremberg Institute of Technology, Keßlerplatz 12, 90489 Nuremberg, Germany
{scheidthauerni63750,rainer.gross}@th-nuernberg.de
[2] FOM Hochschule für Oekonomie and Management gGmbH, Essen, Germany
julian.knoll@fom-net.de

Abstract. During the last decades, the internet has become an increasingly important channel for businesses to sell products and communicate with customers. Web analytics helps companies to understand customer behavior and optimizes processes to satisfy the customer needs but there is still room for improvement in real-time visualization in the context of business content. In this paper, we describe a graph-based visualization showing the entirety of the website activities at a glance. To increase the tangibility of customer behavior, the graph adapts to the website interactions in real time using smooth transitions from one state to another. Furthermore, we incorporate machine learning in our data integration process to deal with the dynamics of change of website content over time. Finally, we conduct an evaluation in the form of expert interviews revealing that our approach is suitable to optimize digitalized business processes, initiate marketing campaigns, increase the tangibility to the customer, and put a stronger focus on customer needs.

Keywords: Visualization · Web analytics · Customer journey · Graph theory · Machine learning

1 Introduction

The COVID-19 pandemic has demonstrated more than ever before that the internet is an essential channel for businesses to engage with their customers. It enables companies to not only sell products in online shops, but also to handle communications in order to manage customer relationships as well as to provide additional after-sales services. These striking advantages come along with some drawbacks, e.g. the alienation of the company's management from its customers. Since nobody can observe the customers' behavior during the process of buying products in a physical shop, an important source of information gets lost.

Web analytics solutions try to cope with this problem by providing the management with key figures about website usage. Based on insights from this area as well as graph

© Springer Nature Switzerland AG 2021
U. R. Krieger et al. (Eds.): I4CS 2021, CCIS 1404, pp. 167–182, 2021.
https://doi.org/10.1007/978-3-030-75004-6_12

theory and other scientific disciplines, we present a prototype which visualizes all website interactions in real time and makes the customers' behavior more tangible for the management.

We make the following main contributions. First, we propose a graph-based visualization which shows the entirety of the website activities at a glance. Second, we include a dynamic setup in which the graph adapts to the customer interactions in real time using smooth transitions from one state to another. Third, we analyze different fuzzy string matching and machine learning approaches to deal with the evolving nature of website content over time and incorporate a real-time prediction step in our data integration process without further manual effort. Fourth, we evaluate our approach by conducting expert interviews in respect to different functions and roles, confirming the potential of our solution.

The remainder of this work is structured as follows. In Sect. 2, we give an overview of the related work. Theoretical background regarding web analytics, graph theory, and data integration is presented in Sect. 3. After describing the implementation of our approach in Sect. 4, we discuss its evaluation in Sect. 5. Concluding remarks and an outlook on our future work are contained in Sect. 6.

2   Related Work

2.1   Literature on Web Analytics and Graph Theory

In their 2020 study, Chitkara and Mahmood [1] assert that very few companies actually recognize the importance of analyzing customer activities on their websites. Nevertheless, web analytics plays a crucial role. In their research they determine the influence of the recording of user behavior, age, demographics, gender and conversions on the optimization of content and decision-making. They come to the conclusion that the analysis of web traffic is not a secondary task, but rather a critical process with the potential to drastically increase website attractiveness for visitors and customers.

In addition to the benefit of introducing web analytics tools, Gupta et al. [2] elaborate on the advantages of a combination of more modern technologies, such as machine learning, with more commonly used analysis techniques from the field of descriptive statistics. To this end, they present a framework that shows the steps to integrate these technologies into existing practices and infrastructures. In addition, the approach shows how companies can gain strategic insights for decision-making and achieving certain business targets.

Filvà et al. [3] and Leitner et al. [4] develop solutions with the aim of optimizing platforms for digital learning environments. One result is that pages can be checked for comprehensibility and clarity by exploiting information about behavioral patterns, such as navigation paths and mouse movements or clicks. Kirsh [5] expands this approach by additionally analyzing the speed and direction of the curser.

With regard to the representation of activity data in the form of graphs, different concepts are presented in the literature. Ostapenko [6] describes a prototype for analyzing web traffic, which is intended to provide an insight into the effectiveness of a company website. The focus of this application is on highlighting the entry page, intermediate pages, and exit page determined by cluster algorithms. Ortega and Aguillo [7] also use a division between entry and exit points when processing visitor data on websites. However, cluster algorithms are not used here, but techniques from the analysis of social networks. Their results suggest that the use of network visualizations is a suitable analysis method to study the behavior of the users of a website.

The transfer of the website structure to a graph has so far only been described to a limited extent in the literature. Ostapenko [6] as well as Ortega and Aguillo [7] focus on the entry and exit pages of a website but do not elaborate on functions or business structures within a website. In this article, we introduce a graphical distinction between main areas and sub-areas and important processes within one graph. Furthermore, we generate the graph in a dynamic setup which enables the management to check changes and developments in real time.

2.2 Literature on Customer Journeys

The customer journey in its full scope maps the path of a customer from the first touch-point to the conclusion of the purchase [8]. These paths are barely linear and differ depending on the person [8]. Lemon and Verhoef [9] emphasize that an entire customer journey is very difficult to oversee and that a subdivision into the three phases of pre-purchase, purchase, and post-purchase is advisable. The various channels through which contact is established differ in terms of benefits and costs, which means that one channel is often more useful than another for a certain phase in the conversion process [9].

According to Liu et al. [10] it is impossible to have an overview of the customer journey in its entirety and analysts instead want to easily identify and highlight the most important paths, the so-called key customer journeys, of website visitors. In addition, dividing the customer journeys into individual segments can help analysts to understand the collected data more quickly [10].

Baumann et al. [11] limit their view to the clickstream data and derive individual customer journeys in the form of graphs from the user sessions. Anderl et al. [12] focus on the analysis of click and purchase behavior of not only successful journeys that end with a conversion, but also those that were never completed. Baumann et al. [11] come to the conclusion that the creation of weighted graphs based on the evaluation of frequently used paths and the consideration of the time spent on certain pages in the representation of the customer journey should still be seen as a research gap.

The aforementioned publications try to select the most interesting and important data and visualize them afterwards. In contrast, we present an approach which incorporates all available data about customer interactions in a clickstream and illustrates all key customer journeys within a website accordingly.

2.3 Related Literature from Other Disciplines

In astronomy, star maps are used to locate astronomical objects such as stars, nebulae, and galaxies. A trained eye can identify certain constellations and areas on a star map at a glance. This variant of the representation of fixed points can be transferred to the field of graphical processing and image recognition. Zhou et al. [13] identify concise key points of similar objects such as the edges of tables and chairs on several images in the form of a star map. The object types can thus be determined from the focus of the clusters. In addition to the static location of elements, the visualization feature of the luminosity of celestial bodies is also displayed on star maps.

In medicine, the visualization of huge amounts of data is also a common issue. For example in the field of neuroscience, Rubinov and Sporns [14] draw each part of the brain in a different color in order to easily recognize the individual functions. Uutela et al. [15] present the brain structures in the form of a Voronoi diagram. Brain activities induced by stimulation are displayed based on a red-yellow color gradient. Depending on the level of activity, the colored area spreads out to neighboring cells and shows a glowing effect.

In mathematics, convex hulls are used as a form of visualization in multidimensional spaces to group objects. Cevikalp et al. [16] utilize convex envelopes in face recognition in order to more efficiently restrict the selection of people in the identification process and to identify groups of similar faces.

In our approach, we transfer the sense of orientation of star maps to the design of graph structure. Moreover, we include visualization techniques from medicine, such as highlighting active nodes in red and using a different color for each area of interest. In addition, we use convex hulls from the field of mathematics to emphasize important graph clusters.

3   Theoretical Background

3.1   Web Analytics

Web analytics takes on an increasingly important role and describes the process of improving the profitability of websites with the help of the evaluation of customer behavior [8]. A central aspect of a web analytics system is collecting and logging data about website visitors in a reasonable quality [17].

There are a variety of techniques for collecting user data, of which page tagging is one of the most common [18]. Page tagging uses the JavaScript (JS) language to track various browser settings and user activities, such as mouse clicks, cursor position, keystrokes, and window size [17]. The JS code is executed on each page load and collects the specified user data and transmits it to a tracking server. A persistent cookie with a unique client ID is placed to recognize an individual user at his or her next visit [17]. Pages that are provided with a page tag can send the collected data to third-party software systems such as Google Analytics or Adobe Analytics. To reduce the workload, separate tag management systems are offered for this purpose, which simplify technical maintenance [17].

To analyze the collected data and convert it into insights, the Web Analytics Association provides a "Definition Framework" which differentiates used metrics into counts, ratios, and KPIs [19]:

- **Count:** Represents the most basic unit of measurement in the form of an integer (Total Visits of a Single Page = e.g., 12,385 visits).
- **Ratio:** Division of two numbers, which can result both from counts and from ratios (Changing Visits of a Page over a Period of Time = e.g., increase of 20%).

- **KPI:** While a count or a ratio can be applied to all pages, a KPI is derived from these metrics and aligned with the company's business strategy.

3.2 Graph Theory

A graph is a simplified representation of a system to reduce the structure to an abstract level by capturing only basic connectivity patterns [20]. Mathematically, a graph is a construct consisting of two main components [21]:

- **Nodes:** Elements of a network, represented by points (also called vertices).
- **Edges:** Connection between the nodes, represented by curves (also called links).

In general, there are only two states between a pair of nodes. Either an edge exists, or it does not. In a weighted graph, nodes and/or edges each have their own attribute, which acts as a strength, value, or weight [20]. Thus, thresholds can be used to form so-called subgraphs (a partial view of a graph) that create a dynamic state of network components. In addition, nodes and edges can be compared and classified based on their weights.

Based on the graph structure, it is possible to calculate many measures and metrics. Prominent concepts are graph centrality, paths, transitivity, or the clustering of network components. In the context of this work, the path (also called edge sequence) is of particular relevance for determining the customer journey. A path in a graph is any sequence of nodes such that each successive pair of nodes in the sequence is connected by an edge [20].

Transferring the concept of graphs to web analytics, the nodes can be seen as pages of a website whereas the edges can refer to the number of customers going from one page to another (clickstream). This is equivalent to the network path of the successive pages of a single visitor. Consequently, the key customer journeys can be formed from the summarized page paths over which all visitors have navigated within a time window.

3.3 Data Integration

Data integration generally involves the organized transfer of data from different upstream systems into data management components of the analytical information systems [22]. This procedure is often divided into the three main tasks of extraction, transformation, and loading (ETL) [22].

In the *extraction* stage of the ETL process, the data is either extracted from the company's internal and external source systems via standardized interfaces or imported in file form (flat files) [23].

The following *transformation* stage processes the raw operational data according to the technical and business requirements. It consists of the following steps [23]:

- **Filtering:** The essential transformation step of filtering involves cleaning the data from syntactic defects (related to code-technical representation) and semantic defects (related to the business content).

- **Harmonization:** The harmonization merges the filtered data to a syntactically and economically consolidated data base.
- **Aggregation:** The aggregation stage adds aggregation structures (e.g., time, region, product groups) to the filtered and harmonized data.
- **Enrichment:** The enrichment calculates the business key figures based on either the harmonization layer or on the aggregation layer.

The *load* stage is the last sub-process that transfers data to the analytical information system where users can build reports or systems handle further processing [23].

4   Implementation

The goal of our implementation is to realize a dashboard which visualizes in real time the customer interactions on a website in a graph. The result resembles a star map and is shown in Fig. 1. We use the concept of nodes and edges described in Sect. 3.2:

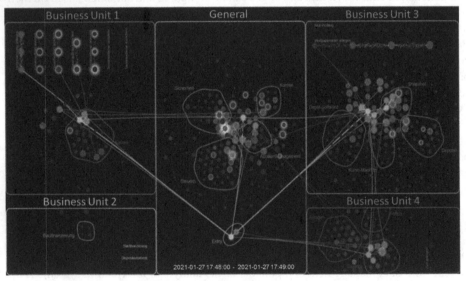

Fig. 1. Dashboard showing a graph with pages and customer movements, as well as business units, subject areas, and processes.

- **Pages**: Each page of the website is represented by one node. The nodes' hue (short-term activity), size (long-term activity), and glow (recent increase of activity) represent their own measures of activity.
- **Customer movements**: The navigations of the customers from one page to another are consolidated, filtered according to their importance, and depicted as the graph's edges. The hue and width of the edge reflect the amount of customers navigating between these pages.

To improve the readability of the dashboard, the following structure elements are incorporated in the graph:

- **Business units**: The graph is split into separate subgraphs, each representing the pages assigned to a business unit of the company.
- **Subject areas**: Convex hulls embrace pages with similar content into a cluster and highlight topics with the most pages.
- **Processes**: Pages which reflect a step in a business process are detached from the graph and moved to a reserved area for processes. Particle streams connect the edges between process steps to make the process flow more tangible.

4.1 Harmonization of the Required Data

The first implementation step is the setup of a basic data foundation. Without the data, no data pipelines can be built, and no calculations can be performed. Basically, a distinction can be made in this project between raw activity data, local configuration data and centrally stored page information.

- **Activity data:** The raw activity data are obtained from a web analytics platform and streamed from an interface in real time. They consist of three variables. The *Contact-Object-Id* identifies the visitor on the website. The *Page* variable represents the page name, and the *Timestamp* indicates the time of page access. A new record is created for each page access by a visitor.
- **Node information**: To place the nodes at the correct positions on the dashboard, additional information is required. This information is loaded into the application from a central database table and joined with the raw activity data. At the beginning, the data set contains a manual classification of the pages to the business units of the website and is extended by individual subject areas. Moreover, there are placeholders for additional information, which are populated during data processing. These include the relative coordinates (between 0 and 1) of the nodes, which are multiplied by the screen resolution to enable the use of monitors of different sizes. On the other hand, there are fields for visitor activities of the last five days, whereby not only the current popularity of a page is visible, but also that of the last days.
- **Process information:** Information on processes is stored in another data set. It is loaded from a central table and indicates which pages represent the individual process steps. In addition, the process name, the business units to which the process is assigned, and the process sequence are stored. In contrast to the node information, the process information is not modified by the application and must therefore be maintained manually.
- A local JSON configuration file contains the **dimensions and placement of the business units** on the dashboard, divided by networks and processes. Additionally, settings for process orientation (vertical or horizontal) and direction (up, down, left, and right) are configurable.
- Finally, another local JSON configuration file sets the **scaling** for each visualization feature such as node size and hue. Different scale types like logarithmic, linear, or ordinal scales with corresponding value ranges can be specified.

4.2 Design of the Data Pipeline

Since all data is made available, the selection of appropriate tools for data processing and visualization is required. Graph frameworks such as Gephi and Cytoscape are not capable of generating the desired graph structures. For this reason, an in-house development is necessary. The primary data integration process is mapped in Python, whereas D3.js acts as an outsourced component to simulate the force layout. Furthermore, PIXI.js is used to render the graph.

Basic System Components. The basic structure of the application can be split into a backend component and an uncoupled webserver. The backend component contains the logic to process the data and to build a graph in the right format. This graph is passed to the webserver on every update and can then be distributed to the browsers. This architecture has the advantage that data only needs to be loaded and processed at a single central location. In addition, we retain the ability to set up multiple distributed webservers to allow horizontal scaling when the number of users increases. Figure 2 illustrates the resulting interaction of the individual components. The described data pipeline shows many parallels to the ETL process from Sect. 3.3.

At the start of the program, the data connector loads the harmonized data into memory and forwards it to the data processor for initial configuration. This includes the local configuration, process, and classification data. This information is crucial for processing the real-time data in subsequent steps. The data connector starts a data poller thread that retrieves the real-time website activity from the Web Analytics interface. It assembles it into 1-min chunks, and places them in a queue that leads to the data processor. The atlas server is another thread launched by the data connector, which receives initial requests from the webservers. It responds with an atlas of the graph as soon as a browser loads the dashboard. The atlas acts as a template and only contains basic information about the nodes and their locations. The application interpolates these nodes and draws edges once an update is ready for transmission. Therefore, the ZeroMQ message library is used for passing data between uncoupled system components.

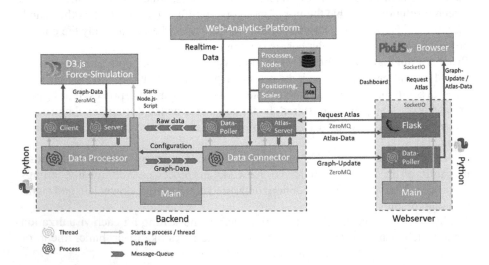

Fig. 2. Architecture of the basic system components including backend and webserver.

Preprocessing of Established Pages. To build a graph from raw data, several data pre-processing steps are required. The first process step is to edit the page names by merging similar pages to reduce the total number of nodes. For example, login and logout pages as well as account settings are combined under "System" to increase clarity in the graph. In addition, the navigated pages are enriched with node information from the initial configuration. This includes page views, business units, subject areas, coordinates on the dashboard, and activity over the last five days.

Classification of Unknown Pages. It is often the case that information is not yet available for many pages because the Web Analytics system does not provide the corresponding business units. One of the reasons lies in the evolving nature of a website. With each campaign or new product, the structures increase. Therefore, classifying unknown pages is a challenge that can be approached in several ways.

We compare two different approaches for predicting the business unit. One way is fuzzy string matching. The Levenshtein distance specifies the difference between two strings based on the minimum number of edit operations of individual characters. The algorithm compares each new page name with all other names of already classified pages. The existing cluster of the name pair with the lowest editing distance is applied to the new page. Slight variations of the Levenshtein distance are tested as well [24].

Alternatively, machine learning will be considered as another approach. Therefore, the Tf-idf measure (Term Frequency, Inverse Document Frequency) is applied, which counts the number of words and scales them according to their weights. Based on the resulting feature matrix, various page classification models can be tested. Promising models and frameworks are the nearest neighbor classifier, random forest, XGBoost, and support vector machine (SVM) with stochastic gradient descent.

A simulation study shows the prediction accuracies of the different models. For this purpose, the weighted F1-Score [25] is used as an evaluation metric. The results show similar scores for both approaches (Table 1). Since this work is a prototype with real-time requirements, it is important to take the execution times of the two approaches into account. Whereas fuzzy string matching takes increasingly more time as the sample rate grows, the machine learning models remain nearly constant. Therefore, the SVM is the best choice for the classification of unknown pages and is used in the implementation of the prototype.

Table 1. Weighted F1-Scores of different models resulting from the simulation study.

Fuzzy		Machine learning	
Model	Score	Model	Score
PartialRatio	0.7823	XGBoost	0.8666
Ratio	0.8785	RandomForest	0.9046
TokenSetRatio	0.8953	KNeighbors	0.9061
TokenSortRatio	0.9149	SVM	0.9436

Building the Graph. After handling unknown pages, all user sessions are extracted from the enriched activity data. The chronological page views of a period are first appended to a session list and can be addressed via the Contact-Object-Id. Thus, the navigation paths of all visitors in the considered time window are sorted in chronologically ascending order and can be processed further. In subsequent periods, old navigation paths are supplemented by new ones. If a session is more than 30 min old, it has expired and is removed from the list.

In the subsequent process step, the application converts the session list to a NetworkX object. It is checked whether the pages within the sessions already exist as nodes in the graph. If this is the case, the weighting and thus the absolute activity is incremented. Otherwise, a new node is created for the page. For the edges, it is determined whether another site was called before the current site in the same session. If the edge in the graph already connects two nodes, the absolute activity of the path increases. If it does not exist yet, a new edge is created between the two sites.

After all elements are added to the NetworkX graph, the application performs several force simulations for each business unit (subgraph) to determine missing coordinates for new nodes. Because no Python package can provide the required customization of forces in the simulation, the d3-force module of the D3.js library handles the calculations by utilizing Node.js. Therefore, a server thread and client thread act as messaging endpoints to transmit and receive the graph.

Table 2 shows the customized forces we used in the simulation to achieve best results. The forces only influence new nodes and do not change the coordinates for already defined nodes. In order to achieve a good network layout, a graph evaluation library measures the resulting network readability of different hyperparameters.

The Node.js application sends the optimal coordinates of the nodes back to the Python backend. Subsequently, the application reduces the edges of the entire network to the top ten most used navigation paths per business unit. Finally, the nodes and edges are transmitted as an update to the Webserver, which immediately forwards them to the browsers.

Table 2. Used forces in the D3.js force layout simulation.

Name	Description
Link Force	Pushes nodes together or drives them apart
Many Body Force	Acts similar to a gravity field and simultaneously influences all nodes by pushing them apart from each other
Center Force	Sets the center of gravity for each subgraph
x and y Forces	Pushes nodes to the center of gravity to increase density
Collision Force	Prevents nodes from overlapping
Cluster Force	Pushes nodes of the same subject together
Box Force	Prevents nodes from drifting out of the visible area

4.3 Visualization of the Interaction Graph

WebGL is used to visualize the network in the web browser because technologies like scalable vector graphics are too inefficient in animating many graphic objects. For 2D applications, the JS library PIXI.js serves as an optimal interface to address WebGL.

Processing Network Elements. After the updated network data is loaded into the JS runtime environment, the nodes and edges are transferred to a task stack. The network's animations are controlled by a subroutine (app ticker) that is called by the web browser at each frame (in this case, 60 times a second). The app ticker moves the nodes and edges from the task stack to a task list until the list is full. Currently, the list is limited to 400 slots, which means that no more than the specified maximum number of items can be processed simultaneously. This has the advantage that performance remains constant. On each call, the app ticker iterates through the task list and performs operations on the items. When it has completely processed certain elements and interpolated their animations, it removes them from the list, causing other nodes or edges to move up and disappear from the stack.

Drawing Network Nodes. When a new node is created, PIXI.js first places a filled circle of the appropriate size and color at the calculated coordinates. Behind each node there is a second circle whose color gradient simulates a glow effect.

If an added node is both part of a network and part of a subject area, a convex hull is drawn around the node group. The function polygonHull of the D3.js library determines the outer nodes of a node cloud, around which closed cubic Catmull-Rom-Splines are drawn in the form of a hull.

Drawing Network Edges. When an edge is drawn, an arc is created along the given coordinates between two nodes in the graph. As changes occur, the program interpolates both the colors and coordinates of the edges and approximates them to the target values with each subsequent iteration.

This approach is not used for edges between nodes that are part of a process. Instead, particles are animated in a constant stream. Different numbers of particles are moved between the process steps in the process direction depending on the activity strength. Based on the edge weighting (the absolute visitor activity), the density and width of the particle stream are determined in the first step using a linear scaling. The number of particles is then calculated from the hypotenuse length of the two nodes multiplied by the density.

5 Evaluation

5.1 Concept

The evaluation examines the acceptance of the dashboard by its main stakeholders. In detail, we investigate the understandability and interpretability of the dashboard, the expected benefits, as well as ideas for optimization. In order to get qualitative feedback on our dashboard, we decided to conduct the evaluation in the form of expert interviews. The experts were selected in a way to be representative for the main stakeholders. Within the framework of the interviews, we discussed three key questions with the experts.

1. Can you understand the dashboard and interpret the visualization features easily?
2. What concrete benefits can the dashboard deliver for your function and for the whole company?
3. Do you see optimization opportunities for the dashboard?

Overall, nine experts were interviewed. They can be divided into four groups: Management - Executive level (3), Marketing - Department level (3), Data Analyst - Department level (2), and Information Technology - Department level (1). The expert interviews were conducted individually and the answers to the key questions have been grouped into topic blocks.

5.2 Responses

Understandability and Interpretability. Almost all respondents stated that the visualization features can be understood without any problems. However, there were also differences in perception. While one respondent from the Marketing group described the dashboard as "easy to understand from the start" and "intuitive", another respondent from the Marketing group described it as "non-trivial, but understandable". One respondent (Data Analyst group) felt that the visualization features are not entirely clear, as "color, size, movement, and differences can only be guessed" and are not easily distinguishable from each other. The similarity of the dashboard to a star map was recognized by many respondents and considered as positive.

Benefits. Looking at the topic blocks with more than two mentions, there are four topic blocks with expected benefits delivered by the introduction of the dashboard (see Fig. 3).

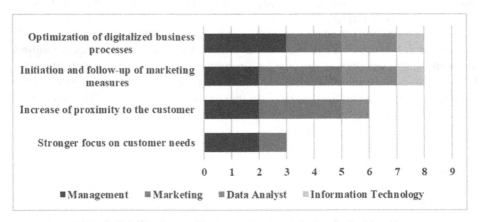

Fig. 3. Absolute mentions for expected benefits by the dashboard.

Almost all respondents shared the opinion that the dashboard can provide starting points for optimizing digitalized business processes. Just by visualizing the use of the main and secondary processes, ideas for process optimization can be gained (respondent from the Information Technology group). For example, the "highly frequented areas of the digital channels" can be distinguished from the less frequented processes. Little activity on certain pages can lead to an "evaluation of user-friendliness, usability, and attractiveness", which can improve the clarity and navigation of the website structure (respondent from the Marketing group). According to a respondent from the Data Analyst group, "levels, paths, aborts, starts, connections and hurdles" can be eliminated or optimized in order to react to the "customer behavior and needs in the digital department stores". The dashboard could also be used to visualize high dropout rates. On the other hand, the dropout rates may be due to an unclear flow of the individual process steps, which can then be examined in a further analysis (one respondent each from the Marketing and Data Analyst groups). One respondent from the Management group confirmed the problem of process aborts by customers and found particular potential in conversion optimization in the context of the "order process".

The dashboard supports the identification of market and campaign influences as well as the initiation of marketing measures. Almost all respondents agreed. When a marketing campaign is launched, the responsible employees can trace the customer reactions in real time. In addition, market influences on the company's business can also be tracked. A respondent from the Marketing group illustrated the importance of recognizing which products are popular for customers at the moment. According to a respondent from the Management group, new trends or problems can be identified at an early stage by analyzing the user behavior.

For six of the nine respondents, the dashboard gave a visual impression of the current customer activities and thus made the relationship with the customer more tangible. One respondent (Marketing group) emphasized "the awareness that a website is a main branch that is open 24 h a day, 7 days a week with a permanent customer presence". A respondent from the Data Analyst group mentioned the quick and comprehensive overview as a way to increase the supply of information to the management. In this context, the respondent explained the advantage of a partially reversed information chain. The management does not have to wait for reports and can directly ask the departments about striking findings discovered on the dashboard.

Another benefit of the dashboard is that it provides a view of the customers' needs (three out of nine respondents). In the long run, the dashboard can help to focus on the essential aspects and promote customer-oriented work.

Optimization Opportunities. Looking at the topic blocks with more than two mentions, there are seven topic blocks with suggestions for optimizing the dashboard (see Fig. 4).

The majority of respondents agreed that a legend should be displayed to prevent misinterpretation by users. Besides the legend, filtering by name or customer segment was the most requested feature. Many users want to be able to see only certain pages, for example by using a search field. One respondent (Data Analyst group) also expressed the wish to compile his own segments in order to compare the behavior between traders, banking customers, or different age groups.

Another preferable function wished by a respondent from the Data Analyst group was the implementation of a time lapse. Users could simulate the course of a day retrospectively in fast-forward or carry out evaluations for predefined periods of time. This

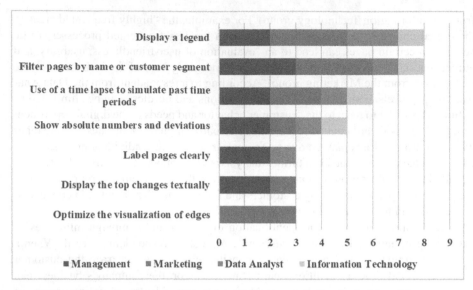

Fig. 4. Absolute mentions for suggestions to optimize the dashboard.

enables them to see the effectiveness of communication measures or changes to the information architecture by directly comparing several time periods.

Furthermore, several respondents mentioned that no absolute numbers, deviations and comparative values can be seen. One respondent (Management group) refers to problems deriving key figures from the visualization. In this context, the lack of page labels is also underscored. More elements should be labelled automatically. In order to be able to quickly recognize striking activity trends, one respondent (Management group) suggested displaying a ticker which lists the top changes in text form. In addition, the respondents from the Marketing group saw optimization potential in the visualization of the edges between the nodes. Accordingly, the flow back from the processes could be depicted in a better way.

6   Conclusions and Future Work

In this article, we demonstrated a prototype visualizing customer interaction of a company's website at a glance. Furthermore, our approach provides a dynamic setup in which the graph adapts to real-time customer interactions using smooth transitions. Our prototype, based on insights from web analytics and graph theory, delivered the following major results: First, it is helpful to incorporate findings from other research areas like medicine, astronomy, and mathematics to generate an innovative visualization approach. Second, operationalizing machine learning is a suitable solution to deal with the evolving nature of website content over time. Third, the expert interviews reveal the potential for optimizing digitalized business processes, initiating marketing campaigns, increasing the tangibility of the customer, and focusing on customer needs in a stronger way.

Future work could be dedicated to examining how a time-lapse can be incorporated into our approach. Furthermore, ways of making our prototype more interactive in order to support not only the management but more operative employees could be evaluated.

References

1. Chitkara, B., Mahmood, S.: Importance of web analytics for the success of a startup business. In: Batra, U., Roy, N.R., Panda, B. (eds.) REDSET 2019. CCIS, vol. 1230, pp. 366–380. Springer, Singapore (2020). https://doi.org/10.1007/978-981-15-5830-6_31
2. Gupta, S., Leszkiewicz, A., Kumar, V., Bijmolt, T., Potapov, D.: Digital analytics: modeling for insights and new methods. J. Interact. Market. **51**, 26–43 (2020)
3. Filvà, D.A., Forment, M.A., García-Peñalvo, F.J., Escudero, D.F., Casañ, M.J.: Clickstream for learning analytics to assess students' behavior with Scratch. Future Gener. Comput. Syst. **93**, 673–686 (2019)
4. Leitner, P., Maier, K., Ebner, M.: Web analytics as extension for a learning analytics dashboard of a massive open online platform. In: Ifenthaler, D., Gibson, D. (eds.) Adoption of Data Analytics in Higher Education Learning and Teaching. AALT, pp. 375–390. Springer, Cham (2020). https://doi.org/10.1007/978-3-030-47392-1_19
5. Kirsh, I.: Directions and speeds of mouse movements on a website and reading patterns. In: Chbeir, R., Manolopoulos, Y., Akerkar, R., Mizera-Pietraszko, J. (eds.) Proceedings of the 10th International Conference on Web Intelligence, Mining and Semantics, Biarritz, New York, pp. 129–138, ACM (2020)
6. Ostapenko, A.: Developing Models to Visualize and Analyze User Interaction for Financial Technology Websites. Polytechnic Institute, Worcester (2020)
7. Ortega, J.L., Aguillo, I.F.: Network visualisation as a way to the web usage analysis. In: Aslib Proceedings, vol. 65, no. 1, pp. 40–53. Emerald Group Publishing Limited (2013)
8. Kamps, I., Schetter, D.: Web-Analyse (Web-Analytics) – messen, analysieren und entschei-den. In: Kamps, I., Schetter, D. (eds.) Performance Marketing. Der Wegweiser zu einem mess- und steuerbaren Marketing - Einführung in Instrumente, Methoden und Technik, pp. 157–174, Springer Fachmedien, Wiesbaden (2017). https://doi.org/10.1007/978-3-658-18453-7_10
9. Lemon, K.N., Verhoef, P.C.: Understanding customer experience throughout the customer journey. J. Market. **80**(6), 69–96 (2016)
10. Liu, Z., Wang, Y., Dontcheva, M., Hoffman, M., Walker, S., Wilson, A.: Patterns and sequences: interactive exploration of clickstreams to understand common visitor paths. IEEE Trans. Vis. Comput. Graph. **23**(1), 321–330 (2017)
11. Baumann, A., Haupt, J., Gebert, F., Lessmann, S.: Changing perspectives: using graph metrics to predict purchase probabilities. Expert Syst. Appl. **94**, 1–21 (2018)
12. Anderl, E., Becker, I., Wangenheim, F.V., Schumann, J.H.: Mapping the customer journey: a graph-based framework for online attribution modeling. SSRN J. 1–36 (2014)
13. Zhou, X., Karpur, A., Luo, L., Huang, Q.: StarMap for category-agnostic keypoint and view-point estimation. In: Ferrari, V., Hebert, M., Sminchisescu, C., Weiss, Y. (eds.) ECCV 2018. LNCS, vol. 11205, pp. 328–345. Springer, Cham (2018). https://doi.org/10.1007/978-3-030-01246-5_20
14. Rubinov, M., Sporns, O.: Complex network measures of brain connectivity: uses and interpretations. NeuroImage **52**(3), 1059–1069 (2010)
15. Uutela, K., Hämäläinen, M., Somersalo, E.: Visualization of magnetoencephalographic data using minimum current estimates. NeuroImage **10**(2), 173–180 (1999)
16. Cevikalp, H., Yavuz, H.S., Triggs, B.: Face recognition based on videos by using convex hulls. IEEE Trans. Circuits Syst. Video Technol. 1–13 (2020)

17. Hassler, M.: Digital und Web Analytics. Besucherverhalten verstehen, Website optimieren, MITP Verlags GmbH, Frechen, Metriken auswerten (2019)
18. Jansen, B.J.: Understanding user-web interactions via web analytics. In: Synthesis Lectures on Information Concepts, Retrieval, and Services, vol. 1, no. 1, pp. 1–102. Morgan & Claypool Publishers (2009)
19. Web Analytics Association: Web Analytics Definitions, Version 4.0, Washington DC (2007)
20. Newman, M.E.J.: Networks. An introduction. University Press, Oxford (2010)
21. West, D.B.: Introduction to Graph Theory, 2nd edn. Prentice Hall, New York (2001)
22. Bange, C.: Werkzeuge für analytische Informationssysteme. In: Gluchowski, P., Chamoni, P. (eds.) Analytische Informationssysteme, pp. 97–126. Springer, Heidelberg (2016). https://doi.org/10.1007/978-3-662-47763-2_6
23. Kemper, H.-G., Mehanna, W., Unger, C.: Business Intelligence — Grundlagen und praktische Anwendungen. Vieweg+Teubner, Wiesbaden (2004)
24. Strika, L.: FuzzyWuzzy: How to Measure String Distance on Python (2019), https://towardsdatascience.com/fuzzywuzzy-how-to-measure-string-distance-on-python-4e8852d7c18f. Accessed 13 Jan 2021
25. Sokolova, M., Japkowicz, N., Szpakowicz, S.: Beyond accuracy, F-score and ROC: a family of discriminant measures for performance evaluation. In: Sattar, A., Kang, B. (eds.) AI 2006. LNCS (LNAI), vol. 4304, pp. 1015–1021. Springer, Heidelberg (2006). https://doi.org/10.1007/11941439_114

A Web Platform and a Context Aware Recommender System for Active Sport Events

Achilleas Achilleos[1]([✉]), Andreas Konstantinides[1], Rafael Alexandrou[1],
Christos Markides[1], Effie Zikouli[2], and George A. Papadopoulos[3]

[1] Frederick Research Center, 7 Filokyprou Street, 1036 Nicosia, Cyprus
{com.aa,com.ca,res.ar,com.mc}@frederick.ac.cy
[2] SportsTraveler76 Ltd., 46 Nikolaou Ioannou Street, 1036 Nicosia, Cyprus
e.zikouli@sportstraveler76.com
[3] Department of Computer Science, University of Cyprus, 2109 Nicosia, Cyprus
george@cs.ucy.ac.cy

Abstract. Customer recommendations have proved to boost sales, increase customer satisfaction and improve user experience, making recommender systems an important tool for businesses. While recommendations of items such as products or movies, when browsing online, are heavily examined and several recommendation algorithms and systems are developed, still recommendation systems for events present unique challenges. This becomes even more challenging when recommending active sport events to users, due to inherent restrictions and limitations. This paper presents a context aware recommender system developed and integrated to the ST76 web platform, which enables for the first time, to the best of our knowledge, to provide recommendations of users that are more likely to participate in an upcoming active sport event. Also, we showcase the importance of the ST76 platform and recommender system for sports tourism, through the analysis of the economic impact of an active sport event hosted on the platform.

Keywords: Active sport events · Context aware · Economic impact ·
Recommender systems · Sports tourism · Web platforms

1 Introduction

Nowadays, end-users have a wide variety of choices to select from and this applies to online store products to buy (e.g., Amazon, eBay), movies and TV shows to watch (e.g., Netflix), restaurants to visit (e.g., TripAdvisor), as well as events to attend. Information systems have a major role to play in terms of "understanding" what customers like in order to help them in their choices, while at the same time increase sales. In fact, due to the huge variety of high-quality items at competitive pricing, businesses need to provide personalised and customer tailored information services to the user. Therefore, information systems help to acquire quickly information from the end-user and meet customers demands in real-time, otherwise there is a direct risk to lose customers [1].

A key subset of information systems is recommender systems (RS), which aim to address the information overload problem faced by customers. These software systems

© Springer Nature Switzerland AG 2021
U. R. Krieger et al. (Eds.): I4CS 2021, CCIS 1404, pp. 183–197, 2021.
https://doi.org/10.1007/978-3-030-75004-6_13

aim to extract information about users, which will allow offering personalised recommendations to the users. Existing research works have demonstrated that recommendations increase sales [2, 3] and customer satisfaction [2], while at the same time can improve user experience [4]. In particular, two distinct categories of recommender systems can be identified from the literature. These are "traditional" RS and context aware recommender systems (CARS). In contrast to "traditional" RS, CARS are designed to incorporate context information (e.g., location, season, time, companion) [5], in order to increase recommendation accuracy [2, 5]. CARS are adopted in this work due to the fact that they provide increased accuracy and because they offer solutions to the unique challenges faced by event-based recommender systems.

RS and CARS have been developed and used extensively in the last two decades to provide solutions in different domains, e.g., web stores, movies, restaurants. While several systems have been developed and widely used in these domains, event-based RS, as aforesaid, present unique development challenges due to the volatile nature of the recommendation items (i.e., events). In fact, RS applied in all domains typically face the cold start problem (i.e., no/limited data at the start), while event-based RS unique constraints are: 1) temporal nature: events are once off, 2) location bound: usually they are not repeated at the same location and 3) time sensitive: happen at a specific time.

This paper focuses on a specific type of events, which refer to active sport events, and presents a web platform and a CARS based on historical context data that can support the organisation and management of these events. Different research works have been performed for event recommendations such as social based event RS and mobile and context-aware event RS. Finally, the key differentiating point of this paper is that it proposes for the first time, to the best of our knowledge, to shift the perspective of recommendations from "a current user to many events" to "a given event recommended to a subset of interested users". The work presented in this paper delivers a commercial platform and CARS for the first time, which enables the delivery of recommendations for active sport events. Also, it examines and presents the economic impact that active sport events can have for sports tourism and the economy of the country in general.

The paper is structured as follows. Section 2 presents the theory and related work on existing web platforms for sport events management. It also presents the theory behind "traditional" RS and CARS, as well as defines related research work on generic RS and RS and CARS for events. The ST76 platform and recommender system are presented in Sect. 3, while the economic impact analysis of an international active sport event is performed in Sect. 4. The final Sect. 5 defines the conclusions and future work.

2 Background Information and Related Work

Sports tourism is becoming increasingly important and can help a tourist destination to differentiate from the norm. In the editorial note "The Growing Recognition of Sport Tourism" [6], the authors clearly state that: "Sport tourism includes travel to participate in a passive (e.g., sports events and sports museums) or active (e.g., scuba diving, cycling, golf) sport event, and it may involve instances where either sport or tourism are the dominant activity or reason for travel." In related research work [7], the nature and evolution of active sport tourism is portrayed. The following subsections present web platforms for sport events management, as well as existing work on RS for events.

2.1   Web Platforms for Sport Events Management

At a national level, there are several information websites[1] that promote the island of Cyprus and enable tourists to identify "things to do", available activities, hotels, etc. Over the last years these websites are complemented by fully-fledged web booking platforms[2], which enable booking hotels, flights or packages and are used mainly by Cypriot and Greek tourists. The only dedicated information website for sports tourism[3] is produced as an effort of a sports fan. Still the events available is rather limited (August 30, 2018 – 9 events: 5 running, 3 sailing, 1 cycling, July 2, 2020 – 1 event: running), providing basic information about a sport event and with no registration and booking solutions.

The most popular national web platform for events[4] has an explicit category related to sports and offers a search functionality for a specific event category, city as well as other parameters. Yet again, a limited number (2–3) of sport events are available, which reveals both the lack of coverage of sport events and the limited number of sport events. Moreover, basic information is provided and links to other pages in order to register.

Finally, at a national level, individual sporting activities, such as three recurring marathons taking place in Cyprus, are promoted and added by the organizers in international websites or web platforms. These systems are dedicated to a specific type of sport[5], while offering only information and instructions on how to buy tickets.

There are several international websites or web platforms that promote passive sport tourism and offer tours and travel packages for sports fans that mainly travel to watch an event. For instance, Sports Traveler[6] features sporting events such as NBA matches, Wimbledon matches, etc., and continues to create tours and travel packages with guaranteed premium tickets, top-quality lodging, transportation, and VIP hospitality access. Similar web platforms[7] exist, a major thing in USA, while when it comes to Europe, it contains mostly football matches, GP and events such as World Championships and Cups (football, Rugby, etc.). These passive sport event management platforms provide packages that include tickets, accommodation and transportation including flights.

On the other hand, Worlds Marathons (See foonote 5) is a major active sports tourism web platform that specializes only on marathon races. It contains more than 4000 races all over the world, and it's a leader for this kind of sporting activity. The website provides all the information uploaded by the organizer. The user can register and pay for the race. There are additional websites promoting active sport tourism, but all of them have limitations such as covering only specific sport types, registering only for the race

---

[1] Cyprus Tourism Portals: http://www.visitcyprus.com, http://www.heartcyprus.com/.

[2] Web-based Holidays Booking Platforms: https://www.pamediakopes.gr/cy/, https://www.topkin isis.com.

[3] Sports Tourism Website: www.runbis.com.

[4] Cyprus Events Website: https://www.cyprusevents.net/.

[5] Worlds Marathons: http://www.worldsmarathons.com/.

[6] Sports Traveler: https://www.sportstraveler.net/.

[7] Sport Event Websites or Web Platforms: http://www.roadtrips.com/, http://www.sportstravel andtours.com/, http://www.sportstraveltours.com/, http://www.globalsports.travel/ and https:// gulliverstravel.co.uk.

without paying, or paying only for the tickets of the race. For instance, Field Sports Travel[8] promotes and supports only fishing, shooting and cricket activity sports.

2.2 Recommender Systems for Events

Recommender systems focusing on events of all kinds offer users a way to easily identify events that they may enjoy. RS for events face explicit challenges. Firstly, events are available to recommend and then they disappear when they are over. Also, if we consider that two events are rarely the same, or at least rarely they take place at the same location, recommendations become harder. Also, events take place at a specific time. Moreover, users' experiences play a role in what events they enjoy and as users grow and mature so does their taste and preferences. Finally, due to the key differences between events (e.g., location), it is more challenging to make recommendations.

In [8], a social-based RS is described as a way to solve these issues. To do so, location is considered as a means of determining the best event to attend. Two datasets were used, regarding the Greater Boston Area, with the first one containing location estimates of one million mobile phone users and the second containing big social events in the same area. Based on the first dataset users' homes could be determined, as well as where they usually go. Recommendations of events were made starting from simple approaches and then trying more complex ones: (i) Most popular, (ii) Closest to users, (iii) Most popular based on where users live, (iv) A calculated score of popular social events in particular home regions that were not popular in other regions, (v) k-nearest locations based on event popularity and (vi) k-nearest events based on events similarity.

In [9], another approach is using social media (i.e., Facebook), to determine event recommendations based on the preferences of a single user and a group of users. It considers that an event is more likely to be attended by a group of friends and attempts to make recommendations that fit all needs. Friends are clustered based on the number of common friends they have on Facebook. Then it considers the Facebook photo tags, which are more personal, the age of the photo and the number of people tagged in the photo to determine the closest friends of the user. Recommendations are the product of the following steps: 1) Events in a specific time period, price range and geographical area are selected. 2) Recommendations for each user and each member of the group are determined. 3) If the recommendation is based on a single user's preferences a group of friends is created for each recommended event that could enjoy the event with the user. If the recommendation is based on a group's preferences a list of events that satisfy everyone will be recommended. 4) To add serendipity, the recommended events are selected by highest rating and uniformly by other classes of events that are not be very accurate but may present an interest for the user which could not be predicted.

Event-based social networks (EBSNs) enable users to create, promote and share upcoming events of any kind with other users. The sheer volume of events available in social networks creates the usual problem of information overload. RS are a natural solution to this problem. The cold start problem is though faced, while events published in social networks are usually short-lived, planned in the future and having limited to no trace of historical data. In [10], the authors propose a CARS to overcome these

---

[8] Field Sports Travel: http://www.fieldsportstravel.com/.

issues, by exploiting content-based information based on the events' description, collaborative information derived from users' RSVPs, social information based on group memberships, location information based on the users' geographical preferences and temporal information derived from the users' time preferences. The authors perform experiments using a large crawl of Meetup.com, which demonstrates the effectiveness of their contextual approach in comparison to existing social based RS for events.

In another work [11], the authors highlight the benefits and challenges of mobile and context-aware event recommender systems. The paper introduces the basics and related work covering the most important requirements for developing event RS, proposes a hybrid algorithm and develops an Android application for context-aware event recommendations. The two-week user study performed by the authors shows clear benefits and accurate recommendations, while the authors based on the findings of their study they outline future challenges related to event-based recommendations.

The work in [12], outlines the first and only research attempt dedicated to sport events and in particular to the World Cup. The authors propose an Ontology-based hybrid system for recommendation of events. The system collects data from various Internet sources (i.e., Mashup), applies Natural Language Processing and Unsupervised Clustering to process raw data, adds semantics to the processed data and to adhere to the defined ontology, in order to provide recommendations based on smart content-based filtering and social-network-based user profiles for sport events. Empirical results by applying the framework to the past World Cup show promising applications.

2.3 Beyond State of the Art

Context can offer a new perspective on what events users enjoy, since it allows taking into consideration context parameters such as when (e.g., season) and with whom (e.g., solo,) they enjoy the events. Therefore, CARS is particularly important for two reasons: 1) the motives of sports tourists when participating in different sports are not at all identical and 2) addressing the cold start problem. In order to design and develop a CARS, context information was gathered explicitly with the use of a questionnaire. The CARS developed in this work is the first attempt, to the best of our knowledge, to provide recommendations of active sport events. It does not display recommended sport events when the user is browsing on the ST76 web platform, due to the fact that there are limited events listed on the platform (i.e., no information overload). Instead recommendations are delivered when the administrator adds a new sport event. In fact, based on the parameters of the new event the administrator will receive recommendations of the top-N users that are more likely to be interested to participate in this event.

3   SportsTraveler76

3.1   The Web Platform

ST76 is the first commercial platform, to the best of our knowledge, that offers the complete set of services for online management and booking of active sport events. The web platform offers to the administrator the capability to manage sport events through the backend. Figure 1 shows on the left pane the entire set of features offered to the administrator of the platform, who apart from managing active sport events, is also able to manage users, manage newsletter clients, etc.

The administrator when creating an event is able to select one of the following event modes: 1) Only tickets – customers are only able to purchase tickets for participating in the races of the event, 2) Only package (hotel) – enables customer to book only hotels for a specific event and 3) Tickets and package (hotel) – enables a customer to book a combined ticket and hotel package price. The first and third mode are the popular options when creating an event using the platform.

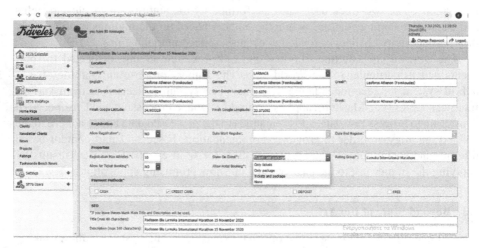

Fig. 1. ST76 web platform – backend

Figure 2 illustrates the end-user view when an event is published, where the customer is able to purchase a ticket or a package based on the type of the active sport event. For instance, in the case the customer selects a package (ticket and hotel) then the user follows a page-by-page wizard where he/she needs to select the number of rooms, the number of athletes, enter each athlete details and finalise the purchase using Six Payment services. Finally, the platform allows creating an event where the hotel and flight ticket can be purchased by company's external collaborators (e.g., travel agency) with the help of iFrames [13] that are integrated in the process flow of the customer registration and purchase wizard.

3.2   The Context Aware Recommender System

The definition and design of the recommendation algorithm and system solves the problem of providing recommendations of existing customers that more likely to be interested to attend the new event that is currently created and published. In this work, a CARS based on historical context data retrieved from a survey, has been designed and implemented for active sport events. The ST76 platform's programming framework (.NET framework) was used for the implementation of the frontend of the CARS system, while

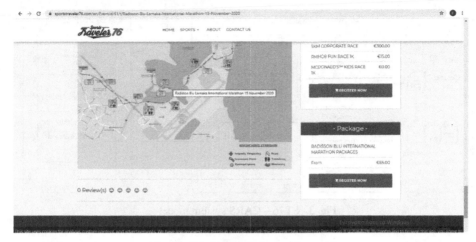

Fig. 2. ST76 web platform – frontend

the CARS system was implemented as a Web API with the help of the Python programming language. In fact, the Python CARS implementation exposes a Web API through which the functionality of the RS can be invoked. In this way, straightforward integration is provided with the ST76 web platform.

System Model

The ST76 platform new feature is the ST76 recommender system (ST76_RS). It is a domain specific solution that aims at providing recommendations of users that are more likely to attend a specific type of event based on the similarity between users' contextual information and events' preferences. In particular, the ST76_RS is used as a Software as a Service (SaaS) to the ST76 web platform. The web service is hosted on the cloud (i.e., Windows Server) and is developed leveraging the .Net Core Framework, which ensures scalability, reliability, and reusability. Additionally, the recommendation algorithm with the K-Means machine learning algorithm, is developed on top of the scikit-learn python library, which ensures valid and efficient operation, as well as high performance; it is also hosted on the same server.

Figure 3 shows the ST76 Recommender System Model: consider a web platform wp (i.e., the SportsTraveler76 web platform) and a web service ws located on server S. Consider a dataset D that contains contextual information of several users clustered into $C1 \ldots Cn$ clusters of users, where Ci is composed of users interested for similar events, using a K-means algorithm. Users contextual information include event type t, event intensity i, event season s, user's companion c and participation's regional information p described by the tuple $CI\{t, i, s, c, p\}$. Additionally, consider a prediction model m stored on S that is able to predict which cluster of users Ci is more suitable to attend a new event e, which is represented by the tuple $CIe\{t, i, s, c, p\}$. In this case, wp sends an HTTP Request to ws for a user recommendation based on CIe and ws responds back with a set of users Su that are most likely to attend event e based on their contextual information.

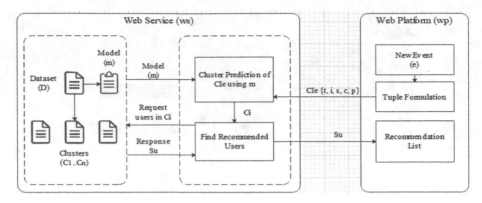

Fig. 3. ST76 – CARS system model

The CARS Algorithm
The ST76_RS algorithmic part is composed of two phases:

i. In the **offline or clustering phase**, the dataset is clustered using the K-Means machine learning algorithm [14]. Each cluster consists of user-related entries that include users' contextual information which refers to specific type of events; Thus, each cluster represents one or more events along with the users that are most likely to attend or have already attended the specific event(s) based on their contextual information. Thus, a prediction model representing the clusters of users and their contextual information is generated using the Joblib python library and stored on a central server.[9]

ii. In the **online or recommendation phase**, the prediction model of the previous phase (i) is used to predict the cluster with users that their preferences and contextual information matches the profile of a new event.

The Dataset
Finally, in order to provide accurate user recommendations to specific events a proper dataset is needed. In the absence of any existing dataset suitable for our needs, we generated our own ST76 dataset by collecting domain specific data from users' contextual information. In particular, the dataset formulated is a result of 68 users answering a Google Forms questionnaire[10], formulated in a way to obtain users' contextual information. The questionnaire was defined in such a way in order for participants to specify their answers including choices (e.g., user attends trails, marathons) and ratings (e.g., with 5/5 trails, 3/5 for marathons) for those choices. The different answers, provided by each participant, produced a resulting dataset of approximately 2 thousand entries, with each entry providing contextual information of a user to a specific event type.

---

[9] Joblib Python Library: https://joblib.readthedocs.io/.

[10] ST76_RS Questionnaire: https://forms.gle/d8Ah7VbeJLuQA3689 (EN version + 19 offline responses), https://forms.gle/6NTYjk8FXuDbBDxcA (GR version).

Contextual information includes information regarding:

1) the type of event (t) (*Official*, *Leisure*, *Domestic*, *Charity*),
2) the intensity of the event (i) (*Scale 1–5*),
3) the season event is scheduled (s) (*Autumn*, *Winter*, *Spring*, *Summer*),
4) the user's companion (c) (*Solo*, $+1$, *Family*, *Team/Friends*), and
5) the event's locality (p) (*National*, *European*, *International*).

As explained above, each user may have multiple entries into the dataset and each entry describes contextual information about a specific event type, which the user has attended presenting a different user's profile perspective. More information on the ST76 platform and recommender system is out of the main context of this paper, but interested readers can refer to project's system specification deliverable[11]. The main contribution of this paper is the examination and analysis of the economic impact of active sport events, through the international active sport (swimming) event that is presented in the following case study.

Evaluation
For the evaluation of the clustering recommendation system a cosine similarity metric was used in order to measure the similarity between and within clusters. The cosine similarity is defined as follows:

$$sim(A, B) = \frac{A \cdot B}{\|A\| \times \|B\|} \tag{1}$$

where A, B are two multi-dimensional vectors representing the attribute values of an item. In particular, the similarity between clusters is defined by the cosine similarity between the cluster centers vectors, where low similarity describes the dissimilarity between clusters.

Also, the similarity within clusters as the average similarity between all vectors included in a cluster compared to cluster centre vector, and is defined as follows:

$$IntraSim(C_i) = \frac{\sum_{n=1}^{m} sim\left(C_n^i, V_{c_i}\right)}{m} \tag{2}$$

where C_i is the corresponding cluster, C_n^i is represents each vector in C_i, V_{c_i} is the vector representing the cluster center, and m is the number of vectors in the cluster.

As part of the evaluation, two experimental studies have been performed in order to examine the recommendation system's accuracy and reliability. In particular, both experiments reveal information regarding similarities between and within clusters, respectively. High similarity within clusters and low similarity between clusters reveal that any recommended cluster will ensure high accuracy in terms of recommended items within the recommended cluster.

Figure 4 presents the results of the first experimental study, that dealt with revealing information regarding the similarity within clusters. As seen in the same figure, every cluster reaches cosine similarity levels above 0.9. This ensures that the items within each

---

[11] System Specification Deliverable: http://mdl.frederick.ac.cy/SportsTraveler76/Main/Results.

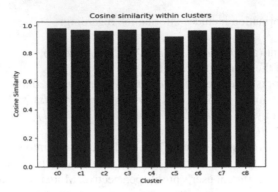

Fig. 4. Cosine similarity within clusters

cluster are highly similar and any cluster recommended will ensure high recommendation accuracy.

During the second experimental study, we evaluated the low similarity or high dissimilarity between all combination of clusters in order to ensure that the clustering process managed to cluster our data in dissimilar clusters. In particular, Table 1 presents the cosine similarities between all clusters' centres. The results show similarity levels between clusters in a range of 0.66–0.83. Given that the dataset used is a rather small dataset, the similarity between clusters can be classified as acceptable and the results reveal satisfying discrimination between the clusters. This ensures the reliability of the clustering process as well as acceptable levels of accuracy on cluster recommendations.

Table 1. Similarity between clusters

	C0	C1	C2	C3	C4	C5	C6	C7	C8
C0	1	0.78	0.76	0.76	0.77	0.73	0.78	0.78	0.81
C1	0.78	1	0.71	0.83	0.71	0.79	0.71	0.69	0.77
C2	0.76	0.71	1	0.7	0.67	0.77	0.73	0.75	0.75
C3	0.76	0.83	0.7	1	0.76	0.69	0.68	0.76	0.68
C4	0.77	0.71	0.67	0.76	1	0.73	0.69	0.72	0.73
C5	0.73	0.79	0.77	0.69	0.73	1	0.81	0.69	0.66
C6	0.78	0.71	0.73	0.68	0.69	0.81	1	0.76	0.73
C7	0.78	0.69	0.75	0.76	0.72	0.69	0.76	1	0.75
C8	0.81	0.77	0.75	0.68	0.73	0.66	0.73	0.75	1

Demonstration
The survey web form of the ST76 platform (see Fig. 5 and Fig. 6) allows new users to complete and submit the static context and profile data that are stored in the database

of the platform using the CARS system's implemented Web Services. In fact, the user completes the first section of the form in order to give the required consent. As soon as the user gives the email and clicks Yes to consent, then the section 2 of the form is enabled (see Fig. 6). The user completes then the different questions and submits the profile data that are stored using the CARS Web Services in the database, while a Web Service generates the static context data that are also stored in the database that are to be used to create the clusters and generate the recommendations when required.

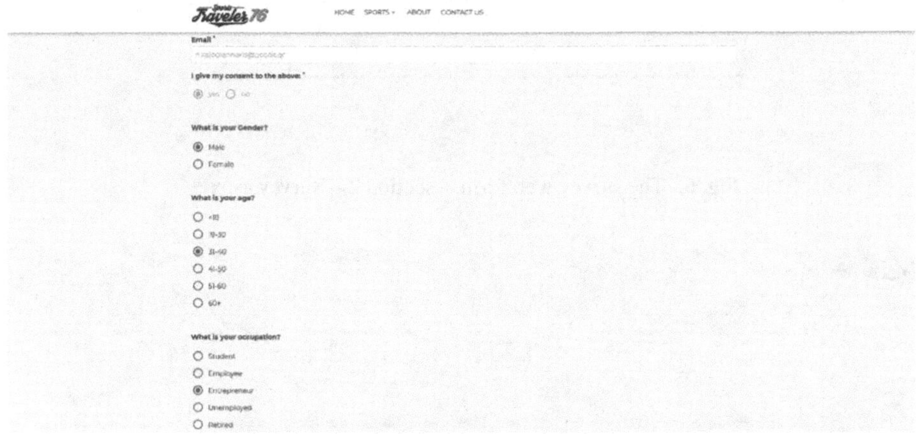

Fig. 5. The survey web form – section 1 – Survey.aspx

The new data records are stored in the database using the Web Services (i.e., Web APIs) provided by the recommender system. A conditional check is performed each time that validates if more than 10 new users have been added in the database, which kicks off the clustering process using the Python scripts that formulate the new clusters, in order to get the updated recommendations, when required by the manager, on the basis of all the information available in the dataset.

In order for the ST76 platform manager and organiser of the new event to get the recommendations of users that are more probable to be interested in the active sport event, the manager needs to complete the following web form by selecting the attributes that best characterise the upcoming event and click Generate to get the list of recommended users by invoking the appropriate service of the CARS system. Note that since during the project the survey was conducted for research purposes the participants that answered the questionnaire had the choice to opt out from providing their email. This was done in order to get as many participants as possible, in order to avoid the cold start problem when developing and testing the recommender system. This is the reason why some of the recommended customers in Fig. 7 are shown with a fake email (e.g., drbpopovic@gmail.com), while the emails of the research survey participants that did provide their emails, are crossed out in this deliverable for confidentiality reasons.

The company can choose to clear the profile and context data of the users that have not provided their emails during the research survey, and since now the email is

Fig. 6. The survey web form – section 2 – Survey.aspx

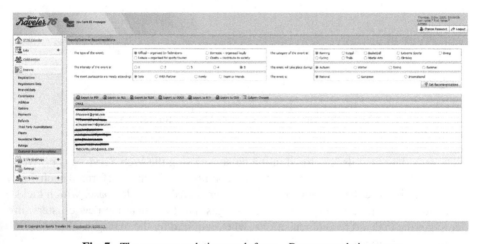

Fig. 7. The recommendations web form – Recommendations.aspx

required by the company in order to complete the survey on the ST76 web platform, the recommender system will continue to work as expected providing the emails of all recommended customers.

4   SportsTraveler76 Case Study

The web platform and recommender system were designed and developed in order to support the organisation and management of active sport events. Complementing the technical contribution of this paper, the economic impact analysis of a sport event is presented. OceanMan is the first international active sport swimming event organized in Cyprus. It attracted 512 active participants (79 from Cyprus), while the 433 international participants arrived from 29 countries.

International visitors are the drivers of economic impact. Hence, only international visitors were considered in the calculation of the economic impact. To estimate the average accommodation cost we rely on rudimentary statistical analysis of questionnaire data. Because most of the responses are given in intervals (i.e. the respondents state whether they have stayed in Limassol between 2 and 4 nights or whether they have spent a sum between €200–300, etc.) we calculate per-person averages using the mean of grouped data formulated as:

$$Mean(Grouped\ Data) = \frac{\sum(Interval\ Midpoint \times Frequency)}{\sum(Frequency)} \tag{3}$$

Based on the data collected from the survey the IMPLAN Input-Output model was applied to calculate the economic impact of the event. In the case of accommodation cost we calculate the average per-person number of nights spent in Limassol and obtain an average cost per night from 2 online travel agencies, namely booking.com and budgetyou rtrip.com. Based on these sources we set an average cost per night equal to €75. Finally, to estimate the economic impact of the entire event we apply the sample ($N = 51$) means of each spending category to the population of visitors ($N = 433$). In fact, based on their responses we estimated their expenditure patterns in the three NACE (Nomenclature of Economic Activities) categories shown in Table 1. This includes accommodation, food and beverages, excursions, transportation and retail shopping.

The Regional Purchase Coefficient (RPC) allows measuring the true economic impact of tourist spending, e.g., when attending an event [15]. In particular, the international visitors that have attended the event purchase goods and services from local businesses. This is in fact, money coming from outside the community that stimulate the region, since tourism is linked with the other sectors of the local economy. Note that some of the spending leaves the community, which is the reason why local purchasing is calculated at the RPC of 65% [15]. Hence, as illustrated in Table 2, *the direct expenditure of international visitors is calculated at € 365,551.92, while local purchasing is calculated at € 237,608.75 that reflects money that stay within the local community.*

Table 2. Estimated expenditure by international visitors

Description	Direct expenditure	(%)	Local purchasing
Accommodation & food	€ 202,621.79	55.43%	€ 131,704.00
Transportation	€ 111,025.64	30.37%	€ 72,167.00
Trade (wholesale and retail)	€ 51,904.49	14.20%	€ 33,738.00
Total	€ 365,551.92		€ 237,608.75

5 Conclusions

Recommendations provide benefits to both the seller and the buyer by recommending the most likely items for which the user may be interested. Several RS have been proposed for various domains (e.g., e-commerce, movies) and demonstrated the benefits they provide. Still, research work on RS for events has been scarce, mostly exploiting social networks, and in many cases event-based RS continue to present unique challenges. In this work, a commercial platform and RS have been proposed, based on the historical context dataset explicitly gathered from customers, in order to avoid the cold-start problem and other event-related challenges (e.g., events commonly happen once). The RS evaluation confirmed the accuracy of the recommendations, while at the same time this paper briefly presents the economic benefits brought on by active sport events.

Acknowledgements. The work presented in this manuscript is performed based on the research funding received from the European Regional Development Fund and the Research Promotion Foundation of Cyprus as part of the Research in Startups SportsTraveler76 project (START-UPS/0618/0049–RESTART 2016–2020).

References

1. Adomavicius, G., Sankaranarayanan, R., Sen, S., Tuzhilin, A.: Incorporating contextual information in recommender systems using a multidimensional approach. ACM Trans. Inf. Syst. (TOIS) **23**, 103–145 (2005)
2. Ricci, F., Rokach, L., Shapira, B., Kantor, P.B.: Recommender Systems Handbook, 1st edn. Springer, New York (2011). https://doi.org/10.1007/978-0-387-85820-3
3. Walter, F., Battiston, S., Yildirim, M., Schweitzer, F.: Moving recommender systems from on-line commerce to retail stores. Inf. Syst. e-Bus. Manag. **10**(3), 367–393 (2012). https://doi.org/10.1007/s10257-011-0170-8
4. Hu, Y., Koren, Y., Volinsky, C.: Collaborative filtering for implicit feedback datasets. In: Proceedings of the 8th IEEE International Conference on Data Mining, pp. 263–272 (2008)
5. Adomavicius, G., Tuzhilin, A.: Context-aware recommender systems. In: Ricci, F., Rokach, L., Shapira, B., Kantor, P.B. (eds.) Recommender Systems Handbook, pp. 217–253. Springer, Boston (2011). https://doi.org/10.1007/978-0-387-85820-3_7
6. Ritchie, B., Adair, D.: Sport Tourism: Interrelationships. Impacts and Issues. Channel View Publications, Clevedon/Buffalo (2004)
7. Gibson, H.J., Lamont, M., Kennelly, M., Buning, R.J.: Introduction to the special issue active sport tourism. J. Sport Tour. **22**(2), 83–91 (2018). https://doi.org/10.1080/14775085.2018.1466350
8. Quercia, D., et al.: Recommending social events from mobile phone location data. In: IEEE International Conference on Data Mining. IEEE (2010)
9. De Pessemier, T., et al.: Social recommendations for events. In: CEUR Workshop Proceedings, vol. 1066 (2013)
10. Macedo, A.Q., Marinho, L.B., Santos, R.L.T.: Context-aware event recommendation in event-based social networks. In: Proceedings of the 9th ACM Conference on Recommender Systems (RecSys 2015), pp. 123–130. Association for Computing Machinery, New York (2015). https://doi.org/https://doi.org/10.1145/2792838.2800187
11. Herzog, D., Wörndl, W.: Mobile and context-aware event recommender systems. In: Monfort, V., Krempels, K.-H., Majchrzak, T.A., Traverso, P. (eds.) WEBIST 2016. LNBIP, vol. 292, pp. 142–163. Springer, Cham (2017). https://doi.org/10.1007/978-3-319-66468-2_8
12. Nguyen, Q., Huynh, L., Le, T., Chung, T.: Ontology-based recommender system for sport events. In: Lee, S., Ismail, R., Choo, H. (eds.) IMCOM 2019. AISC, vol. 935, pp. 870–885. Springer, Cham (2019). https://doi.org/10.1007/978-3-030-19063-7_69

13. World Wide Web Consortium (W3C): HTML Living Standard, The iFrame Element. https://html.spec.whatwg.org/#the-iframe-element. Accessed: 22 July 2020
14. Forgy, E.W.: Cluster analysis of multivariate data: efficiency versus interpretability of classifications. Biometrics **21**, 768–769 (1965)
15. Stynes, D.J.: Economic Impact of Tourism: A Handbook for Tourism Professionals. University of Illinois, Tourism Research Laboratory, Urbana (1997)

Technology Empowers Industry Processes

5G Network Quality of Service Supporting Adequate Quality of Experience for Industrial Demands in Process Automation

Karl-Heinz Lüke[1]($\boxtimes$), Dirk von Hugo[2], and Gerald Eichler[2] ⓘD

[1] Ostfalia University of Applied Sciences, Siegfried-Ehlers-Str. 1, 38440 Wolfsburg, Germany
ka.lueke@ostfalia.de
[2] Deutsche Telekom AG, Technology and Innovation, Deutsche-Telekom-Allee 9, 64295 Darmstadt, Germany
{dirk.von-hugo,gerald.eichler}@telekom.de

Abstract. Future converged communication systems have to fulfil challenging tasks, promised to be delivered by the fifth generation (5G) of mobile networks. 5G shall enable services on the move with both well-known and new emerging performance requirements, while preserving high security and privacy levels to the customers' diverse devices and applications. The applications typically demand a specific quality level end user expectation, measured by Quality of Experience (QoE). To enable QoE, the network has to provide the corresponding end-to-end Quality of Service (QoS), described in terms of technical key performance indicators. The capability to offer different services, covering variable use cases for customer groups in a resource efficient manner, is denoted as network slicing. Addressed services shall cover a broad range of vertical business applications. This contribution will focus on selected solution concepts, rated by potential customers, to enable a set of exemplary industrial applications with demanding requirements in terms of throughput, latency, and device density. Such QoE levels are typically demanded by the automotive industry and car manufacturers to achieve cost-efficient production e.g., by wireless process control. Within the empirical survey of selected use cases of 5G in the automotive industry, the topics Remote Access and Predictive Maintenance, Design and Operation of Mobile Sensor Networks, Wireless Process Monitoring, and Wireless Control and Monitoring of Production Logistics receive the highest approval ratings.

Keywords: Next generation mobile network · Quality of service · Quality of experience · Standardization bodies · Automation industry · Automotive

1 Quality of Service versus Quality of Experience

Classical communication networks experience a long-period design phase, based on an extensive list of technical and operational requirements. In many cases, such a specification considers Quality of Service (QoS) aspects as a nice-to-have add-on. Looking at IP fixed line based networks, often quality by quantity is a sufficient solution. This implies an over-dimensioning of network nodes and links.

© Springer Nature Switzerland AG 2021
U. R. Krieger et al. (Eds.): I4CS 2021, CCIS 1404, pp. 201–222, 2021.
https://doi.org/10.1007/978-3-030-75004-6_14

One can note a paradigm change, when it comes to Next Generation Networks (NGN). This trend is even stronger for Next Generation Mobile Networks (NGMN) as frequency ranges assigned to operators of such networks are a limited and expensive resource. Representative user scenarios guide the design of NGMN. Looking at the fifth generation (5G) mobile networks, four such core scenarios have been identified:

- Extreme/Enhanced Mobile Broadband (xMBB/eMBB),
- Ultra-Reliable Low Latency Communications (URLLC),
- Massive Internet of Things (MIoT)/Machine-Type Communications (mMTC), and
- Vehicle-to-anything (V2X)

While QoS describes the technical approach for network operations, Quality of Experience (QoE) steps in for a customer-centric view (Fig. 1). A user story is broken down to several use cases. Later on, such use cases are evaluated by user satisfaction. Industry-specific, early studies can help to mediate between customer expectations and network design. The term *Human-centred Technology* emphasises this. Therefore, typical user stories are written and broken down to single use cases.

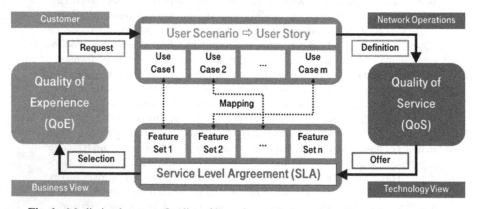

Fig. 1. Mediation between Quality of Experience (QoE) and Quality of Service (QoS).

Section 2 of this contribution focuses on 5G and its QoS network offers, while Sect. 3 describes user expectations for QoE. Use cases for the automotive industry are collected in Sect. 4, whereas Sect. 5 evaluates the results of a customer survey. Section 6 finally concludes with insights and proposes issues for upcoming investigations.

2   Flexibility of Next Generation Mobile Networks

The evolution of digital mobile communication systems worldwide has occurred within the roughly last 40 years with continuous performance gains thanks to technological improvements and new or enhanced system concepts allowing for new services and network features. Starting to provide fixed line communication services i.e., mainly voice calls also to humans on the move, the benefit of mobile data exchange has accelerated growth of radio data applications and traffic volumes. Nature of wireless access both fosters ease of usage as it remains the cause of transmission errors and degradation due to limitations in performance of over-the-air signal propagation. Nowadays a broad variety of different mobile oriented services are commonly in use with wireless connected end user terminals e.g., smart mobile phones, being highly popular. While mobile data rate and throughput approach the figures available by wireline technology, the overall traffic volume is still fixed network dominated. Both types of access networks do inter-operate and evolve in parallel to each other in terms of underlying technology and design principles to achieve more efficient and customer-oriented service provisioning. This trend is reflected in the fact that with every new generation an enhanced trend towards integration and convergence can be observed.

2.1 Evolution and Development Towards 5G

Early use of mobile phone systems started in 1950s as mainly proprietary technologies e.g., in Germany with so-called A- and B-Netz, which were introduced 1958 and 1972, respectively. True cellular networking with automatic switching and mobility support via handover between base stations was enabled in the 1980s with C-Netz. Further examples for such 1st Generation (1G) standardized systems are included in Table 1 as well as characteristics of the following generations based on digital technologies (2G–5G).

The evolution of the Global System for Mobile communication (GSM) and corre-sponding data capable extension General Packet Radio Service (GPRS) via Enhanced Data Rates for GSM Evolution (EDGE) towards 3rd generation (3G) systems as Uni-versal Mobile Telecommunication System (UMTS) is documented in detail in terms of Technical Specifications (TSs) by 3rd Generation Partnership Project (3GPP)[1].

3G enhancement towards High-Speed Packet Access (HSPA) for both up- and down-link (HSUPA/HSDPA) applies higher order modulation, multi-carrier aggregation, and advanced antenna concepts as Multiple Input Multiple Output (MIMO). Long Term Evolution (LTE) and Orthogonal Frequency Division Multiple Access (OFDMA)-based Evolved UMTS Terrestrial Radio Access (E-UTRA) as 4G packet switched technology is followed by current 5G with New Radio (NR) access which again is designed in terms of the global system for International Mobile Telecommunication (IMT) for 2020, exceeding performance of prior systems by factors of up to 100, shown in Fig. 2.

Since the last decade, the goal to support specific demands from various business services for vertical industries led to specification of flexible modular networks. Beside challenging requirements towards higher peak and average data rates in up- and downlink in Gbps range, better spectral efficiencies of up to 30 bps/Hz and latencies down to few milliseconds also new frequency bands offering between 100 MHz and up to 1 GHz range shall be foreseen[2,3] – covering also radio frequencies even beyond 6 GHz.

---

[1] https://www.3gpp.org/.

[2] https://www.etsi.org/technologies/mobile/5g/.

[3] https://www.itu.int/dms_pub/itu-r/opb/rep/R-REP-M.2410-2017-PDF-E.pdf.

Table 1. Exemplary systems, technologies, and exemplary performance figures of different generations of mobile communication, together with year of first commercial operation.

| | Year | Services | | | Multiplex | Switching | | Name | Region | Peak data rate [Mbps] | Mean data rate [Mbps] | Spectral efficiency [bps/Hz] |
		Voice	SMS	Data		Circuit	Packet					
1G	1981	X			FDMA	X		NMT	Scandinavia	n/a	n/a	n/a
	1983	X			FDMA	X		AMPS	North America			
2G	1991	X	X		TDMA	X		GSM	Europe	0.058	0.010	0.05
	1993	X	X		TDMA	X		IS-54 IS-136	North America			
2.5G	1999	X	X	X	CDMA	X	X	IS-95B	Asia	0.171	0.027	0.11
	2000	X	X	X	TDMA	X	X	GPRS	Europe			
2.9G	2003	X		X	TDMA	X	X	EDGE	Europe, North America	0.384	0.256	0.24
3G	2001	X		X	W-/TD-CDMA	X	X	UMTS	Europe	2.0	0.384	0.40
	2002	X	X	X	CDMA	X	X	CDMA 2000	North America			
3.5 + G	2005			X	CDMA	X	X	HSDPA, HSUPA	Global	7.2–42	4.0–11	1.44–8.4
4G	2009			X	OFDMA		X	LTE, E-UTRA	Global	100–300	34.5–150	16–30
5G	2020			X	OFDMA		X	NR	Global	10^4	500	35

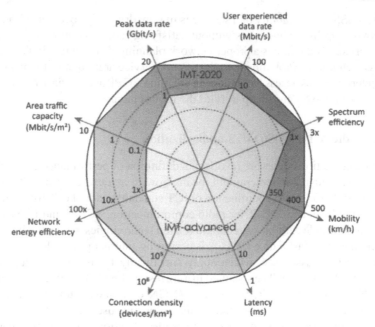

Fig. 2. Comparison of 4G IMT-Advanced key capabilities with 5G IMT-2020 according to ITU (https://www.itu.int/rec/R-REC-M.2083/en/).

2.2 Quality of Service Parameters for Mobile IP Networks

The overall quality of a telecommunication service suffers from the joint impact of the performance of factors as *operability, accessibility, retainability, integrity,* and other service-specific ones. Service integrity often requires a minimum throughput of successfully transmitted data packets per time unit which in mobile environment is mainly limited by the capabilities of the air interface as described in the preceding section. In case the available bandwidth does not meet the required one, e.g., due to congestion, a delayed data delivery will result. Queuing delay may be caused by on-path signal processing, e.g., Forward Error Correction (FEC) encoding and decoding to make the radio signal robust to propagation distortions. Also, re-transmissions in case of lost or faulty delivered packets cause latency. Any variation in latency contribute to jitter which further degrades the service performance.

To avoid time consuming re-transmissions, some applications can survive a certain loss rate or apply corrective actions on higher layers e.g., FEC causing overhead due to added redundant bits. Fault tolerant applications, like voice and video, suffer more from delay and exhibit correspondingly relaxed requirements.

In packet switched IP networks the order of arrival of subsequent packets cannot be taken for granted: taking routes via different paths exhibiting different delays requires measures to detect out of order arrival and execute re-ordering. For the scenario where multiple radio paths are included to enhance the throughput or increase the transmission reliability by, e.g., multi-path access, the re-ordering feature becomes important [1]. This feature is required by 3GPP's 5G Access Technology Steering, Switching, and

Splitting (ATSSS)[4]. Availability of a service is mainly driven by coverage of the mobile access network. Filling white spots without satisfying radio reception is a continuous effort of operators and requires a proper network planning. 5G will rely both on NR and LTE access technology. Providing complementary service areas thanks to integration of multiple heterogeneous access technologies, e.g., non-3GPP access via a Wireless Local Area Network (WLAN), may help to fulfil the requirements.

2.3 State of the Art in QoS/QoE Standardization

Various standardization bodies are involved in definition of performance parameters for service quality, their measurement, and means how to achieve the values technically. ITU is responsible for global coordination of ICT standards with ITU-T for the telecommunication standards and ITU-R for radio communication. 3GPP[5] and ETSI work on specification of mobile cellular systems and related technologies, respectively, while the Internet Engineering Task Force (IETF)[6] is designing Internet protocols.

Aspects of QoS assurance, which apply specifically for industrial internet in the framework of IMT-2020 shall be specified in a corresponding ITU-T Recommendation[7]. ITU-T in NGN Global Standards Initiative (NGN-GSI) have studied QoS issues in terms of basic criteria for QoS evolution being 'subjective user satisfaction' e.g., *speed*, *accuracy*, *reliability*, and *security*. This involves identification of parameters that can be directly observed and measured at the point at which the service is accessed by users and network providers. Flexibility within the global end-to-end (E2E) in NGMN is essential to allow for each operating agency's different regulatory environment, service offerings, geographic span, and network infrastructure. These factors need to be taken into account when agreeing on parameters for, and levels of, QoS for NGMN.

3GPPs system architecture for 5G in TS 23.501 (See footnote 4) specifies the 5G QoS model, which is based on QoS flows, controlled by a Core Network (CN) function for session management (SMF) and may be preconfigured or established per Packet Data Unit (PDU) session. A PDU session is responsible for transport of the application data between e.g., User Equipment (UE) and the corresponding network-based Application Function (AF). The QoS profile includes the QoS characteristics, i.e., a set of parameters, e.g., *Resource Type* (e.g., Delay-critical Guaranteed Bitrate, GBR), *Priority Level*, *Packet Delay Budget* (PDB, due to AN and CN), and *Packet Error Rate* (PER). The profile is provided by the SMF to the Access Network (AN) via the Access Management Function (AMF) or preconfigured in the AN. 3GPP describes 26 standardized profiles, each associated with a 5G QoS Identifier (5QI). One or more QoS rules or corresponding QoS parameters are provided to User Equipment (UE) and/or derived by UE of the received downlink signal. This feature is denoted as Reflective QoS control and describes how a UE can decide on applicable uplink QoS parameters by measuring downlink performance. Alternative QoS Profiles (AQP) represent sets of QoS parameters as delay,

---

[4] https://www.3gpp.org/DynaReport/23501.htm.

[5] https://www.3gpp.org/ - editor of Technical Standards TS #.

[6] https://www.ietf.org/ - editor of Request For Comments RFC #.

[7] https://www.itu.int/md/T17-SG13-C-0973/.

error rate, and data rate, to which an application traffic can adapt. Corresponding notification by the network via a Network Exposure Function (NEF) allows to prevent service disruption and cope with some degradation smoothly.

IETF started to specify network element behaviour, required to deliver QoS terms of guaranteed delay and bandwidth on the Internet back in the 1990s. The Resource ReSerVation Protocol (RSVP) describes Integrated Services (IntServ) trying to rebuild capacity assignment as known from circuit switched networks in the packet switched internet. While being applicable in an E2E manner within dedicated domains, in the public Internet, however, the Differentiated Service (DiffServ) approach gained more attraction and is widely used. QoS specific Differentiated Services Code Points (DSCP) in a packet header and Per-Hop Behaviour (PHB) to be followed by each node on the path have to be mapped at domain borders. For details see RFC 5977 and RFC 7657[8].

In addition, the IETF is active on the topic of *low latency, low loss,* and *scalable throughput* (L4S), which is also covering Congestion Control (CC) in terms of Explicit Congestion Notification (ECN) [2]. While 3GPP networks increasingly rely on and re-use IETF protocols, the basic architecture and procedures for cellular networks are laid out in own technical specifications which shall grant worldwide interoperability, also with non-3GPP technologies and networks, requiring however correspondingly defined gateway functions e.g., the Non-3GPP Interworking Function (N3IWF) towards a WLAN-connected UE. Since E2E connectivity between a UE and the Application Server (AS) includes increasingly also non-3GPP transport networks and other IP networks, a consistent mapping of session QoS parameters in adaptive manners is required.

2.4   Trends and Requirements for Next Generation Mobile Networks

Operators of NGMNs will offer specifically tailored services according to customer requirements with on-demand provided QoS laid down in SLAs (Service Level Agreements)[9]. In addition to means and functional entities as described in Sect. 2.3 further 5G characteristics are required to offer higher value to mobile services sustainably and efficiently without exceeding infrastructure investments. To deliver such services affordably the network must be operated cost- and resource efficiently with respect to, e.g., scarce radio spectrum and energy. The latter is consumed both by the access domain (radio towers) and in terms of processing power in the CN data centres. These data centres will host network functions implemented as software on standard computation hardware allowing for Software Defined Networking (SDN) and Network Function Virtualization (NFV), promising to additionally enable a high level of automation and flexibility by self-organized networking with re-configurable entities. Such flexibility is required to, e.g., assign resources dynamically as a function of changing demand in terms of traffic volume and performance requirements. Also distributed execution of modular network functionalities as well as provision of storage and processing capacity in the cloud (e.g., in terms of Multi-access Edge Computing[10], MEC) is a technology to allow for traffic

---

[8] https://www.rfc-editor.org/rfc/rfc5977.html, https://tools.ietf.org/html/rfc7657/.

[9] https://www.ngmn.org/.

[10] https://www.etsi.org/committee/1425-mec/.

shaping (load balancing) according to actual needs and to reduce the E2E latency and thus improve the network QoS.

To efficiently apply the appropriate QoS measures, the physical network infrastructures resources as transmission, processing, and storage capacity have to be properly assigned to the service flows according to their demand. Such an assignment or slicing of resources for specific service classes or sets of applications is like separating the overall network into logical sub-networks, commonly denoted as network slicing in 5G.

Whereas bandwidth and throughput increase are well-handled today, the main challenge to provide optimum QoE per slice is to establish countermeasures to reduce E2E latency caused by interruption due to cellular handover, increased distance to ASs due to mobility, processing delay due to more complex application features, and latency increase due to application of error recovery to grant high reliability.

3 Usage-Driven Performance and Quality Requirements

Communication network operators' success increases with customers' satisfaction or even excitement when the experienced service performances meet their expectations at a reasonable cost-performance ratio. To achieve an efficient and sustainable operation, the provider needs to optimize the amount of effort and resources spent per customer. Especially, the means of "over-provisioning" in fixed networks to grant QoS is not applicable to services including radio paths with scarce resources. The main business model of IP networks to offer "best effort" quality led to the fact that applications on user and server side try to counteract varying performance, e.g., due to congestion, to reach acceptable execution of applications. Ability of the network to automatically reconfigure in case of degradation and/or provide application-specific add-on information on network characteristics would improve the situation considerably[11].

In case the network is able to react to application requests in an effective and efficient way the customer will benefit most from such a method. In the following we will describe the components and underlying concepts on the level of network, application, and the customer as main drivers of QoE provisioning in detail.

3.1 Network-Centric Approach

In a properly planned and maintained communication network, the incapability to fulfil all customer requests under normal operating conditions is just a question of correct assignment of resources to the services in need. Managing the network resources effectively requires monitoring of the network status on all levels with the right granularity. Proper analysis methods allow to decide on the required measures which cover, e.g., re-routing of traffic in congested data paths or scheduling radio resources within a single and across multiple cells (to balance the load) in a dynamic way e.g., by means of interference cancellation. To assist the network in such intelligent decisions 3GPP has specified for 5G the NetWork Data Analytics Function (NWDAF), which interworks with all entities of network management, control, and user plane functionalities (See

---

[11] https://www.3gpp.org/common-api-framework-capif/.

footnote 4), e.g., with Operations, Administration, and Maintenance (OAM), but potentially also external entities as AS via a NEF (see also Fig. 3). The situation is obviously more complex for a system, serving real mobile applications with continuous change of location and radio signal quality, compared to a stationary environment.

3.2 Application-Centric Approach

Providing the required quality to the end user devices irrespective of the current environment where the device is located todays providers of Over-The-Top (OTT) services follow an application-centric approach. E.g., for video delivery to applications installed on a smartphone in a client-server mode, the International Organization for Standardization (ISO) has specified a standard[12] which is in widespread use. However, without cooperation with network entities e.g., MEC infrastructure, the performance is inferior especially for high resolution video: leveraging context information on both the content characteristics and radio propagation conditions can improve QoE as could be shown by [3]. Another popular example of such an approach is performance of original TCP protocol conceived for fixed IP networks over radio paths. Packet loss increase is interpreted as congestion-driven which to cope by transmission bit rate reduction. However, radio propagation may cause short term signal attenuation thus TCP performance without such network-related knowledge degrades dramatically[13].

3.3 Consumer-Centric Approach

A true customer or consumer-oriented provision of QoE according to the user expectations shall consider detailed information on the user context, i.e., data such as UE capabilities, current RAN performance, usage and content history etc. These depend on the location, the current speed and direction, and maybe even communication and transaction history, Type of User etc. Based on extensive investigations on customer QoS requirements including a broad range of industrial use cases, 3GPP[14] has developed and is enhancing both 5G architecture and technologies.In smart combination of network originated information as, e.g., prediction of the situation and potential QoS change in the next few seconds or distance units according to users' speed (e.g., pedestrian or vehicular), and concurrent application specific data (content volume to be transmitted), a best experience for the customer could be achieved.

In addition, the specified Common API Framework (CAPIF) (See footnote 11) allows for 3rd parties' (verticals') Application Programming Interfaces (APIs) to interwork with dedicated network provided clients and corresponding servers. These expose network capabilities on a Service Enabler Architecture Layer (SEAL) or Vertical Application Layer (VAL) and in addition can support edge computing application enabling services.

Customized slice provisioning includes different QoE relevant features as, e.g., definition of consumer-tailored and -instantiated network service functions, including measures for security, monitoring, data analytics, etc. A 5G system to serve and assure

---

[12] Moving Pictures Expert Group - Dynamic Adaptive Streaming over HTTP (MPEG-DASH), https://www.iso.org/standard/71072.html and http://dashif.org/.

[13] https://tools.ietf.org/html/rfc3481/.

[14] https://www.3gpp.org/DynaReport/22261.htm.

multiple fine-grained QoS levels concurrently for multiple verticals' needs is in scope of global research and standardization programs and of current network deployments.

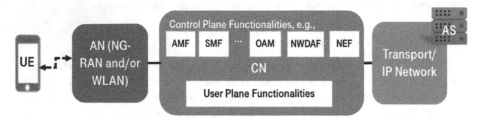

Fig. 3. E2E QoS provision between application on UE and corresponding AS in the internet.

Based on the above-described considerations and enhancements, a feature set of 5G provided service capabilities can be derived and applied to serve requirements of actual industrial application areas as detailed in the following and summarized in Sect. 6.1 (Fig. 9). The high-level view on E2E QoE provisioning based on future converged 5G system features is depicted in Fig. 3. Consistent measures to achieve QoS are applied to the user session between UE via AN and CN that applies control and assurance by corresponding functionalities, towards the application hosted on an (external) AS. In order to understand, which use cases in the industry, especially in the automotive industry, are relevant for 5G, a detailed analysis of the survey is carried out in Sect. 4 and Sect. 5.

4   Scenarios for Automation in the Automotive Industry

4.1   Use Case Definition

The automotive industry is characterized by significant changes such as increased competitive pressure, radically technological and political changes. The companies of the automotive and automotive supply industry keep looking for product as well as process innovations, consequently [4]. In particular, for automation in production in the automotive industry, 5G technology offers a wide range of technological improvements in terms of lower latency, higher bandwidth as well as the focus on machine-to-machine (M2M) communication [5–9].

The 5G Alliance for Connected Industries and Automation (5G-ACIA) has developed basic use cases for automation in the manufacturing industry [6, 7]. Taking into account industry-specific requirements, ten 5G use cases have been developed to describe the characteristics of automation in the automotive industry [4, 6, 10].

1. *Wireless Motion Control of Industrial Robots:* With the control of motion sequences in quasi "real time", the industrial robots must be provided continuously with information about changes in the direction of motion.
2. *Wireless Control and Monitoring of Production Logistics:* The term production logistic is characterised by planning, control and monitoring of a company's internal

transport, storage, and handling processes. In order to optimise the internal material flow, control and monitoring information (e.g. localisation) should be exchanged permanently with the production infrastructure.

3. *Mobile Control Panels for Operation of Machines:* Mobile control panels are used by workers when spatial flexibility is required for operating, controlling, and monitoring of machines. For example, machines need to be configured and emergency stop buttons need to be activated.

4. *Wireless Control of Mobile Robots:* Mobile robots are intelligent, programmable systems that can move independently, can transport materials, and can ensure a high degree of flexibility in industrial production. Driverless transport systems, a sub-category of mobile robots, are used for internal transport of materials.

5. *Design and Operation of Mobile Sensor Networks:* Mobile sensor networks are used in industrial production wherever sensors are required to measure physical variables (e.g., air pressure, temperature, humidity, torque) or other operating states (e.g., determining the position of the work piece).

6. *Remote Access and Predictive Maintenance:* Remote access is the possibility of accessing a remote network from a local computer or a mobile device. For example, remote maintenance access from a mobile device to the production facilities can be realised via the 5G networks. Accordingly, regular service updates can be operated and data for predictive maintenance can be generated.

7. *Wireless Operation of Augmented Reality (AR):* Augmented reality is a computer-based representation in which the real world is enhanced by virtual elements. In the production area, the use of AR glasses can be used to display additional information on the employees' field of vision in order to improve instructions for manual production and ad-hoc assistance for support.

8. *Wireless Control of Production Processes:* For cost-efficient production processes, sensors are used to measure physical variables (e.g., air pressure, temperature) and other operating states (e.g., position and angle of the robot arm), and to coordinate the production systems with each other. In particular, the data on the current operating state of a production system is constantly compared with a predefined reference variable (target value).

9. *Wireless Process Monitoring:* In order to monitor the current production process, data is be collected along the process chain and stored in databases (or in the cloud). Relevant process information (information cockpit) are available on monitors or mobile devices and context information can be used for data analysis e.g., creation of trends for failure rates.

10. *Plant Asset Management:* Plant Asset Management is the management and optimisation of the use of production facilities. Therefore, the collection of plant data (e.g., sensor data) and the provision of information for decision support is a relevant task. Results of data analysis can be used to evaluate the current status (diagnosis), further development (forecast), and optimisation approaches for the plants.

As automation is very diverse in industrial production, the use cases presented above can be assigned to five different application areas (Table 2) [6]:

1. The area *factory automation* covers the optimisation, monitoring, and automated control of processes within a manufacturing plant.
2. *Process automation* refers to the management and control of production. A fundamental goal of automation is to rationalise production processes, increase safety, and reduce energy consumption.
3. *Human-machine interfaces (HMIs)* cover various devices to improve the interaction between production systems and people. HMIs can include standard IT devices (e.g., tablet PC or smartphones) as well as augmented and virtual reality systems (AR/VR), which will play an important role in the future.
4. The term *logistics and warehousing* can be defined as the control and organisation of the flow of materials and the storage of materials in industrial production. Particularly, in logistics, tracking, positioning, and monitoring of goods play a crucial role.
5. *Monitoring and predictive maintenance* can be considered as the monitoring of specific processes, involving condition monitoring and predictive maintenance based on sensor data.

Table 2. Use cases and application areas mapping onto fields of production [6].

Use case	Application area				
	Factory automation	Process automation	Human machine interfaces (HMI)	Logistics and warehousing	Monitoring and predictive maintenance
Wireless Motion Control of Industrial Robots	X				
Wireless Control and Monitoring of Production Logistics	X			X	
Mobile Control Panels for Operation of Machines			X		
Wireless Control of Mobile Robots	X	X		X	X
Design and Operation of Mobile Sensor Networks	X	X			X
Remote Access and Predictive Maintenance					X
Wireless Operation of Augmented Reality (AR)			X		X
Wireless Control of Production Processes		X			
Wireless Process Monitoring		X			
Plant Asset Management		X		X	

4.2   Questionnaire Methodology and Evaluation Criteria

In order to investigate the significance of the presented use cases in an industrial context, an online questionnaire was developed for an empirical survey. This online survey on the "Application scenarios of 5G technology in the field of automation (automotive industry)" was conducted in the period from December 2019 to January 2020. 240 participants from the automotive industry took part (respondent rate 2.93%), 187 questionnaires were evaluated. One criterion for assessing the sample is the composition of the population [11]. The data from Institute for Production Management (IPM AG[15]) was used as the panel. This panel characterizes very well the composition of representatives of the German automotive industry in middle and top management. Therefore, even with a low response rate for online surveys, it can be assumed that the sample is representative. Figure 4 shows an example of Use Case 6 "Remote Access and Predictive Maintenance". The scale of the response options from "do not agree at all" (1) to "agree completely" (5) is based on the explanations of item scales. In general, it can be assumed that the Likert scale used here (a type of item scale) corresponds sufficiently well to the requirements of interval scaling [11].

6. Remote Access and Predictive Maintenance					
Remote access is the possibility of accessing a remote network from a local computer (or a mobile device). The 5G networks can be used e.g. to perform remote maintenance access from a mobile device on the production facilities. Accordingly, regular service updates can be operated and data for predictive maintenance can be generated.					
Change with 5G: 5G has the potential to perform service updates wirelessly on production equipment and significantly improve maintenance flexibility. With 5G, data for predictive maintenance analyses can be disseminated reliably and without delay.					
Questions on the application scenario (use case): Remote Access and Predictive Maintenance	do not agree at all	rather not agree	partly/ partly	partly agree	agree completely
The implementation of these use cases with 5G is interesting for my company	☐	☐	☐	☐	☐
If 5G is available, I can very well imagine implementing the use case in my	☐	☐	☐	☐	☐
The implementation of this use case with 5G improves the processes in production	☐	☐	☐	☐	☐
The implementation of this use case with 5G simplifies the control of production processes	☐	☐	☐	☐	☐
My company provides the necessary resources (e.g. financial resources, infrastructures) for this use case	☐	☐	☐	☐	☐

Fig. 4. Part of the questionnaire for use case "Remote Access and Predictive Maintenance".

Based on the Unified Theory of Acceptance and Use of Technology (UTAUT) analysis, the user acceptance of the application scenarios (use cases) for process automation is analysed. The model of the UTAUT analysis is based on an extensive literature analysis

---

[15] http://www.ipm.ag/.

[12–14] and combines the predominant technology acceptance models in the literature e.g., Technology Acceptance Model (TAM), in a redundancy-free model.

Originally, the UTAUT analysis was developed for acceptance surveys of technologies. As 5G technology is not yet widely available for industrial applications, the UTAUT analysis approaches are used for the acceptance studies of the application scenarios. For this purpose, significant influencing factors are identified and a corresponding question is formulated for each use case. In the UTAUT analysis [12, 13], significant factors influencing behaviour intention and use behaviour are identified: *performance expectancy*, *effort expectancy*, *social influence* and other *facilitating conditions*.

Social influence refers to individual perceptions of what relevant people around a technology user think about their use or non-use of the system. If social influence happens on a voluntary basis, this effect can be neglected [13]. As the use of 5G by companies is voluntary, the social influence is not considered so far.

Table 3. Assignment of questions and significant influencing factors of UTAUT analysis.

Question	UTAUT factor	Characteristic
The implementation of these use cases with 5G is interesting for my company	Behavioural intention	Dependent variable
If 5G is available, I can very well imagine implementing the use case in my company	Use behaviour	Dependent variable
The implementation of this use case with 5G improves the processes in production	Performance expectancy	Independent variable
The implementation of this use case with 5G simplifies the control of production processes	Effort expectancy	Independent variable
My company provides the necessary resources (e.g. financial resources, infrastructures) for this use case	Facilitating conditions	Independent variable

In Table 3, the significant influencing factors of the UTAUT analysis are taken into account by corresponding questions, which are applied to each use case. Normally, several items (here questions) can be used per influencing factor to examine different facets of a construct [11]. In this survey, preliminary research on the questionnaire showed that focusing on one item per influencing factor can describe the construct well.

5 5G Use Cases Study Results

5.1 Profile of the Survey

The detailed profile of the survey can be seen in Fig. 5. This study focuses on companies in the automotive and automotive supply industry. The turnover of 40.1% of the participating companies is between 1 billion € and 50 billion €. More than 50% of the study participants have between 501 and 5.000 employees. In terms of their position in the supply chain, 23.27% of the companies belong to the Original Equipment Manufacturer (OEM) category, while almost 50% are 1st-tier and 2nd-tier suppliers.

40.39% of the study participants stated that their company has not yet engaged with 5G technology. For slightly more than a third of the participants, the topic of 5G has been addressed already in the corporate context for more than a year.

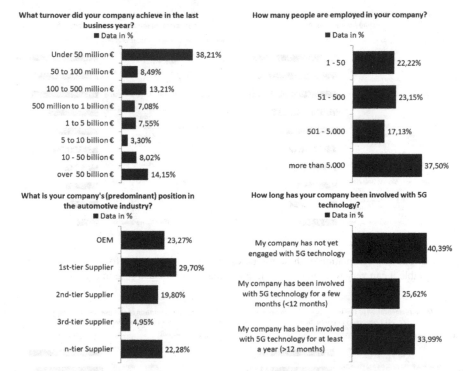

Fig. 5. Profile of the study "Application scenarios of 5G technology in the field of automation (automotive industry)".

5.2 Specific Evaluation of Use Cases

An example of the ranking of the use cases on the question "The implementation of these use cases with 5G is interesting for my company" is shown in Fig. 6(a). The following statements can be derived from this:

- High approval ratings are achieved for *Remote Access and Predictive Maintenance* (3.92), *Design and Operation of Mobile Sensor Networks* (3.87), and *Wireless process monitoring* (3.86).
- Low approval ratings are observed for *Plant Asset Management* (3.42), *Wireless Control of Production Processes* (3.51), *Wireless Operation of Augmented Reality (AR)* (3.51), and *Wireless Control of Mobile Robots* (3.51).

Figure 6, Fig. 7, and Fig. 8 show the results of the survey for the individual fields of the UTAUT analysis. In detail, these are (Table 3): Behaviour intention, use behaviour, performance expectancy, effort expectancy, and the facilitating conditions [12, 13]. The ranking of the use cases for each field is based on the weighted mean values of all answers of the study participants across all customer segments. The values of agreement range from "do not agree at all" (1) to "agree completely" (5).

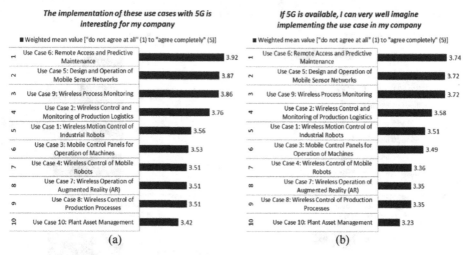

Fig. 6. (a) The implementation of these use cases with 5G is interesting for my company. (b) If 5G is available, I can very well imagine an implementation of the use case in my company.

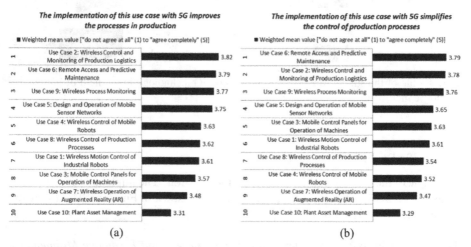

Fig. 7. (a) The implementation of this use case with 5G improves the processes in production. (b) The implementation of this use case with 5G simplifies the control of production processes.

The results of the other rankings can be seen in Fig. 6. Across all relevant question categories, the four use cases *Remote Access and Predictive Maintenance, Design and Operation of Mobile Sensor Networks, Wireless Process Monitoring,* and *Wireless Control and Monitoring of Production Logistics* receive the highest approval ratings in the automotive and automotive supplier industry. The lowest approval rating by far is achieved by the use case *Plant Asset Management.*

5G seems to have the potential, especially in the use case *Remote Access and Predictive Maintenance* that service updates can be carried out wirelessly on the production plants and maintenance work can be designed more flexibly. With 5G, data can also be distributed reliably, flexibly, and wirelessly for predictive maintenance analyses.

The use of 5G also improves the integration of different sensor types into a mobile sensor network with a high sensor density in the use case *Design and operation of mobile sensor networks.* 5G also simplifies the installation and operation of these networks through a uniform standard.

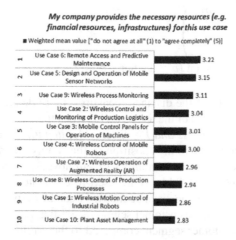

Fig. 8. The implementation of this use case with 5G simplifies control of production processes.

In order to monitor the production process, the use of 5G in the use cases Wireless Process Monitoring and Wireless Control and Monitoring of Production Logistics allows data to be collected along the process chain, stored in databases or possibly also in the cloud, and made available to employees as an information cockpit. Process monitoring can be realized with a high degree of reliability, high availability, short signal runtimes, and at a high data rate without cables.

5.3 Customer Specific Evaluation

As the variables in the present survey have a metric structure, so-called distance measures can be used to calculate similarities and dissimilarities. A well-known distance measure is the Minkowski metric [4, 15, 16]. If the calculation of the distance measure between two objectives (a, b) is lower than between two other objectives (a, c), a higher similarity (a, b) is assumed. If, on the other hand, the calculation of the distance measure is higher (a, c), there is less similarity between the objects.

$$b_{k,l} = \left[\sum_{m=1}^{M} |x_{k,m} - x_{l,m}|^{p} \right]^{\frac{1}{p}} \tag{1}$$

$b_{k,l}$:   distance value of the objects k and l
          $b_{k,l}^{max} = max\{b_{1,1}, \ldots, b_{k,l}, \ldots, b_{n,n}\};$
          $b_{k,l}^{min} = min\{b_{1,1}, \ldots, b_{k,l}, \ldots, b_{n,n}\}; \forall k \neq l$
          $b_{k,l} = b_{l,k}; b_{k,l} = 0 \forall k = l;$ number of objects n ($n = 1, \ldots, N$)
$x_{k,m}, x_{l,m}$: value of the variable (weighted mean value) m of objects
          k, l ($m = 1, \ldots, M$)
A: distance matrix
          $$A = \begin{pmatrix} b_{1,1} & \cdots & b_{1,n} \\ \vdots & \ddots & \vdots \\ b_{n,1} & \cdots & b_{n,n} \end{pmatrix}$$
p: Minkowski constant ($p \geq 1$), here: $p = 2$

From these calculations of the distance measures, more detailed statements can be made about the evaluation level of the use cases between the customer segments. In this case, the use case *Remote Access and Predictive Maintenance* is used to examine the customer segments with regard to the "position in the supply chain" ("OEM", "1st-tier supplier", etc.) and "company size" (number of employees, "1–50", "51–500", etc.). The independent variables (see Table 3) are used to calculate the Minkowski-Metric. The following statements from the distance matrix A can be derived from the Table 4(a) and Table 4(b). In Table 4(a), the customer segments 3rd-tier supplier and n-tier supplier are combined into one customer segment compared to the original survey for reasons of different group sizes.

Table 4. Minkowski Metric for use case *Remote Access and Predictive Maintenance* in two different customer segments: (a) "position in the supply chain" (left), (b) "company size" (right).

	OEM	1st-tier	2nd-tier	3rd-n-tier		1-50	51-500	501-5.000	> 5.000
OEM	0.00	0.23	1.71	1.53	1-50	0.00	0.43	0.49	1.66
1st-tier		0.00	1.54	1.34	51-500		0.00	0.34	1.30
2nd-tier			0.00	0.41	501-5.000			0.00	1.21
3rd-n-tier				0.00	> 5.000				0.00

          (a)   (b)

The following conclusions can be derived from Table 4:

- Table 4(a): The customer segments "OEM" and "2nd-tier" show the highest distance $\left(b_{k,l}^{max}\right)$ in the evaluation of the use case *Remote Access and Predictive Maintenance* (1.71). The customer segments "1st-tier" and "2nd-tier" (1.54) and "OEM" and "3rd-tier and n-tier" (1.53) differ in terms of the evaluation almost on the same level. The lowest distance $\left(b_{k,l}^{min}\right)$ can be observed between the customer segments "OEM" and "1st-tier" (0.23). Overall, it can be determined that there is a positive tendency between the distance level and the position in the supply chain, i.e. the more closely the supply levels are coordinated, the more similar is the evaluation for the use case.
- Table 4(b): (1.66) is the highest distance level $\left(b_{k,l}^{max}\right)$ between the customer segments "1–50" and "more than 5000". If the customer segment "51–500" is compared with "501–5000", the lowest distance value $\left(b_{k,l}^{min}\right)$ should be noted (0.34). It can be seen that there is a strong tendency between the distance value and the size (number of employees) of a company. If the companies have roughly the same size, measured by the number of employees, the distance values become lower.

6 Insights and Further Work

The approach of identifying groups of customer segments with similar demands as detailed above incites the 5G typical Network Slice (NS). Configuring NSs permits to flexibly separate resources and functional entities between vertical customers thus providing an isolated scalable and optimized communication system to each of them as mentioned in Sect. 3.3 as was investigated in [17]. In the following an exemplary feature set tailored according to the needs of application areas in terms of 5G use cases described in Sect. 4 and 5 is chosen to illustrate a 5G NS based efficient service offering.

6.1 Recommended Feature Set Quantification

As a key result the selected eight-parameter QoS feature set, derived in Sect. 2.1, is high-level quantified on a high-medium-low requirements scale per single parameter. It can be divided into three clusters as shown in Fig. 9:

- Network parameter: *peek data rate, E2E latency,*
- Operation parameter: *reliability/availability, security/integrity, energy efficiency,*
- Topology parameter: *device mobility, localization accuracy, device density.*

On a contractual level, appropriate SLAs clearly need to negotiated, covering measurable values. The requirements for *Factory and Process Automation* have been combined, as these application areas are technically similar.

Based on the QoS feature set described above, a basic set of requirements can also be defined at the use case level. For example, in the highly ranked use case *Design and Operation of Mobile Sensor Networks*, the basic 5G requirements (see Fig. 9) of Factory and Process Automation, Logistics and Warehousing, and Monitoring and Predictive Maintenance are defined taking into account the assignment in Table 2.

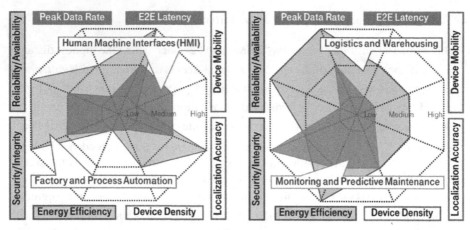

Fig. 9. Application specific QoS feature sets required from and provided by mobile networks.

6.2 Future Network Evolution

The ITU and research initiatives worldwide already consider use cases and requirements for further progress in communication technologies to allow for even more efficient and service specific networking, including information-centric communication and deterministic networking[16]. True heterogeneous network's integration is foreseen in 5G as inclusion of cellular technologies and so-called non-3GPP access as WLAN for fixed-mobile convergence (FMC) but also satellite and other non-terrestrial connectivity and interoperation with non-public networks. Such a seamless interoperation of different access networks within a 5G core controlled E2E session maintenance will be next step of intelligent or smart communication for the well-being of all, following the ITU sustainable development goals. Furthermore, the following trends have been noted:

- Seamless wireless network **convergence** between 5G, WLAN, and Bluetooth,
- Increased **interoperability** by open, worldwide standards e.g., open RAN,
- Better environmental and cost **efficiency** by Green IT and self-configuring networks,
- Efficient **slicing** for class of service bundling and service-decentralization,
- Global network **monitoring** to enable dynamic resource management, and
- Enhanced **analytics** for reliability by predictive maintenance.

6.3 Use Case Blueprints

Future use cases might be mapped onto the evaluated ones. Across all user groups the following use cases experienced the highest interest, which can be seen as blueprints:

- Remote Access and Predictive Maintenance,
- Design and Operation of Mobile Sensor Networks,
- Wireless Process Monitoring and Wireless Control, and
- Monitoring of Production Logistics.

---

[16] https://tools.ietf.org/html/rfc7476/ and https://tools.ietf.org/html/rfc8578/.

However, for *Remote Access and Predictive Maintenance*, there are some evaluation differences between the customer segments "OEM" and "2nd-tier". High evaluation differences can be recognized. The same holds for *Remote Access and Predictive Maintenance*, in this case depending on the number of employees.

Currently 5G networks are rapidly improving to use built-in flexibility and efficiency to provide specifically tailored solutions fitting demanding industrial requirements as low latency and high reliability in a broad range of application scenarios, e.g., in terms of Campus deployments and specified non-public networks (NPNs).

References

1. Amend, M., Hugo, D.: Multipath sequence maintenance, draft-amend-iccrg-multipath-reordering-01, November 2020. Work in progress
2. De Schepper, K., Briscoe, B.: Identifying modified explicit congestion notification (ECN) semantics for ultra-low queuing delay (L4S), draft-ietf-tsvwg-ecn-l4s-id-12, November 2020. Work in progress
3. Ge, C., et al.: QoE-driven DASH video caching and adaptation at 5G mobile edge. In: Proceedings of the 3rd ACM Conference on Information-Centric Networking (ACM-ICN 2016) (2016). https://doi.org/10.1145/2984356.2988522
4. Lüke, K.-H., Walther, J., Wäldchen, D., Royer, D.: Innovation management methods in the automotive industry. In: Lüke, K.-H., Eichler, G., Erfurth, C., Fahrnberger, G. (eds.) I4CS 2019. CCIS, vol. 1041, pp. 125–141. Springer, Cham (2019). https://doi.org/10.1007/978-3-030-22482-0_10
5. Sarfaraz, A., Hämmäinen, H.: 5G transformation – how mobile network operators are preparing for transformation to 5G? In: CTTE 2017, pp. 1–9. IEEE (2017)
6. 5GACIA (A): 5G for Automation in Industry, White Paper (2019). https://www.5g-acia.org/. Accessed Jan 2021
7. 5GACIA (B): Exposure of 5G Capabilities for Connected Industries and Automation Applications, White Paper (2020). https://www.5g-acia.org/. Accessed Jan 2021
8. von Hugo, D., Eichler, G., Rosowski, T.: A holistic communication network for efficient transport and enhanced driving via connected cars. In: Lüke, K.-H., Eichler, G., Erfurth, C., Fahrnberger, G. (eds.) I4CS 2019. CCIS, vol. 1041, pp. 11–24. Springer, Cham (2019). https://doi.org/10.1007/978-3-030-22482-0_2
9. von Hugo, D., Eichler, G.: Location-aware network function execution for new challenging location based services in next generation converged 5G communication networks. In: Proceedings of the 12th Location-Based Application and Services, LBAS 2016, Logos Verlag, Berlin (2016)
10. 5GACIA (C): 5G for Connected Industries and Automation, White Paper (2019). https://www.5g-acia.org/. Accessed Jan 2021
11. Kuß, A.: Marktforschung, 4th edn. Springer, Wiesbaden (2012). https://doi.org/10.1007/978-3-8349-3853-4
12. Venkatesh, V., Davis, F.D.: A theoretical extension of the technology acceptance model: four longitudinal field studies. Manag. Sci. **46**(2), 186–204 (2000)
13. Venkatesh, V., Morris, M.G., Davis, G.B., Davis, F.D.: User acceptance of information technology: toward a unified view. MIS Q. **27**(3), 425–478 (2003)
14. Venkatesh, V., Thong, J., Xu, X.: Unified theory of acceptance and use of technology: a synthesis and the road ahead. J. Assoc. Inf. Syst. **17**, 328–376 (2016)
15. Backhaus, K., Erichson, B., Plinke, W., Weiber, R.: Multivariate Analysemethoden. Springer, Heidelberg (2016). https://doi.org/10.1007/978-3-662-46076-4

16. Lüke, K.-H., Walther, J., Wäldchen, D.: Innovation management methods in the aviation industry. In: Hodoň, M., Eichler, G., Erfurth, C., Fahrnberger, G. (eds.) I4CS 2018. CCIS, vol. 863, pp. 161–177. Springer, Cham (2018). https://doi.org/10.1007/978-3-319-93408-2_12
17. Yousaf, F.Z., et al.: Network slicing with flexible mobility and QoS/QoE support for 5G networks. In: International Conference on Communications (ICC 2017), 5GARCH WS, Paris (2017)

Raising Awareness of SMEs for Real-Time Locating Systems (RTLS) in Intralogistics
A Workplace Learning Approach

David Gutewort(✉) [ID], Arlett Semm [ID], and Christian Erfurth [ID]

Department of Industrial Engineering, University of Applied Sciences Jena,
Carl-Zeiss-Promenade 2, 07745 Jena, Germany
{David.Gutewort,Arlett.Semm,Christian.Erfurth}@eah-jena.de

Abstract. Digital transformation in small and medium-sized enterprises (SMEs) is progressing only slowly. In addition to scarce resources, there is often a lack of the necessary IT or technology knowledge and acceptance among employees. In this paper, we present a possible approach for introducing a specific technology, real-time location, in an intralogistics scenario. Together with a pilot company, load carriers are equipped with tags for tracking in an exemplary scenario. The potential of the technology and its concrete application are demonstrated in a teaching and learning concept specially developed for the employees of SMEs. The selection of the technology, the procedure for setting up the scenario and the conception of the workplace learning approach are described in detail.

Keywords: Real-Time Locating Systems · Workplace learning · Indoor localization · Small to medium-sized enterprises · Employee development · Digital transformation

1 Introduction

Increasing digitalization of central areas in society and economy is leading to new opportunities and challenges. In order to keep pace in international competition a conversion of production, logistics and offered services is required. To create new structures, it is necessary to look at changes in work processes and qualifications. The consideration of the knowledge, creativity and demands of employees are the key factors for the success of digitalization. SMEs often need guidance and assistance on the way to the successful digitalization of their business processes. Mostly SMEs have only limited possibilities and resources to take care of their strategic development. Besides the day-to-day business, there is usually no room for improvements. In the project "ZeTT - Center for Digital Transformation Thuringia"[1], these problems are being addressed and solutions are being developed. The introduction of SMEs to new technologies in the context of the digital transformation is described in more detail below. Therefore, the focus is on intralogistics[2] with the introduction of a real-time localization solution.

---

[1] https://zett-thueringen.de/.

[2] The internal material flow and transport of a finished product or equipment in the production area of a factory or in the local company is intralogistics.

© Springer Nature Switzerland AG 2021
U. R. Krieger et al. (Eds.): I4CS 2021, CCIS 1404, pp. 223–236, 2021.
https://doi.org/10.1007/978-3-030-75004-6_15

Real-Time Locating Systems (RTLS) are typically found in large companies, for example in the automotive industry. There, usually enough budget is available to purchase the required expertise and to develop solutions specifically according to the intern requirements. In contrast, access to RTLS-based technology solutions for SMEs is more difficult due to the factors mentioned above. Knowledge and skills are required to understand RTLS and its advantages for intralogistics.

The contribution of this paper is to ensure awareness, provide information of all potentials, and use case scenarios of RTLS in intralogistics. To supply employees in SMEs with the necessary specialist knowledge about the implementation and applications of RTLS, together with companies, the project is developing a modular training program to be launched later in 2021. Taking into account the active participation of employees, the approach of a learning concept is presented in the following. It should be noted that the full learning material has not yet been developed and training has not yet taken place.

In the related work section, the current state of research regarding to RTLS and learning in SMEs is shown. The methodology and research results, including a workplace learning approach are then presented. A discussion of the results follows, regarding to the applicability in SMEs. Finally, a conclusion is given and approaches for further research are pointed out.

2 Related Work

2.1 Intralogistics

The logistics industry is open to new technologies. However, the economic profitability of a technological improvement is a fundamental requirement for the customers [1]. The ambition of the companies goes in the direction of an increase in profit. This plays an increasingly important role in the company and has become an important starting point for digital optimization. Therefore, sources of loss should be identified and eliminated. These include excessive inventory, unnecessary waiting times, transports or employee motion. In this context, just-in-time delivery to the right place (e.g. milk run concept, which is a delivery method where mixed loads are transported from different suppliers to one customer), as well as tracking of persons and objects with knowledge of the respective location, plays an important role [2–4]. The implementation of indoor localization systems can be a solution for this. In addition to warehouses and production areas, this makes sense in office buildings, hospitals, stores or museums [3, 5].

2.2 Real-Time Locating Systems (RTLS)

The first location-based services for localization were intended for outdoor use. These are mostly based on satellite positioning systems such as GPS (Global Positioning System), in which the object to be located determines its position itself in the form of self-location. Inside buildings, the GPS signal is significantly weakened. In addition, there are numerous extra objects that also interfere with the signal. For this reason, this technique is not useful for Indoor Positioning Systems (IPS) [4–6].

Moreover, most indoor positioning scenarios require high precision in the low one-meters range for their purpose. Indoor Location Based Services (ILBS) are used for indoor environments, which can determine the location of a mobile device using special location methods. In this case, the position of the object or person in a certain areas is usually determined of an external location. A special form of locating and tracking things is real-time localization by using a Real Time Location System (RTLS) [5–7].

In this context, real-time does not necessarily mean real-time. It is sufficient if the positioning information is available within the specified time in order not to slow down processes. The following steps are part of the implementation of a solution approach. First of all, a site plan must be created or provided. Then the map material is enriched with digital information, such as points of interest. After that, an appropriate positioning system is integrated, e.g., using Ultra-Wideband (UWB). The actual positioning is then performed using various algorithms such as trilateration. For these, special forms of geometric analysis are used in relation to fixed landmarks, such as angular information the Angle of Arrival (AoA) or travel time information such as Time of Arrival (ToA) or Time Difference of Arrival (TDoA) [5, 6].

Indoor Location Systems. Indoor location systems, such as RFID (Radio Frequency Identification), ZigBee, Wireless LAN (Wifi), image processing systems, Bluetooth Low Energy technology (BLE), iBeacon from Apple, and Ultra-wideband (UWB). Because the performance of the systems varies widely, selecting an appropriate technology requires a comprehensive evaluation of the site conditions and the necessary parameters. The requirements for the planned scenario, such as the necessary accuracy and flexibility, should be set in relation to effort and cost [1, 3–6, 8].

RFID technology is already widely used in the warehouse sector because it is very robust. Radio waves are used to read data and information from the RFID tag. However, since it was not originally intended for use in localization scenarios, it is often not accurate enough and cannot be used in 3D applications.

In image processing systems, special installed cameras are attached, which locate objects by means of images and corresponding evaluation programs. The exact position of the cameras must be adjusted, and optimal lighting must be ensured. The setup is done by expensive specialized employees. The positions can be shifted by physical impacts, then the cameras must be adjusted again.

WLAN is already available in many companies, but in addition to location tracking, it is used for file transfer, e-mails and the Internet. The most important problem is the accuracy of the localization in the range of 5–15 m. This is not accurate enough in a building [8].

UWB is a potential technology in the field of indoor localization with short ranges and high localization accuracy of 5–30 cm. 3D positioning with a vertical accuracy of 1–2 m is also possible. The Time of Flight (ToF) method is used for this. In this method, the distance between the transmitter object and the receivers (anchors) is measured by means of the time required for the signal to travel this distance. This is based on the fact that the electromagnetic waves used move at a constant speed. However, this requires suitably equipped hardware at the transmitter and receiver with high precision synchronized clocks. Furthermore, it is not compatible with current smartphones [5, 6, 8, 9].

Bluetooth Low Energy (BLE) is currently the most widely used positioning method. The sensors are less cost-intensive, have low power requirements and are flexible. The distances to at least three permanently installed nodes (anchors) must be known. The localization tags (small BLE transmitters) are attached to each object to be located and transmit their identity (IDs) to the anchors at fixed time intervals and can achieve a range of up to 30 m in the process. From the received IDs and the values of the received signal strength, the Received Signal Strength Indicator (RSSI), the position of the object in two-dimensional space can be determined using the trilateration algorithm. The BLE tags are given a certain area, which is displayed as a circle with a radius of the estimated distance. The current position is located in the area of the crossing point of the three circles. Signal spreading in BLE is very sensitive to interference, for example by reflections and attenuation of the radio signal at barriers and existing radio noise in the environment. In [4], reference measurements are used to show the fluctuations in signal strength depending on distance. This shows that a high localization accuracy is possible up to 2 m. Up to 5 m distance error is between 0.5 and 4 m. Therefore, the RSSI values must be filtered and smoothed to minimize the noise. With increasing distance, the error also increases significantly. Since the API does not provide an angle value for the BLE tags, triangulation cannot take place. This method measures angles instead of distances. Therefore, this can be used in 3D space [4–6].

Another more accurate way is to use scene analysis in the form of fingerprinting. A map of measurement vectors is created over the entire space. Each measured vector with the signal strength RSSI is stored as a fingerprint in a radio map together with its location. When the object is localized, its measured value RSSI is then compared with the vectors of the present neighbors. The best matching vector is suggested as the location. This promises high precision. However, the associated manual effort to create the measurement map in the calibration phase is very high. This is not possible for very large buildings. Furthermore, when there are changes in the mapped environment, the radio map has to be recreated [5, 6].

Since RTLS generates enormous amounts of data, which must be processed and understood, artificial intelligence (AI) and data mining methods are used in addition to the algorithms to generate position data for intralogistics from the raw data. In the paper of Rácz-Szabó et al. [3], a literature review on data analysis techniques related to areas of RTLS based application was conducted. Web applications were used for management, i.e., data processing, data analysis, position visualization and for executing required actions [4, 8].

The gained knowledge from the RTLS data enables numerous optimizations such as the management of the stock and the ordering, a higher efficiency due to less standing and search times in the production process [10].

One problem area that has received little attention is location spoofing. In this case, attempts are made to manipulate location procedures in order to cause damage or to get access to sensitive data. This can be internal or external manipulation. Internal manipulation can be caused, for example, by the loss or stealing of a mobile device. This should be considered when implementing such a system. In the paper by Decker, an overview was given from the literature on the possible manipulations of location systems and procedures for preventing spoofing [7].

2.3 Learning in SMEs

Focusing on the employees, knowledge and skills are one of the most important factors for success in a digital change effort [11]. In addition to digitalization, there are a number of other drivers for training of employees. For most employers, training is an activity required to ensure that employees have the skills necessary to do their jobs effectively. It implies that a training need is likely to be triggered by some change in the business environment, work practices, technology, or personnel. The most commonly mentioned drivers for training are [12]:

- the recruitment of new staff
- significant changes in technology in the workplace
- new product or service development
- the introduction of new regulations relating to work practices
- radical changes in work organization

Related to the workforce's digital capabilities, in large companies human resource departments (HRD) are responsible for the further development of employees. Compared to SMEs, scaled-down versions of large organizations methods could be unsuitable. Instead of HRD, the terms "learning" and "training" are more commonly used in SMEs [13]. In this context, a differentiation can be made between "what employers do (offer training)" and "what employees do (learn)" [14].

Large Companies Versus SMEs. Therefore, learning in SMEs needs to be viewed differently. In addition, SMEs should not be considered as a homogeneous group [12]. Learning environments are likely to be very different in a micro SME, with less than ten employees, to such requirements in a small enterprise from 10–49 employees, and different again in a medium-sized company with almost 50 up to 250 employees [15, 16]. In addition to the size of a company, it is also important to consider other aspects that influence corporate learning. Factors such as the skills and infrastructure needed to develop and support learning environments are probably very different. It is expected that the sector/industry and the mindset of the owner will also influence this [13].

The lack of homogeneity in SMEs leads to further complexity in the observation. This results in SMEs developing their own habits and language. The perceived lack of learning in SMEs can also result from the nature of SMEs. This means that learning take place as part of everyday, operational business. This lead Wenger [17], while researching SMEs as Communities of Practice, to observe that "learning is an integral part of our everyday lives". In summary learning in SMEs is socially situated, informal and social learning dominate. SMEs are also typically seen as informal organizations [18], which is reflected in their learning, although employees often seem to believe that "only formal training is "real" training" [19]. Consequently, the ubiquity and continuous nature of learning in SMEs can result in not being recognized as a learning process [20, 21].

Barriers to Employee Training in SMEs. After reflecting on the complexity of learning in SMEs, barriers to employee training in SMEs are outlined below. The differences of learning and training between SMEs and large companies have already been discussed above. There are different factors that influence the supply and demand of training. On the other hand, there is a lack of awareness among small business owners of the importance of skills development training as well as the training opportunities available [12, 22].

List of barriers to training and learning in SMEs [22]:

- Lack of time for training and learning activities.
- Limited financial resources for training provision.
- High cost of external training provision.
- Lack of external training programs tailored to the specific needs of SMEs.
- Small firm owners' negative attitudes towards employee training (lack of awareness by small business owners of the importance of training for firm success).
- Lack of awareness by small business owners of the training opportunities available.
- Fear of "poaching".
- A low-cost business strategy.
- Lack of employee desire for training and learning.
- Problematic training needs analysis.
- Poor quality of external training vendors.

Lifelong Learning and SMEs. The research findings suggest that SMEs are significantly less likely than larger employers to provide or fund formal training that leads to qualifications for employees. The learning that takes place in most SMEs tends to be informal, on the job, and related to short-term business problems. The nature of work and the skills it requires are changing at such a rapid and unpredictable pace that employees and employers must be able to adapt flexibly to change. The concept of lifelong learning is coming into focus. Learning must take place throughout a working lifetime. An important implication of this analysis is that learning activities need to take place while people are working. The need to adapt to technological change, increased competition, new regulations and other changes in the economy and society means that workers must constantly learn new skills [12].

Practice of workplace learning [23]:

- *Self-initiated:* Employees have to find learning opportunities by themselves in the workplace. If an employee does not actively want to learn, nothing happens.
- *Non-structured:* There are no ready-to-use learning programs; instead, employees create their own learning formats depending on what they have available in the workplace. Learning practices tend to be spontaneous, individual, interpersonal, and without limitations.
- *Job related:* Most learning practices relate to work. Employees use learning resources customized to their work assignments.
- *Team driven:* Workplace learning in a team context to leverage employee resources (knowledge and skills) and save time. Informal learning through interaction with colleagues (sharing of experiences and group discussions among the team members) remains a key component of learning in this rapidly changing environment.

- *'more is fewer':* Offering too many learning opportunities in the workplace can be counterproductive, as employees find it difficult to take advantage of them due to their busy work life and time pressure. Multiple learning opportunities can result in employees limiting their learning practices to quick approaches such as self-study, asking close colleagues at work, or learning from acquaintances in their professional network.

In this context, e-learning is a learning format that covers many of the requirements listed for learning in SMEs. The flexible learning, where the time, the place and the duration can be determined by the learner, is ideal for learning close to the workplace. E-learning as a digital learning opportunity should be adapted to the needs of the learners as far as possible. Since the attention span in this case determines the learning success, digital learning content should be prepared in the form of short learning nuggets (micro-learning). A modular structure of the e-learning modules ensures that content can be compiled and adapted as needed. Finally, this learning format enables a highly individualized learning experience [16, 18, 24].

3   Method and Results

The first task was to define a suitable scenario together with the pilot company. After visiting the production site, possible scenarios were discussed in workshops. At the same time, technological possibilities were explored. To keep up with the latest trends in RTLS an extensive research phase was necessary. In this context the focus was on the discussions with experts, particularly with logistic service providers, manufacturing industries and RTLS solution providers. The results provided a basis for the development of the learning concept.

The research activities are still in the beginning of creating prototypes and learning concepts. For a selected scenario, a prototype as well as a teaching and learning concept for the employees are to be developed in the funded transfer project. Together with a pilot company, possible approaches to value-adding digitalization would be investigated. The discussions revealed a need for a more precise level of information on progress in processing customer orders.

3.1   RTLS Use Case Scenarios in Intralogistics

A custom order passes through various workplaces in the company. Thereby custom orders are moved between the processing stations with the help of load carriers. An order can be divided among several load carriers. During the processing of orders, the start and end of each work step is confirmed at the processing station in the ERP system (Enterprise-Resource-Planning).

During the discussion of the process, the following requirements emerged, which can currently only be answered by a time-consuming search on site:

- Where are the load carriers currently located for a particular order?
- Are the landing carriers already available at the next processing station?
- How could an employee be assisted in finding the load carriers for further processing?

Real-time tracking of load carriers assigned to customer-specific orders promises an adequate answer to the questions arising from the requirements. Together with the pilot company, a prototype for tracking load carriers is being built iteratively. Suitable sensor technology is attached to the load carriers, which is used to locate their position. In addition to the proof of feasibility, the necessary efforts in setup, maintenance and costs must be weighed up. The required knowledge and skills should also be clarified. All findings are incorporated into the development of the learning concept.

3.2 Common RTLS Technologies

In the context of IoT (Internet of Things), interest in localization capabilities within buildings have grown in recent years. Various methods, as shown in the related work section, are applicable and suitable technologies are available. Zafari et al. [25] present a detailed description of different indoor localization techniques and technologies. Short- and medium-range technologies, such as BLE, Zigbee, WiFi, UWB, etc., are available for use and support high data rate often required by applications. Zafari et al. [25] used an evaluation framework to investigate metrics such as energy efficiency, accuracy, scalability, reception range, cost, latency and availability.

The requirements for accuracy and real-time are moderate in the context of the scenario. An accuracy of the localization below one meter and an update frequency of about ten seconds is sufficient. In preparation for a learning scenario, differences between technological solutions should be highlighted too. This is also useful for transferability to other application areas. Therefore, two implementation approaches were chosen for the prototype: UWB can be used to represent increased precision and update frequency requirements. BLE is well suited to cover the moderate requirements in the sample scenario. In addition, the lower costs and low power consumption of the tags are advantageous. Market maturity can be observed for both variants, with higher adoption of BLE in the industry.

3.3 RTLS Demonstrator

To build the prototype, the necessary infrastructure must be created and the processes to be considered in the scenario must be implemented. Essential infrastructure elements are the tags that are attached to the load carriers and the anchors for locating these tags. The anchors must be networked with a computer that processes the tracking data analytically and makes it available for further use, e.g., visualization, event handling and linking with ERP data. For example, a software application can visualize the localization information in a stored building plan. This information can be made available on mobile devices to support routing to the location of the load carrier.

In addition to localization, movements of the load carriers are also of interest. From these, conclusions can be drawn about the progress of the processing of an order. Likewise, movement patterns can be recognized and, with sufficient data material, also optimized. In addition, the movement event can be used as a trigger for automatisms in the ERP system. A virtual division of the shop floor into areas, for which suitable triggers are defined when entering or leaving the areas (geofencing), enables an improved level of information in the ERP system. This can contribute to the simplification of (manual) processes. An enrichment of existing data sets, the automatic documentation of production processes or further algorithmic processing e.g., for a better understanding of the processes or for optimizations hold further potentials.

3.4 Learning Concept

To raise awareness of RTLS among employees and to provide them with knowledge, a workplace learning approach is presented below. The learning concept considers the special aspects of learning activities in SMEs as described above. Such as the required flexibility of employees and the general informal learning readiness. As the target group, the manufacturing industry is considered. Basically, the learning concept can be transferred to all industries. To begin, the learning concept will be rolled out and evaluated in the pilot company.

To meet the different needs of the SMEs (different workplaces, number of employees or preferences in the learning context), the concept is based on a mix of methods. Conventional face-to-face training, webinars (online seminars), workshops and e-learning modules (web-based trainings) are used for knowledge transfer. For hands-on experience the RTLS demonstrator is set up in the pilot company. Therefore, a learning station is installed at the workplace. This combination of methods is intended to provide an individualized and demand-oriented learning experience for the employees. All modules can also be combined as a blended learning approach.

The learning concept primarily aims to raise awareness of RTLS among executives and employees. It is expected to help understand the technology as well as to show possible implementations. This should help to determine the expected benefits of RTLS for the company and it will help to transfer the needed knowledge. If required, it can help with the preparation and implementation of the technology.

The learning modules are divided into categories according to their content. The basic content teaches the fundamentals of RTLS, including the technology and scenarios (Table 1). Depending on the requirements of the employer, the basic training is recommended as a classroom training or webinar. On the other side, an individual workshop is conducted in the advanced course (Table 4). Therefore, internal processes are analyzed regarding to possible RTLS scenarios. Customized application possibilities are developed from this. Additionally, e-learning modules are offered for the employees. In the e-learning module "RTLS learning cards" (basic course), employees can inform themselves about basic terms and contexts in the field of RTLS (Table 2). The digital module "Implementation steps of a Bluetooth indoor positioning system in SMEs" (advanced curse) presents the entire process of implementing a Bluetooth indoor positioning system using an illustrative storyline (Table 3).

The learning concept can also be used as a completely independent learning setup in the company, as shown in Fig. 1. Therefore, the RTLS prototype is set up with a learning station in the working environment of the employees, including tablets or laptops for consuming the e-learning modules. The training station, equipped with RTLS prototypes and e-learning elements, allows employees to get hands-on experience and knowledge about several use case scenarios. In addition, learning posters are developed that give an overview of the topic and initiate discussions between the employees. The employees can learn and acquire knowledge independently and with a high flexibility at

Table 1. Course description "RTLS essentials for SMEs".

RTLS essentials for SMEs (basic)	
Learning objectives	• The participants are familiar with current RTLS technologies and know their advantages and disadvantages • The participants understand the functionality of RTLS systems • The participants know the required components of a RTLS system • The participants know possible applications and their added value
Content	• RTLS technologies • Basics of RTLS • RTLS use-case scenarios • Hands-on lab with the demonstrator
Course format	Classroom training, webinar
Duration	2 h

Table 2. Course description "RTLS learning cards".

RTLS learning cards (basic)	
Learning objectives	• With the help of short learning nuggets, the participants get to know important terms and contexts • For example: indoor positioning system, geofencing, locating and positioning, locating and tracking, angle of arrival, time of arrival
Content	• Explorative approach • Explanation of RTLS terms • Point out of typical use-case scenarios
Course format	E-learning module
Duration	Short learning nuggets (max. 5 minutes per unit)

Table 3. Course description "implementation steps of a BLE indoor positioning system in SMEs".

Implementation steps of a BLE indoor positioning system in SMEs (advanced)	
Learning objectives	• The participants know the basics of real-time localization and are familiar with the technology and application scenarios • The participants know and understand the entire process of implementing a Bluetooth indoor positioning system • The participants understand the complexity of an implementation • The participants understand the financial investment and can compare costs and benefits
Content	• Step by step description of the implementation of a Bluetooth indoor positioning system • Illustration on the basis of a user story
Course format	E-learning module
Duration	20 min

Table 4. Course description "RTLS requirements analysis and scenarios".

RTLS requirements analysis and scenarios (advanced)	
Objectives	• The participants analyze their current workflows and evaluate the use of RTLS in this context • The Participants jointly develop relevant application scenarios of RTLS for their company
Content	• Point out actual situation (without RTLS) • Show up application possibilities • Develop individual RTLS scenarios
Course format	Workshop
Duration	3 h

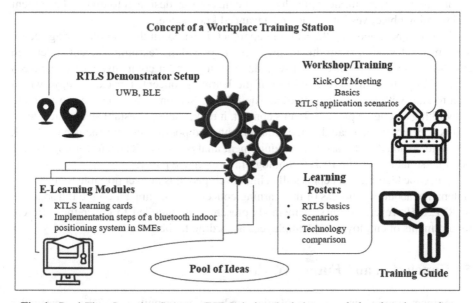

Fig. 1. Real-Time Locating Systems (RTLS) in intralogistics – workplace learning station

the workplace learning station. By coming together in this process, the informal learning process between employees is triggered. The last promotes the formation of communities to shape the introduction of RTLS together with the employees.

The learning concept can either be used, if the company has no experience or ideas about the use of RTLS yet. Or it can be used specifically in the implementation of RTLS to qualify employees and involve them in the digital change effort.

4   Discussion

As part of the digital transformation, a digital assistance system for intralogistics was presented above. The real-time localization of elements in the production environment opens up a wide range of possible applications. Understanding this technology requires a broad spectrum of knowledge from different disciplines. Such as IT skills, technical understanding, entrepreneurial thinking but also the willingness to be supported by digital solution offerings. The learning concept approach presented here was developed to meet these requirements.

While companies with high percentages of well-educated and skilled workers have a relative advantage in ICT (information and communications technology) adoption [26]. The level of digital maturity of SMEs varies widely. Entrepreneurs who are involved in the day-to-day business usually have little time to take care of strategic developments in their company [27]. New technologies or digital services must therefore be presented as simple and relevant for SMEs as possible. By preparing relevant knowledge content as compactly and comprehensibly as possible, for example in the context of RTLS, employees can check the usage of a technology for their work processes. In order to ensure the required simplicity, the learning concept was designed to divide the content and learning objectives into basic and advanced knowledge.

It should be noted that the learning approach is based on the manufacturing sector. This means that before introducing the technology and the learning concept, a detailed situation analysis is required, as it was done with the pilot company. This is the basis for deciding about the scope and use of the learning concept. For example, in which area to start with the implementation. The training station should be used to promote networking among employees. In this context, it makes sense to establish a project team that is specifically dedicated to the requirements and possibilities for the use of RTLS. It should be noted that, based on a requirement analysis, other RTLS technologies may be more suitable than the BLE technology favored in the paper.

Since the learning concept is still being developed, it is not yet possible to make any statements about the success of the learning concept and its impact on the introduction of RTLS. However, the mix of methods presented is intended to cover the different requirements of employers and employees according to their needs.

5   Conclusion and Future Work

In-company training on new technologies can be an opportunity for SMEs in particular to drive forward the digital transformation. An important factor here is a low-threshold and practicable approach to imparting knowledge. Goals and potentials must not only be named, but must also be accessible to the employees themselves. The approach presented in the article promises a suitable transport of knowledge through the combination of haptic elements such as the prototype, face-to-face and digital learning elements. Employees are able to understand new technology and acquire new skills. Even more they are integrated in the process of changes actively.

Employers and employees in all sectors who are looking for assistance systems in intralogistics can benefit from this approach. It will be easier for them to understand the technology and to identify suitable deployment scenarios.

It is assumed that additional support such as guidelines and roadmaps can be useful. These and other approaches may be of interest for future research. The usage in other sectors or in other scenarios, outside intralogistics, could be considered in more detail.

For example, the localization of people and the associated possibilities such as triggering events (through geofencing) could be interesting. A community driven approach can foster the exchange and networking of people.

Acknowledgement. The project "ZeTT - Center for Digital Transformation Thuringia" is funded by the German Federal Ministry of Labor and Social Affairs (BMAS) under the grant number 2019010726 and the European Social Fund as part of the funding guideline "Future Centers - Supporting SMEs, Employees and the Self-Employed in Developing and Implementing Innovative Design Approaches to Mastering the Digital Transformation".

References

1. Kessler, R., van der Ahe, F., Suske, J., Marx Gómez, J.: Einbindung von intelligenten Ladungsträgern in Prozesse der Intralogistik. HMD **56**, 574–586 (2019). https://doi.org/10.1365/s40702-019-00527-4
2. Osieczko, K., Gazda, A.: The use of intralogistic systems in the enterprise. In: Proceedings CLC 2018 - Carpathian Logistics Congress, pp. 682–687 (2018)
3. Rácz-Szabó, A., Ruppert, T., Bántay, L., et al.: Real-time locating system in production management. Sensors (Basel) **20** (2020). https://doi.org/10.3390/s20236766
4. Mekki, K., Bajic, E., Meyer, F.: Indoor positioning system for IoT device based on BLE technology and MQTT protocol. In: 2019 IEEE 5th World Forum on Internet of Things (WF-IoT). IEEE, pp. 787–792 (2019)
5. Estel, M., Fischer, L.: Feasibility of Bluetooth iBeacons for indoor localization. In: Zimmermann, A., Rossmann, A. (eds.) Digital Enterprise Computing (DEC 2015): June 25–26, 2015, Böblingen, Germany, pp. 97–108. Ges. für Informatik, Bonn (2015)
6. Roehrig, C., Lategahn, J., Müller, M.: Anwendung von Real Time Locating Systems (RTLS) in der Sicherungstechnik - Verfahren und Technologien von Bluetooth Low Energy (BLE) bis Ultra Wide Band (UWB). In: Conference Innosecure (2015)
7. Decker, M.: Ein Überblick über Ansätze zur Vermeidung der Manipulation von Ortungsverfahren. In: Bick, M. (ed.) Mobile und ubiquitäre Informationssysteme - Entwicklung, Implementierung und Anwendung: Proceedings zur 4. Konferenz Mobile und Ubiquitäre Informationssysteme (MMS 2009), 3. März 2009 in Münster, Germany. Ges. für Informatik, Bonn, pp. 53–66 (2009)
8. Halawa, F., Dauod, H., Lee, I.G., et al.: Introduction of a real time location system to enhance the warehouse safety and operational efficiency. Int. J. Prod. Econ. **224**, 107541 (2020). https://doi.org/10.1016/j.ijpe.2019.107541
9. Zhang, C., Kuhn, M.J., Merkl, B.C., et al.: Real-time noncoherent UWB positioning radar with millimeter range accuracy: theory and experiment. IEEE Trans. Microwave Theory Tech. **58**, 9–20 (2010). https://doi.org/10.1109/TMTT.2009.2035945
10. Shamsuzzoha, A., Helo, P.: Real-time tracking and tracing systems: potentials for the logistics network. In: Proceedings of the 2011 International Conference on Industrial Engineering and Operations Management, pp. 22–24 (2011)
11. de La Boutetière, H., Alberto Montagner, A.R.: Unlocking success in digital transformations (2018)
12. Steve, J.: Lifelong learning and SMEs: issues for research and policy. J. Small Bus. Enterp. Dev. **9**, 285–295 (2002). https://doi.org/10.1108/14626000210438607
13. Short, H.: Learning in SMEs. Hum. Resour. Dev. Int. **22**, 413–419 (2019). https://doi.org/10.1080/13678868.2019.1658368

14. Kitching, J.: Regulating employment relations through workplace learning: a study of small employers. Hum. Resour. Manage. J. **17**, 42–57 (2007). https://doi.org/10.1111/j.1748-8583.2007.00019.x

15. Chartered Institute for Personnel and Development: Making Maximum Impact as an HR Professional in an SME (2005)

16. Attwell, G.: The Challenge of E-learning in Small Enterprises: Issues for Policy and Practice. Office for Official Publications of the European Communities, Luxembourg (2003)

17. Wenger, E.: Communities of Practice: Learning, Meaning, and Identity. Cambridge University Press, Cambridge (1998)

18. Roy, A.: The training process of SMEs: what motivates SMEs to use e-learning. Int. J. Adv. Corp. Learn. (iJAC) **2** (2009). https://doi.org/10.3991/ijac.v2i3.991

19. Coetzer, A., Perry, M. (eds.): Factors influencing employee learning in small businesses. Educ. Train. **50**(8/9), 648–660 (2008)

20. David, H., Coral, A.: Learning to learn: a case for developing small firm owner/managers. J. Small Bus. Enterp. Dev. **18**, 43–57 (2011). https://doi.org/10.1108/14626001111106424

21. Geldenhuys, D., Cilliers, F.: Transforming a small business: a learning intervention. SA J. Ind. Psychol. **38**, 147–155 (2011). https://doi.org/10.4102/sajip.v38i2.1028

22. Antonios, P.: Barriers to employee training and learning in small and medium-sized enterprises (SMEs). Dev. Learn. Organ. Int. J. **25**, 15–18 (2011). https://doi.org/10.1108/14777281111125354

23. Steven, T., Gray David, E.: The practice of employee learning in SME workplaces: a micro view from the life-cycle perspective. J. Small Bus. Enterp. Dev. **23**, 671–690 (2016). https://doi.org/10.1108/JSBED-07-2015-0099

24. Roy, A., Raymond, L.: Meeting the Training Needs of SMEs: Is e-Learning a Solution? (2008)

25. Zafari, F., Gkelias, A., Leung, K.K.: A survey of indoor localization systems and technologies. IEEE Commun. Surv. Tutorials **21**, 2568–2599 (2019). https://doi.org/10.1109/COMST.2019.2911558

26. Giotopoulos, I., Kontolaimou, A., Korra, E., et al.: What drives ICT adoption by SMEs?: evidence from a large-scale survey in Greece. J. Bus. Res. JBR **81**(2017), 60–69 (2017)

27. Wolf, M., Semm, A., Erfurth, C.: Digital transformation in companies – challenges and success factors. In: Hodoň, M., Eichler, G., Erfurth, C., Fahrnberger, G. (eds.) I4CS 2018. CCIS, vol. 863, pp. 178–193. Springer, Cham (2018). https://doi.org/10.1007/978-3-319-93408-2_13

Future Community Support

General Requirements and System Architecture in Local Micro Smart Grid

Steffen Späthe$^{(\boxtimes)}$ and Peter Conrad

Friedrich Schiller University Jena, Jena, Germany
{steffen.spaethe,peter.conrad}@uni-jena.de

Abstract. Integrating electromobility and local energy generation based on renewable energy sources into commercial housing poses a challenge for network operators, tenants, as well as the housing industry itself. This paper analyzes the general technical and organizational requirements to establish a local micro smart grid within the framework of the research project *Winner Reloaded*. Starting from a general analysis of the requirements, a suitable architecture design is derived, focusing on four main, high-level components for data collection, system control, billing, and tenant information. Further this paper describes each component in more detail and discuss the resulting system's viability, taking both technological and organizational viewpoints into account.

Keywords: Smart grid · Charging infrastructure · Tenant electricity model · System architecture

1 Introduction

Efforts to protect the climate and the associated need to increase energy efficiency and incorporate renewable energies present the society with new challenges. In parallel, the goal of having 7 to 10 million electric vehicles on Germany's roads by 2030 also requires extensive construction measures and long-term investments. As a key player in the management of residential neighborhoods and the provision of private housing, the housing industry plays a central role here and must rise to these challenges. The combination of renewable energies and electromobility in the neighborhood leads to the need for locally controlled smart grids. Since to date there are no generally applicable blueprints for the housing industry on how to achieve such goals, new, integrated solutions must be created with regard to the construction and operation of local micro smart grids.

One potential consequence of these developments are landlord-to-tenant electricity models, which aim for local generation and consumption of energy by the tenants whenever possible. By including charging points for communally used electric vehicles, this creates opportunities to enable and promote electromobility while simultaneously using energy in a climate-friendly way within the residential neighborhood.

© Springer Nature Switzerland AG 2021
U. R. Krieger et al. (Eds.): I4CS 2021, CCIS 1404, pp. 239–250, 2021.
https://doi.org/10.1007/978-3-030-75004-6_16

The implementation of such a landlord-to-tenant electricity model requires a reconsideration of the power grid's operation in terms of the distribution of available energy. Furthermore, the legal registration as an energy supplier as well as the billing aspects of electricity consumption must be reconsidered. Due to volatile energy generation and consumption peaks caused by fast charging processes, the energy production costs fluctuate, which can and will also affect pricing in the future.

For instance, regarding the supply of solar energy, there is a high availability of energy on sunny days. In contrast, little to no energy could be generated on cloudy days or at night. At the same time, the supply can change by the minute depending on the weather. Similarly, usage of energy on the tenant side is also variable. For example, it could be expected that there would be higher demand in the mornings, late afternoon, and evenings than at night or during regular working hours, while possibly the use of electric cars would also follow similar temporal patterns. Such variability between supply and demand, which also affects energy rates, needs to be considered, and a sensible allocation of the available energy to tenants, domestic systems, and the charging points, possibly with the assistance of the public power grid, needs to be carried out and also billed accordingly. Our research project *Winner Reloaded* [3] examines such a local micro smart grid model and is engaged in the discussion and implementation of the necessary hardware infrastructure as well as software components. In this paper, we discuss our overall requirements and propose a system architecture for building and operating the described local micro smart grid model. We thereby highlight the main components and go into more detail about their individual requirements.

The contribution of this paper is a presentation of high level requirements to a micro smart grid ICT system, an architectural design and a discussion about its feasibility in the context of the housing industry.

This paper is structured as follows: The paper proceeds with Sect. 2 to contextualize the presented requirements and proposed solutions within existing work. Section 3 presents an overview of the overall system goals and the smart grid ICT system' derived main requirements. Following Sect. 4 presents more details for each of the main components of the proposed architecture. Finally, Sect. 5 discusses the viability of our presented architecture, taking into consideration the impact on and the novel requirements for the housing industry. In Sect. 6 the paper closes with a conclusion.

2   Related Work

Electricity grids are undergoing significant changes, primarily due to the increase in distributed, renewable energy sources, among other factors. To meet these upcoming challenges, the previously hierarchically structured and operated power grid must be converted into a smart grid. Fundamental approaches and ideas of smart grids are presented by Santacana et al. in [10]. As discussed by Santacana there are four technology layers in a smart grid: power distribution/consumption, sensor/actuator layer, communication layer, and decision intelligence layer. As will be illustrated later, these layers are also reflected in local micro smart grids.

As presented by Kristov et al. in [8] the overall optimization process and market design is going to change as well. For example, a dynamic pricing model is briefly discussed in which the locational energy price is derived from the instantaneous generation price plus additional influencing factors such as distribution system losses, congestion, and other characteristics [8].

An overview over various residential demand response systems, strategies an load-scheduling techniques is given by Haider et al. in [6].

A survey over the potentials of distributed ledger technology for transactive energy exchanges in energy markets is given by Siano et al. in [11]. Furthermore, it is shown by Di Silvestre et al. in [4] that distributed ledger technology can be used for distributed decision making for technical operations in microgrids. They give a brief overview about blockchain technology and distributed ledger implementations usable for energy transactions in micro grids as well.

In their literature review Dutta and Mitra have compiled a list of various electricity pricing policies with their economic implications [5]. A field test in Germany about flexible energy tariffs and resulting domestic customer behavior is described by Ifland et al. in [7].

The spectrum of application of big data and artificial intelligence methods in the context of smart buildings to realize energy management and improve energy efficiency are shown by Marinakis in [9].

3   Requirements Overview

As previously outlined, the development and integration of distributed energy power plants based on renewable energy sources, and the expansion of electromobility are key political objectives. As the housing industry operates residential neighborhoods, they are also in a position to actively move these two objectives forward by building photovoltaic systems and providing charging points for tenants. Going one step further, under these circumstances, electric power can be offered directly to tenants. This concept is called the landlord-to-tenant electricity supply model. Here, the housing company becomes not only the landlord, but also the electricity provider and system operator.

The installation and operation of a local smart grid in a residential neighborhood is a really sensitive undertaking. Maintaining a safe operation and trouble-free supply of electrical power to the occupants is a top-priority requirement. This implicates a fundamental requirement for all controlling and controlled infrastructure components: Safety first. Local activities must always be carried out in safe value ranges. If external control variables are implausible or missing over a certain period of time, it is automatically necessary to switch to a safe mode.

In addition to this foundation, other main objectives must be achieved in order to achieve economical and technically beneficial operation of the local smart grid. Obvious main objectives are:

- Local energy generation and consumption must be coordinated as good as possible to minimize expensive energy purchases from the higher-level grid.
- Charging processes of electrical vehicles at non-public, personalized charging points must be coordinated in a reliable manner, so that all charging processes run in accordance with the contract and priority even when electrical capacity is limited.
- Local energy consumption, as well as local energy generation and external energy procurement, must be recorded in a highly reliable, audit-proof manner and stored for later billing.
- All tenants must have insight into their neighborhood's energy performance and, if desired, their own energy use in near real time, to ensure transparency.

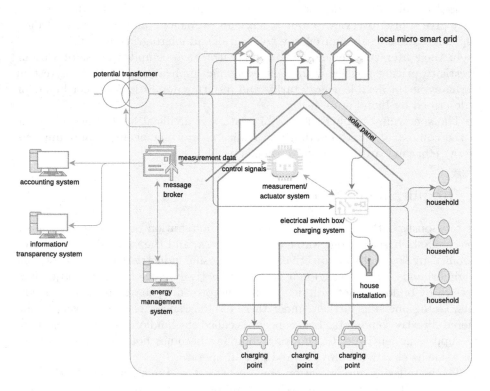

Fig. 1. An illustration of the complete system. Data flows are shown in green and power flows in red. (Color figure online)

With respect to the outlined objectives the overall smart grid ICT system can be divided into the following three main components:

1. *Dynamic load and charge management.* The local energy management component has to supervise and optimize the operation of the smart grid. This requires all current energy consumption and generation to be known by this

component. Due to the high variability of supply and demand, a highly dynamic control system is required that balances, at high temporal resolution, the demand for energy of the tenants, the charging processes, and the supply of energy from local energy sources and the higher-level power grid, taking mobility priorities into account. Since it is not intended to actively control individual households directly, the power consumption of several households can be measured summarily. Same is true for other electricity consumers and producers. Thus, a high temporal, but a low spatial measurement resolution is required.

In order to optimize the operation, forecasts of future energy generation as well as energy consumption are necessary in addition to measured real-time information. Additional external information, such as weather, electricity price or vehicle usage forecasts, may have to be included in the calculation of optimal operation schedules.

2. *Accounting data gathering.* With volatile power generation and dynamic control of power flows comes the problem of energy pricing. While classically a fixed electricity price has been the basis for billing, it seems reasonable to use a dynamic pricing model in the local smart grid. Up to now, energy billing for the end customer has usually taken place retrospectively on a balance sheet basis. With dynamic electricity pricing based on current locally available energy, such a billing model is not adequate.

Therefore, the energy quantities must be recorded for each individual end consumer (household, charging point, general electricity), each local generator, and the transfer point of the local smart grid to the higher-level power grid in a time-resolved manner. Since energy prices fluctuate only slightly compared to instantaneous power, a somewhat lower temporal resolution is sufficient for these measured values. In contrast to the measurements required by the energy management component, the individual consumers and producers cannot be summarized, since the energy quantities must be clearly and individually allocated and billed accordingly. Continuous, distributed, and high-resolution acquisition raises questions about the correctness and tamper-resistance of such information. Distributed ledger technology and smart contracts built on top of it offer a possible solution to this particular challenge.

3. *Transparency towards the tenant.* Due to the technical innovations in the neighborhood and the dynamic pricing model approach, which is based on local consumption, production and external grid purchase, transparency for the end user, i.e., the tenant, is very important.

For this purpose, energy consumption data should also be collected and made available for real-time verification in the form of an information portal. Since this part of the system is neither relevant for safety nor billing, the data does not need to have the same high temporal resolution as the energy management component or be stored in a tamper-proof manner. However, the individual tenant must only be provided with data that is and may be of interest to him. This includes the energy balance of his neighborhood and his house, as well as his personal energy consumption.

To homogenize the infrastructure and avoid redundant equipment, a fourth main system component is necessary. The *measurement and control infrastructure* has to provide all required measurement data out of the local smart grid installation, and must convert the logical control commands into physical actions.

An overview of the designed local smart grid setup in the neighborhood is given by Fig. 1. It includes the dynamic measurement and control system within the local micro smart grid, a system for storing accounting data, and a system for visualization. Connected to each house are a photovoltaic system as well as non-public charging infrastructure with multiple charging points. Depending on the local energy consumption and production, power can be drawn from or supplied to the public power grid when necessary.

In cooperation with partners from the housing industry, the project *WINNER Reloaded* not only determines theoretical requirements and develops software. In a housing complex in the city of Chemnitz, the infrastructure is actually built and tested, thus verifying the functionality in a real scenario. In this research setup, operation is envisioned within the following approximate scales:

- 100 households with associated electricity meters.
- 10 house meters (1 per residential building)
- 10 solar power systems (1 per residential building)
- 1–2 combined heat and power plants
- 80 non-public charging points for tenant electric cars
- 10 public charging points with high performance chargers

4   Details of the System Architecture

This chapter will take a closer look at the technical details of our proposed architecture and highlights some details from a high level perspektive. Both the hardware and software requirements will be examined in more detail. Figure 2 provides an overview of the technical building blocks and the main communication paths.

4.1   Dynamic Load and Charge Management

Dynamic load and charge management is at the heart of controlling the infrastructure. Its task is to determine the supply and consumption of energy and to make intelligent decisions regarding its distribution. Due to the high variability, we consider a sampling rate of one Hertz to be necessary. Several components are used for this purpose, which must be deployed locally for security reasons and to ensure low latency and must not depend on connection to the Internet. This is accompanied by the requirement for a high level of fail-safety, since a faulty system can only be maintained locally.

At a high level, load and charge management can be divided into three interconnected components: *measurement and actuator system* (MaAS), *charging point control system* (CPCS), and *energy management system* (EMS).

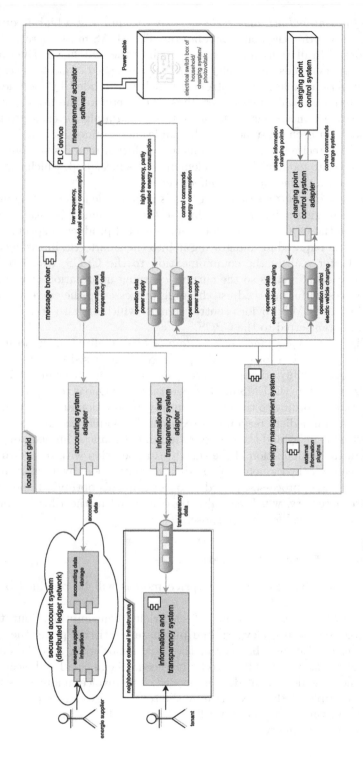

Fig. 2. Conceptual sketch of the complete system architecture.

The *measurement and actuator system* (MaAS) acquires at a high-frequency measurement data within the house installation. The MaAS must operate at the level of the house installation and be integrated into the switchgear. Due to the consequently high demands on stability, resilience and speed of data processing, the use of a programmable logic controller, which is extended by modules for current measurement of all three power phases, is therefore the most suitable solution. The current measurement is carried out separately for each producer and, if requested, for each consumer, which enables fine-grained data acquisition and control. This precise spatial measurement resolution requires the purchase of additional separate modules for each element to be measured, which can lead to challenges in data privacy and cost effectiveness.

The *charging point control system* (CPCS) is responsible for operating multiple, non-public charging points per building, so there are multiple inside a local smart grid. Since the CPCS is an independent, finished product, a specific software component is required for integrating it into the smart grid infrastructure. This CPCS adapter realizes the communication to the CPCS, translates the provided protocols, and makes so the current charging information available to the EMS in processed form. To adjust charging processes to the current overall energy situation, the EMS provides control signals, which are also translated by the adapter and transferred to the CPCS.

The intelligent *energy management system* (EMS), realized in the form of a software service, takes decisions regarding energy usage based on the received data, forecasts and possibly other parameters and sends them back in the form of control signals. Therefore the EMS has two central tasks: One is to ensure instantaneous operation according to the current supply, production and consumption information. If an immediate response is required, individual consumers can be deactivated without delay and the energy requirement reduced immediately. On the other hand, the optimization of the smart grid operation with regard to economic and/or ecological parameters by predictive control, e.g. by accelerating or slowing down charging processes. In order to perform this optimized operation, predictions are necessary, which can also be calculated in the EMS. A plugin structure will be provided for this purpose.

4.2 Capturing of Accounting Data

The basis for billing based on dynamic price models will be provided by the system for collecting accounting data.

In conjunction with the invoicing of electricity consumption, four time-dependent progressions are relevant: The purchase electricity price, the retail electricity price, total energy balance of the local smart grid, and the energy consumption of the single consumers to be invoiced. In classical fixed electricity price models, no time-dependent data is needed. The invoice amount is simply calculated by multiplying the fixed price by the total energy consumption of the billing period. As time-based price tariffs are now to be tested, the basis for calculating the invoice changes.

The retail electricity prices will be calculated on the basis of the overall energy production costs. The energy production costs themselves depend on the short-term generation and consumption in the local smart grid as well as the current electricity price for which additional energy is purchased or surplus energy is sold.

In order to make all these calculations possible, the recording of the following data over time out of the smart grid is required:

- data on power generation (by photovoltaic systems and combined heat and power plants)
- data on electricity balance (purchased from and fed into the public grid)
- data on electricity consumption per tenant or charging point

The data have to be supplemented with the course of the electricity purchase price. Based on all this data, the energy provider can calculate the dynamic retail price and perform the billing.

Special attention must be paid to the traceability and tamper-proofness of all the recorded data. In addition, the system must ensure that no captured data can be lost at any point during transport or processing.

For these reasons, we propose the operation of the billing system using decentralized distributed ledger technologies. Particular attention should be paid to the interface areas where information must be collected, signed, serialized, and stored in blocks. Building on this system, settlement processes may run automatically by accessing the captured information.

As various protocols and frameworks are available for implementing applications on this technology, their evaluation and selection are subject of ongoing research activities. The most promising candidate is currently the Hyperledger Fabric framework [2]. This framework supports smart contracts, which are needed to realize the master data management and data access with role based access control, as well as private data storage, which will be used to store the time series data.

4.3   Information and Transparency System

The goal of the transparency system is to inform the tenant about the own current energy consumption and the overall electric power situation in the own neighborhood. For this purpose, the data collected inside the local smart grid by the measurement and actuator system are to be stored outside and by thus made available to the tenant in the form of an information portal. Compared to EMS, the data collection can be done at a lower frequency (e.g. once every minute). Even this enables the tenant to monitor the overall consumption of the neighborhood as well as optional his own consumption in almost real time. The criticality is lower than that of the billing system, both in terms of data reception and operation: a temporary failure of the transparency system does not entail any serious consequences. Also some missing data points can be retrospectively interpolated with new values or, if necessary, requested again. Since the data is still not relevant for billing, storage in a conventional database is sufficient.

For the transparency system, an implementation as a web application to which tenants can log in is a suitable option, although given a suitable design of the API, access via a smartphone app could be offered as well.

Obviously, certain security aspects must be taken into account, e.g., to prevent access to energy consumption data by other customers or non-customers and to protect the privacy of users. The transparency system can be operated as a global cloud system and is not tied to a specific local micro smart grid, thus achieving an increase in cost efficiency. Special security measures should be taken here, both at the transition points and for the system itself, to prevent infiltration of the smart grid network from the outside or unauthorized access to data.

5 Discussion

The system architecture outlined here lays the technological foundation for operating a local smart grid while promoting electromobility. It is envisioned that the model described here can contribute to climate protection and pave the way to a more ecological future. For actual implementation, however, there are several challenges that must be overcome. These challenges exist on both the technological/organizational and legal sides.

The technological and organizational aspects include the fact that the housing industry's business area is expanding and that the actual implementation will involve a non-negligible amount of work. In addition to its core business, the housing industry now has to offer its own electricity and mobility services and set up and maintain the necessary technological infrastructure. These additional tasks may entail higher operating costs and administrative expenses. Furthermore, the interaction of the individual system components results in a higher level of complexity as a whole, which should not be underestimated. While the individual components meet the requirements for functionality and quality and the architecture has been developed with industrial standards and components in mind, numerous wide-ranging technological decisions have to be made for the specific implementation in detail. These range from the choice of suitable hardware (e.g., the PLC for the measurement/actuator system), decisions for underlying software technology (e.g., suitable database systems for storing energy consumption data), the design of the interfaces of each system along with the selection of a suitable data format for communication, the securing of communication at the interfaces between the systems (e.g., by configuring and applying suitable firewall technology), up to the prevention of system failures (e.g., by containerization).

The legal problems arise primarily due to dynamic control and the dynamic energy pricing model. Under German law, for example, it is possible and desirable for energy suppliers to offer time-variable electricity tariffs [1, §40(5)], although it is not further specified to what exact degree these tariffs may vary, so further clarification of the legal situation is needed here. The situation is further complicated by the fact that the measurement technology used by the measurement/actuator system at least in Germany cannot be used for billing purposes under calibration law. A way out of this situation might be to use a reimbursement model in which the consumer is charged a static tariff metered by a conventional electricity meter, which estimates and limits the expected energy price from above. The difference to the amount determined by the billing system can subsequently be refunded to the consumer.

For the above reasons, the actual feasibility of local micro smart grid projects with the corresponding implementation of the required infrastructure has yet to be demonstrated in practice initially. Projects in this form are still uncharted territory, with correspondingly great challenges and many questions still to be answered. In the closer future, the *Winner Reloaded* project will focus on the actual construction of a local micro smart grid infrastructure and investigate the question of feasibility in more detail.

Last, it should be pointed out that the local micro smart grid is only one building block on the way to a climate-friendly future. Even though the LMSG aims at local energy generation and consumption, it is still necessary to draw energy from the parent grid to balance load peaks when local generation is too low. Thus, for maximum effect, the development of local micro smart grids ideally occurs in parallel with an expansion of renewable energy use.

6 Conclusion

The outlined system architecture fulfills the presented functional requirements as well as the quality requirements. The subsystems are designed to meet the specific needs and objectives of each main objective. However, the combination of the components presented results in a widely distributed, complex overall system. The proposed techniques, apart from the block-chain technology, are well known and industry proven. However, when evaluating the appropriateness, it must be taken into account that the overall system must be installed, operated and maintained in the housing industry environment.

By setting up a local smart grid and providing non-public charging infrastructure, the housing industry is taking on additional tasks outside its core business. In this way, the housing company becomes an electricity producer, electricity supplier, and mobility provider. In addition to the operation of the smart grid infrastructure, there are system administration and IT network security tasks.

From the perspective of the research project, the proposed system structure and the outlined infrastructure represent a viable starting point for the flexible testing of various scenarios. Thus, the creation and billing processes of generation- and load-dependent tariffs can be evaluated. Likewise, different optimization strategies can be mapped in smart grid operation.

The upcoming pilot operation will show whether it is feasible and practicable to transfer the system to regular operation from both a technical and an organizational perspective.

Acknowledgements. We would like to take this opportunity to thank the partners of the research project. The research project *WINNER Reloaded* [3] is funded by the Federal Ministry for Economic Affairs and Energy of Germany under project number 01ME19001E.

References

1. Gesetz über die Elektrizitäts- und Gasversorgung (Energiewirtschaftsgesetz (EnWG)) (07 2005), zuletzt geändert durch Gesetz vom 21.12.2020 (BGBl. I S. 3138) m.W.v. 01.01.2021
2. Androulaki, E., et al.: Hyperledger fabric: a distributed operating system for permissioned blockchains. In: Proceedings of the Thirteenth EuroSys Conference (EuroSys 2018), Association for Computing Machinery, New York, NY, USA (2018). https://doi.org/10.1145/3190508.3190538
3. Chemnitzer Siedlungsgemeinschaft eG: WINNER Reloaded (2021). https://winner-projekt.de
4. Di Silvestre, M.L., Gallo, P., Ippolito, M.G., Sanseverino, E.R., Zizzo, G.: A technical approach to the energy blockchain in microgrids. IEEE Trans. Industr. Inf. **14**(11), 4792–4803 (2018). https://doi.org/10.1109/TII.2018.2806357
5. Dutta, G., Mitra, K.: A literature review on dynamic pricing of electricity. J. Oper. Res. Soc. **68**(10), 1131–1145 (2017). https://doi.org/10.1057/s41274-016-0149-4
6. Haider, H.T., See, O.H., Elmenreich, W.: A review of residential demand response of smart grid. Renew. Sustain. Energy Rev. **59(C)**, 166–178 (2016). https://doi.org/10.1016/j.rser.2016.01.01. https://ideas.repec.org/a/eee/rensus/v59y2016icp166-178.html
7. Ifland, M., Exner, N., Westermann, D.: Influencing domestic customers' market behavior with time flexible tariffs. In: 2012 3rd IEEE PES Innovative Smart Grid Technologies Europe (ISGT Europe), pp. 1–7 (2012). https://doi.org/10.1109/ISGTEurope.2012.6465638
8. Kristov, L., Martini, P.D., Taft, J.: A tale of two visions: designing a decentralized transactive electric system. IEEE Power Energ. Mag. **14**, 63–69 (2016). https://doi.org/10.1109/MPE.2016.2524964
9. Marinakis, V.: Big data for energy management and energy-efficient buildings. Energies **13**(7), 1555 (2020). https://doi.org/10.3390/en13071555
10. Santacana, E., Rackliffe, G., Tang, L., Feng, X.: Getting smart. IEEE Power Energ. Mag. **8**(2), 41–48 (2010). https://doi.org/10.1109/MPE.2009.935557
11. Siano, P., De Marco, G., Rolán, A., Loia, V.: A survey and evaluation of the potentials of distributed ledger technology for peer-to-peer transactive energy exchanges in local energy markets. IEEE Syst. J. **13**(3), 3454–3466 (2019). https://doi.org/10.1109/JSYST.2019.2903172

Energy Storage Scheduling: A QUBO Formulation for Quantum Computing

Frank Phillipson[✉], Tariq Bontekoe, and Irina Chiscop

TNO, The Hague, The Netherlands
frank.phillipson@tno.nl

Abstract. Energy storage systems and home energy management and control systems will play an important role in reaching the Paris Agreement on climate change. Underlying scheduling mechanisms will lead to a computational burden when the size of the systems and the size of the control space increase. One, upcoming alternative to overcome this computational burden is quantum computing. Here a quantum computer is used to solve the scheduling problems. In this paper an approach of using the D-Wave quantum annealing to solve an energy storage scheduling problem is proposed and used to solve a small example. The example shows the potential that quantum computing can have in this area in the future.

Keywords: Quantum annealing · Energy storage scheduling · Home energy management

1 Introduction

The Paris Agreement states that the maximum global average temperature rise has to be kept as close as possible to 1.5 °C [1]. Decarbonisation of our energy supply is an important component to achieve this target, because 65% of the world's CO_2 emissions are due to burning fossil fuels. Photovoltaics and wind energy are key technology options for implementing the shift to a decarbonised energy supply. A problem here is that these technologies exhibit high fluctuations in production over time. This means that electricity generated by these technologies will probably not match the energy demand and can cause over- or underproduction of electricity. Solving this discrepancy is of great importance.

A first approach in matching supply and demand is to adjust the supply side. There is a wide range of different types of energy models with different approaches and objectives known in literature. The review papers [14] and [15] give a good overview of energy models presented in the literature. In [15] an overview is given of energy models that have been emerging over the last few years. The following types of energy models are discussed: energy planning models [2,18], energy supply-demand models [8], forecasting models [5], optimisation models [6,14,22,32], energy models based on neural networks [17] and emission

© Springer Nature Switzerland AG 2021
U. R. Krieger et al. (Eds.): I4CS 2021, CCIS 1404, pp. 251–261, 2021.
https://doi.org/10.1007/978-3-030-75004-6_17

reduction models [16]. For local initiatives on distributed generators this is a tactical planning problem that can be solved by optimisation models [4, 27].

A second approach is managing the demand side, so called demand-side management (DSM) [29]. In a smart grid environment users's consumption can be scheduled directly, where the peak period demand is shifted to a non-peak period. Alternatively, users can be incentivised by tariff schemes, using home energy management systems. Within these schemes the price per energy unit changes depending on the aggregated load of all users [12, 24, 33, 34]. However, these approaches interfere with the routines of users leading to dissatisfaction [20] and the problem that users might not want to give away their freedom [29].

Then a third approach arises, where energy storage systems, such as a battery, are used to shift the peak load. Energy, supplied when there is not enough demand, is put in the storage and used later. This might come with inefficiencies by the loss occurred when charging or de-charging a battery. Again, tariff schemes can help here, where the (communicated) price is low when the (expected) supply is high, and a scheduling mechanism can optimise the cost of energy of a system. A wide range of scheduling approaches exist in literature, based on (stochastic) mathematical programming solutions [13, 19, 20, 23], game theoretic approaches [29] and (meta-) heuristic approaches [9, 26, 35]. The heuristic approaches are employed to overcome the computational burden when the size of the problem increases.

In this paper an alternative approach is proposed to overcome the computational burden using quantum computing. Quantum computing is the technique of using quantum mechanical phenomena such as superposition, entanglement and interference for doing computational operations. The type of devices which are capable of doing such quantum operations are still being actively developed and are called quantum computers. We distinguish between two paradigms of quantum computing devices: gate-based quantum computers and quantum annealers. Gated based quantum computers are just as classical computers that have data stored in registers using machine-level commands based on primitive functions of binary logic. Only, on a quantum computer, the data is stored in quantum bits (qubits) and there are powerful commands that classical computers do not have – such as 'write all possible values into my register simultaneously' or 'entangle two qubits' – and that looking at your data can influence what is in your register. A qubit is the quantum mechanical analogue of a classical bit. In classical computing the information is encoded in bits, where each bit can have the value zero or one. In quantum computing the information is encoded in qubits. A qubit is a two-level quantum system where the two basis qubit states are usually written as $|0\rangle$ and $|1\rangle$. A qubit can be in one of these states or (unlike a classical bit) in a linear combination of both states. The name of this phenomenon is superposition. Entanglement means that the quantum state of two qubits are dependent and the measurements of those qubits will always be correlated. Making gate-based quantum computers is hard for multiple reasons. One of the reasons is that qubits are very sensitive and can quickly become useless due to small interactions with the environment.

Quantum annealers are different. On their hardware, energy minimisation problems can be embedded. In quantum annealers, each state can be represented as an energy level. These states are simulated in a short time by taking advantage of the superposition and entanglement properties of qubits and the lowest energy result is obtained. The lowest energy state gives the optimal solution or the most likely solution.

A practically usable quantum computer is expected to be developed in the next few years. In less than ten years quantum computers will begin to outperform everyday computers, leading to breakthroughs in artificial intelligence, the discovery of new pharmaceuticals and beyond[1]. Currently, various parties, such as Google, IBM, Intel, Rigetti, QuTech, D-Wave and IonQ, are developing quantum chips, which are the basis of the quantum computer [30]. The size of these computers is limited, with the state-of-the-art being around 70 qubits for gate-based quantum computers and 5000 qubits for quantum annealers. In the meantime, progress is being made on algorithms that can be executed on those quantum computers, on the software (stack) itself and quantum software engineering processes [28] to enable the execution of quantum algorithms on quantum hardware. The main impact of quantum computing [7], next to the impact on cryptography, is in optimisation, machine learning [25] and simulation of quantum systems, for example in drug design.

In the remaining of this paper we introduce an energy storage scheduling problem and model this as a Quadratic Unconstrained Binary Optimisation problem, which is the standard format for the quantum annealer. In Sect. 2, the problem definition is given. In Sect. 3, the problem is translated to a QUBO problem. The results of solving this QUBO and further discussion is given in Sect. 4.

2   Problem Definition

In this paper a relatively simple problem is proposed. We assume that we have a number of tasks that require electricity. These tasks can be induced by household appliances, such as a fridge or washing machine, or by industrial processes. These tasks cause a demand for electricity d_t at discrete time t. At time t the price of one unit electricity is p_t. The electricity is imported from the grid or discharged from a battery. When the price is low, a battery, can be charged to optimise the total costs. Charging the battery is done with rate r^+ and discharging, using the electricity, with rate r^- with a charging and discharging efficiency η^+ and η^- respectively, leading to an efficiently stored amount of electricity of $\eta^+ r^+$ and an efficiently used amount of electricity when discharging of $\eta^- r^-$. We now have to decide on discrete time steps when the battery is charged and when the battery is discharged, leading to the decisions variables:

$$x_t = \begin{cases} 1 & \text{if battery is charged at time } t \\ 0 & \text{otherwise,} \end{cases} \tag{1}$$

---

[1] Quote from Jeremy O'Brien (2016).

and

$$y_t = \begin{cases} 1 & \text{if battery is discharged at time } t \\ 0 & \text{otherwise.} \end{cases} \tag{2}$$

To meet the demand d_t at time t, we need to import:

$$I_t = \begin{cases} d_t - \eta^- r^- & \text{if battery is discharged at time } t \\ d_t & \text{otherwise,} \end{cases} \tag{3}$$

leading to

$$I_t = d_t - y_t \eta^- r^-. \tag{4}$$

The load of the battery at time t can be expressed by

$$B_t = B_{t-1} + x_t \eta^+ r^+ - y_t r^-, \tag{5}$$

namely, the amount on the previous time interval plus the effectively charged amount minus the discharged amount. This all together leads to the binary optimisation problem for a time range $t = 1, ..., T$, formulated by:

$$\min \sum_{t=1}^{T} p_t (I_t + r^+ x_t), \tag{6}$$

$$\text{such that} \quad B_t = B_{t-1} + x_t \eta^+ r^+ - y_t r^-, \qquad t = 1, ..., T, \tag{7}$$
$$I_t = d_t - y_t \eta^- r^-, \qquad t = 1, ..., T, \tag{8}$$
$$x_t, y_t \in \{0, 1\}, \qquad t = 1, ..., T, \tag{9}$$
$$B_t \geq 0, \qquad t = 1, ..., T, \tag{10}$$
$$B_0 = 0. \tag{11}$$

Note that we do not require $I \geq 0$, meaning that we allow to feed back into the grid and receive a compensation for that.

3   QUBO Formulation

The standard problem formulation on the quantum annealer is the QUBO. We now give the definition of the QUBO-problem [11] and propose the formulation of the QUBO for the problem as stated in the previous section. The QUBO is expressed by the optimisation problem:

$$\text{QUBO: } \min/\max y = x^t Q x, \tag{12}$$

where $x \in \{0, 1\}^n$ represents the decision variables and Q is a $n \times n$ coefficient matrix. QUBO problems belong to the class of NP-hard problems [11]. Another formulation of the problem, often used, equals

$$\text{QUBO: } \min/\max H = x^t q + x^t Q x, \tag{13}$$

or a combination of multiple of these terms

$$\text{QUBO: min/max } H = A \cdot H_A + B \cdot H_B + \cdots, \qquad (14)$$

where $A, B, \ldots$ are weights that can be used to tune the problem and include constraints into the QUBO. We will use this representation.

For already a large number of combinatorial optimisation problems the QUBO representation is known [11, 21]. Many constrained binary programming problems can be transformed easily to a QUBO representation. Assume that we have the problem ($x \in \{0, 1\}^n$)

$$\min c^t x, \text{ subject to } Ax = b, \qquad (15)$$

then we can bring the constraints to the objective value, using a penalty factor λ for a quadratic penalty:

$$\min y = c^t x + \lambda (Ax - b)^t (Ax - b). \qquad (16)$$

Using $P = Ic$, the matrix with the values of vector c on its diagonal, we get

$$\min y = x^t P x + \lambda (Ax - b)^t (Ax - b) = x^t P x + x^t R x + d = x^t Q x, \qquad (17)$$

where the matrix R and the constant d follow from the matrix multiplication and the constant d can be neglected, since it does not influence the optimisation problem.

To convert the problem formulated by Eq. (6)-(11), the constraints have to be modelled into the objective function. This means that I_t is directly inserted in the objective and that an alternative for B_t has to be found. A first step is to rewrite the problem as:

$$\min \sum_{t=1}^{T} p_t(d_t - y_t \eta^- r^- + r^+ x_t), \qquad (18)$$

$$\text{such that } \sum_{s=1}^{t} (x_s \eta^+ r^+ - y_s r^-) \geq 0 \qquad t = 1, \ldots, T, \qquad (19)$$

$$x_t, y_t \in \{0, 1\}, \qquad t = 1, \ldots, T, \qquad (20)$$

where Eq. (19) makes sure the battery level is non-negative for all time steps. Now the last step is to convert the inequality of Eq. (19) to an equality by introducing binary $T \times K$ slack variables z_{tk}:

$$\min \sum_{t=1}^{T} p_t(d_t - y_t \eta^- r^- + r^+ x_t), \qquad (21)$$

$$\text{such that } \sum_{s=1}^{t} x_s \eta^+ r^+ - y_s r^- - \sum_{k=1}^{K} 2^{k-1} z_{tk} = 0, \quad t = 1, \ldots, T, \qquad (22)$$

$$x_t, y_t, z_{tk} \in \{0, 1\}, \quad t = 1, \ldots, T, k = 1, \ldots, K \qquad (23)$$

The overall solution for this QUBO is now given by:

$$\min \quad A \cdot H_A + B \cdot H_B, \tag{24}$$

$$\text{with } H_A = \sum_{t=1}^{T} p_t (d_t - y_t \eta^- r^- + r^+ x_t), \tag{25}$$

$$H_B = \sum_{t=1}^{T} \left(\sum_{s=1}^{t} (x_s \eta^+ r^+ - y_s r^-) - \sum_{k=1}^{K} 2^{k-1} z_{tk} \right)^2, \tag{26}$$

where A and B denote penalty coefficients to be applied such that the constraints will be satisfied. The parameter K is given by $K = \log_2 \left(\min \left(\sum_{t=1}^{T} d_t, T\eta^+ r^+ \right) \right)$. The battery load cannot be higher than the total demand or the total amount that can be charged in T time steps. Note that the number of slack variables can be reduced by taking $K(t^*) = \log_2 \left(\min \left(\sum_{t=1}^{t^*} d_t, t^* \eta^+ r^+ \right) \right)$ and summing over $k = 1$ to $K(t)$ in Eq. (26). When determining the penalty coefficients, we can set $A = 1$ and look for a good value for B. Rule of thumb is that the gain of violating a constraint must be lower than the cost of the objective.

Table 1. Parameters for a Tesla (inspired) battery storage system.

Variable	Value
η^+	0.958
η^-	0.958
r^+	3.3 kW/h
r^-	3.3 kW/h

4   Example and Discussion

In this section an example is given and the results thereof are discussed. The case that is under consideration, comprises the energy demand of two flats [20] and 10 T (inspired) Powerwall 2 battery systems, using the parameters as depicted in Table 1 [29]. The efficiency variables η^+ and η^- are calculated under the assumption that charging and discharging contribute to equal amounts towards the given round-trip efficiency of $0.918 = \eta^+ \cdot \eta^-$. The demand and the electricity price for a day ($T = 24$) are depicted in Fig. 1. Note that the size of the problem here is quite small, due to the current state of the quantum technology. The optimal schedule for this problem can easily be calculated by a conventional solver and is depicted in Fig. 2. The total cost of this solution is \$151.40.

To solve the QUBO on D-Wave's hardware, we need to set the value of B as indicated in the previous section. First we define p_t in dollar cents instead of dollars. Two meta-search loops using the simulated annealing (using num_reads = 1000, which indicates the number of states or output solutions to be read from the solver) result in the relation between B and the total cost of the solution as shown in Fig. 3. A value for B too small ($B < 0.03$) gives a set of solutions that are all violating constraint (22). A value for B around 0.07 seems to give the best results.

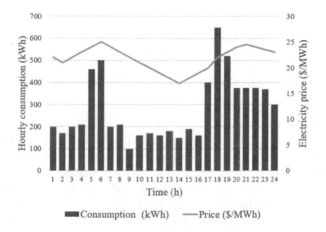

Fig. 1. Electricity demand and price during the day.

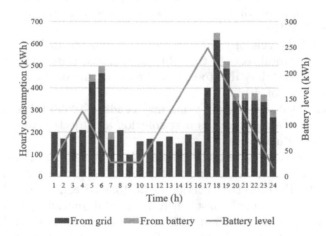

Fig. 2. Electricity provision and battery level during the day.

Next, the chain strength has to be determined. Because of the limited connectivity of the chip, a problem variable has to be duplicated to multiple (connected) qubits. Those qubits should have the same value, meaning the weight of their connection should be such that it holds in the optimisation process. All these qubits representing the same variable are part of a so-called chain, and their

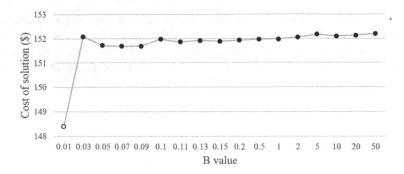

Fig. 3. Relation between B and the total cost of the solution. The open dot is an infeasible solution.

edge weights are called the chain strength (λ), which is an important value in the optimisation process. In [3], Coffrin gives a thorough analysis. He indicates that if λ is sufficiently large, optimal solutions will match $\lambda \geq \sum_{ij} |Q_{ij}|$. However, the goal is to find the smallest possible value of λ, to avoid re-scaling of the problem. Coffrin also indicates that finding the smallest possible setting of λ can be NP-hard. Also other research has been performed on selecting an optimal choice for this chain strength [31], but at the moment there is no solid criterion for choosing a value. A rule of thumb indicated in the D-Wave documentations [2] is $\lambda = \max_{ij} Q_{ij}$. It may be necessary to use the quantum annealer with multiple values of the chain strength in order to determine which value for λ is optimal for a given problem [10].

For $B = 0.07$ the rule of thumb results in $\lambda = 3506$. In Fig. 4 the relation between λ and the total costs of the solution is shown using **num_reads** = 100, so with (much) uncertainty due to the stochastic nature of the results. A value for $\lambda > 2000$ seems sufficient.

A call to the D-Wave annealer using **num_reads** = 10000 takes 1.62 seconds of QPU access time and returns as best solution an objective value of \$151.84, \$0.44 above the optimal value.

Concluding, the QUBO formulation and the implementation are successful. However, the found solution is not that good. The problem at hand has as outcome range for the objective function [\$135.15, \$168.88], the first found when all $y_t = 1$ and all $x_t = 0$, the last when all $y_t = 0$ and all $x_t = 1$. However, the trivial solution of all $y_t = 0$ and all $x_t = 0$ results in an objective value of \$151.66, which is better than the best solution found before. This means that the real range of interest is [\$151.40, \$151.66], which is quite small and apparently too small for a meta-heuristic to (quickly) find a solution in this area. Adding obvious cuts, like

$$x_i + y_i \leq 1,$$

as it makes no sense to charge and discharge the battery in the same time unit, and

$$(1 - \eta^+) \sum_{i=1}^{T} x_i - (1 + \eta^-) \sum_{i=1}^{T} y_i \geq 0,$$

as the (dis-) charging losses have to be charged and the total charging has to be more or equal than the total discharging, do not lead to better results and but do lead to a higher complexity due to more scaling parameters within the QUBO that have to be tuned. The size of this problem reaches the maximum of the chip (5000 qubits). It is possible that for a bigger problem the solution is relatively better, as is expected that the calculating time scales linearly and the interval of interest may grow.

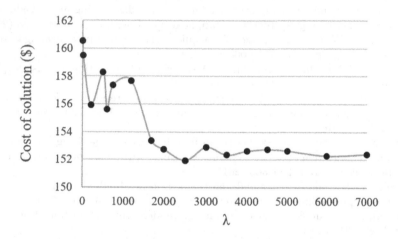

Fig. 4. Relation between λ and the total cost of the solution.

Further research is recommended in scaling of the data and the QUBO parameter to make it more easy for the quantum annealer to find a good solution. Also, finding other cuts that reduce the search space more efficiently is an interesting research direction.

References

1. Arantegui, R.L., Jäger-Waldau, A.: Photovoltaics and wind status in the European Union after the Paris Agreement. Renew. Sustain. Energ. Rev. **81**, 2460–2471 (2018)
2. Belyaev, L.S.: Pay-off matrix technique. Energy **15**(7/8), 631–643 (1990)
3. Coffrin, C.J.: Challenges with chains: testing the limits of a D-Wave quantum Annealer for discrete optimization. Technical Report. Los Alamos National Laboratory, USA (2019)

4. Croes, N., Phillipson, F., Schreuder, M.: Tactical congestion management: the optimal mix of decentralised generators in a district. In: Integration of Renewables into the Distribution Grid, CIRED 2012 Workshop, pp. 1–4. IET (2012)
5. Cuaresma, J.C., Hlouskova, J., Kossmeier, S., Obersteiner, M.: Forecasting electricity spot-prices using linear univariate time-series models. Appl. Energ. **77**(1), 87–106 (2004)
6. De Musgrove, A.: A linear programming analysis of liquid-furl production and use options for Australia. Energy **9**, 281–302 (1984)
7. de Wolf, R.: The potential impact of quantum computers on society. Ethics Inf. Technol. **19**(4), 271–276 (2017). https://doi.org/10.1007/s10676-017-9439-z
8. Esmaili, M., Firozjaee, E.C., Shayanfar, H.A.: Optimal placement of distributed generations considering voltage stability and power losses with observing voltage-related constraints. Appl. Energ. **113**, 1252–1260 (2014)
9. Faisal, M., Hannan, M., Ker, P.J., Rahman, M.A., Begum, R., Mahlia, T.: Particle swarm optimised fuzzy controller for charging-discharging and scheduling of battery energy storage system in mg applications. Energ. Rep. 6, 215–228 (2020)
10. Foster, R.C., Weaver, B., Gattiker, J.: Applications of quantum annealing in statistics. arXiv preprint arXiv:1904.06819 (2019)
11. Glover, F., Kochenberger, G., Du, Y.: A tutorial on formulating and using QUBO models. arXiv preprint arXiv:1811.11538 (2018)
12. Haider, H.T., See, O.H., Elmenreich, W.: Dynamic residential load scheduling based on adaptive consumption level pricing scheme. Electri. Power Syst. Res. **133**, 27–35 (2016)
13. Hemmati, R., Saboori, H.: Stochastic optimal battery storage sizing and scheduling in home energy management systems equipped with solar photovoltaic panels. Energ. Buildings **152**, 290–300 (2017)
14. Hiremath, R., Shikha, S., Ravindranath, N.: Decentralized energy planning; modeling and application - a review. Renew. Sustain. Energ. Rev. **11**, 729–752 (2007)
15. Jebaraj, S., Iniyan, S.: A review of energy models. Renew. Sustain. Energ. Rev. **10**(4), 281–311 (2006)
16. Kang, J., Ng, T.S., Su, B.: Optimizing electricity mix for CO2 emissions reduction: a robust input-output linear programming model. Eur. J. Oper. Res. 287(1), 280–292 (2020)
17. Khalil, A.J., Barhoom, A.M., Abu-Nasser, B.S., Musleh, M.M., Abu-Naser, S.S.: Energy efficiency predicting using artificial neural network (2019)
18. Labys, W.C., Kuczmowski, T., Infanger, G.: Special programming models. Energy **15**(7/8), 607–617 (1990)
19. Li, Y., Yang, Z., Li, G., Zhao, D., Tian, W.: Optimal scheduling of an isolated microgrid with battery storage considering load and renewable generation uncertainties. IEEE Trans. Ind. Electron. **66**(2), 1565–1575 (2018)
20. Longe, O.M., Ouahada, K., Rimer, S., Harutyunyan, A.N., Ferreira, H.C.: Distributed demand side management with battery storage for smart home energy scheduling. Sustainability **9**(1), 120 (2017)
21. Lucas, A.: Ising formulations of many np problems. Front. Phys. **2**, 5 (2014)
22. Mashhour, E., Moghaddas-Tafreshi, S.: Integration of distributed energy resources into low voltage grid: a market-based multiperiod optimization model. Electr. Power Syst. Res. **80**(4), 473–480 (2009)
23. Merdanoğlu, H., Yakıcı, E., Doğan, O.T., Duran, S., Karatas, M.: Finding optimal schedules in a home energy management system. Electr. Power Syst. Res. 182, 106229 (2020)

24. Mohsenian-Rad, A.H., Wong, V.W., Jatskevich, J., Schober, R., Leon-Garcia, A.: Autonomous demand-side management based on game-theoretic energy consumption scheduling for the future smart grid. IEEE Trans. Smart Grid **1**(3), 320–331 (2010)

25. Neumann, N., Phillipson, F., Versluis, R.: Machine learning in the quantum era. Digitale Welt **3**(2), 24–29 (2019)

26. Pedrasa, M.A.A., Spooner, T.D., MacGill, I.F.: Coordinated scheduling of residential distributed energy resources to optimize smart home energy services. IEEE Trans. Smart Grid **1**(2), 134–143 (2010)

27. Phillipson, F.: Multi objective approach for tactical capacity management of distributed generation. In: Eichler, G., Erfurth, C., Fahrnberger, G. (eds.) I4CS 2017. CCIS, vol. 717, pp. 155–166. Springer, Cham (2017). https://doi.org/10.1007/978-3-319-60447-3_11

28. Piattini, M., et al.: The Talavera manifesto for quantum software engineering and programming. In: QANSWER, pp. 1–5 (2020)

29. Pilz, M., Al-Fagih, L., Pfluegel, E.: Energy storage scheduling with an advanced battery model: a game-theoretic approach. Inventions **2**(4), 30 (2017)

30. Resch, S., Karpuzcu, U.R.: Quantum computing: an overview across the system stack. arXiv preprint arXiv:1905.07240 (2019)

31. Rieffel, E.G., Venturelli, D., O'Gorman, B., Do, M.B., Prystay, E.M., Smelyanskiy, V.N.: A case study in programming a quantum Annealer for hard operational planning problems. Quantum Inf. Process. **14**(1), 1–36 (2014). https://doi.org/10.1007/s11128-014-0892-x

32. Satsangi, P., Sarma, E.: Integrated energy planning model for India with particular reference to renewable energy prospects. In: Energy options for the 90's: proceedings of the National Solar Energy Convention held at Indian Institute of Technology, pp. 596–620. Tata McGraw Hill, New Delhi (1988)

33. Soliman, H.M., Leon-Garcia, A.: Game-theoretic demand-side management with storage devices for the future smart grid. IEEE Trans. Smart Grid **5**(3), 1475–1485 (2014)

34. Wang, Y., Saad, W., Mandayam, N.B., Poor, H.V.: Load shifting in the smart grid: to participate or not? IEEE Trans. Smart Grid **7**(6), 2604–2614 (2015)

35. Zhao, Z., Lee, W.C., Shin, Y., Song, K.B.: An optimal power scheduling method for demand response in home energy management system. IEEE Trans. Smart Grid **4**(3), 1391–1400 (2013)

Author Index

Printed in the United States
by Baker & Taylor Publisher Services

Printed in the United States
by Baker & Taylor Publisher Services